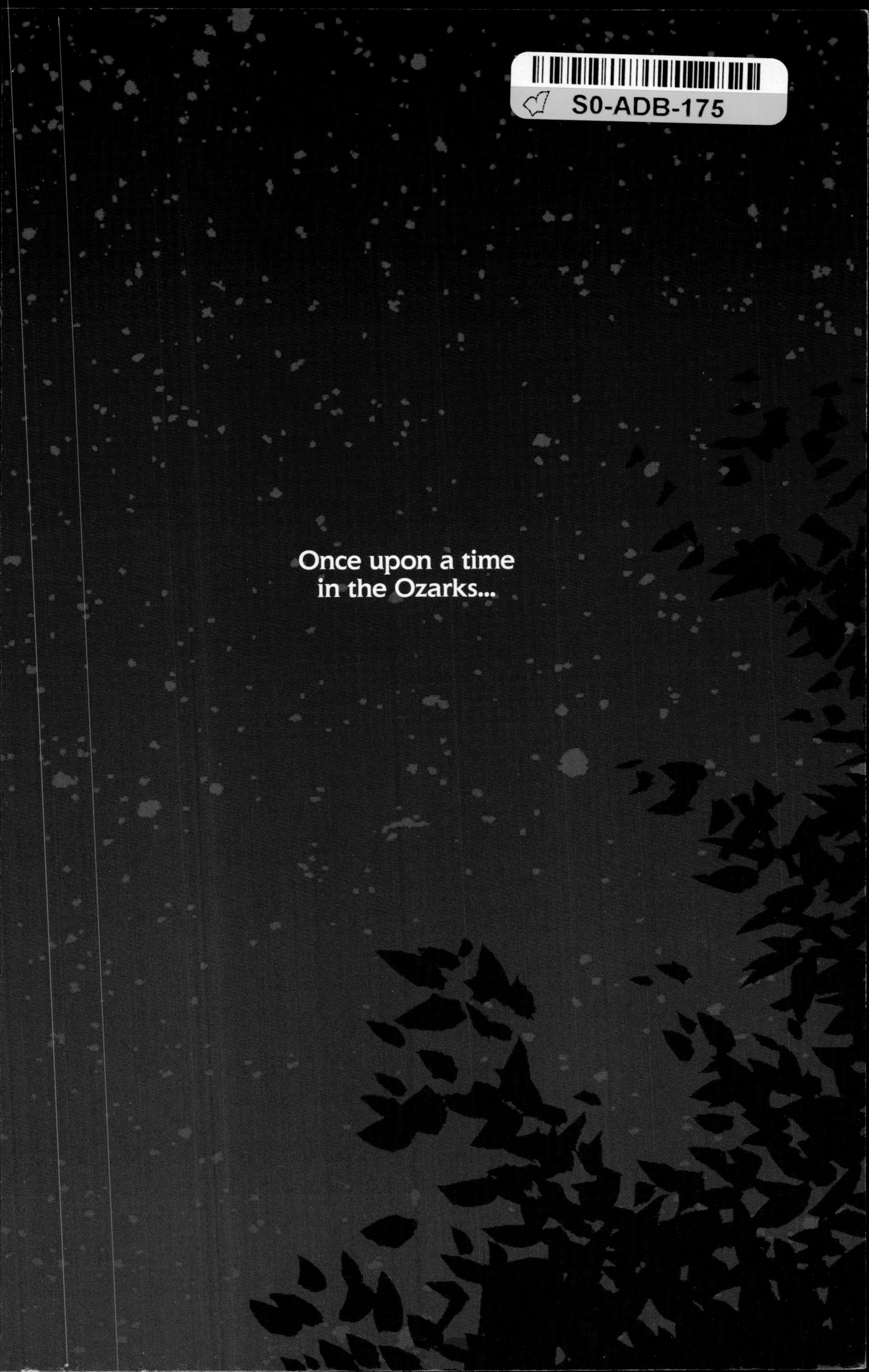
Once upon a time
in the Ozarks...

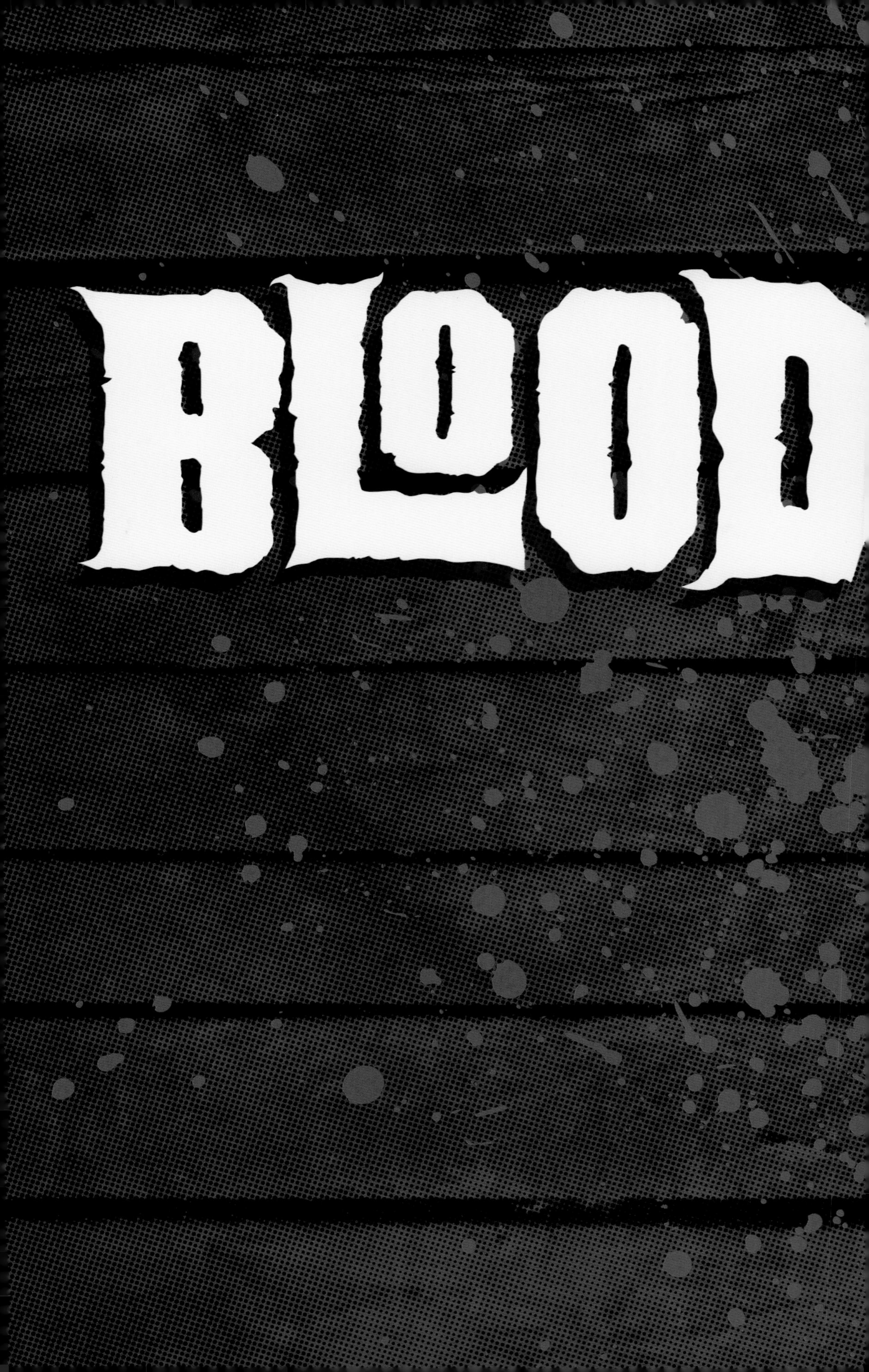
BLOOD

FEUD

WRITTEN BY **CULLEN BUNN**
ILLUSTRATED BY **DREW MOSS**
COLORED BY **NICK FILARDI**

DESIGNED BY **DYLAN TODD**
LETTERED BY **CRANK!**

EDITED BY **CHARLIE CHU**

AN ONI PRESS PUBLICATION

PUBLISHED BY ONI PRESS, INC.
Joe Nozemack PUBLISHER
James Lucas Jones EDITOR IN CHIEF
Andrew McIntire V.P. OF MARKETING & SALES
Cheyenne Allott DIRECTOR OF SALES
Rachel Reed PUBLICITY COORDINATOR
Troy Look DIRECTOR OF DESIGN & PRODUCTION
Hilary Thompson GRAPHIC DESIGNER
Jared Jones DIGITAL ART TECHNICIAN
Ari Yarwood MANAGING EDITOR
Charlie Chu SENIOR EDITOR
Robin Herrera EDITOR
Bess Pallares EDITORIAL ASSISTANT
Brad Rooks DIRECTOR OF LOGISTICS
Jung Lee LOGISTICS ASSOCIATE

onipress.com
facebook.com/onipress
twitter.com/onipress
onipress.tumblr.com
instagram.com/onipress

cullenbunn.com / @cullenbunn
facebook.com/DrewerdMoss / @drew_moss
@nickfil
bigredrobot.net / @bigredrobot
@ccrank

THIS VOLUME COLLECTS ISSUES #1-5 OF THE ONI PRESS SERIES **BLOOD FEUD**.

FIRST EDITION: JUNE 2016

ISBN 978-1-62010-317-3
EISBN 978-1-62010-318-0

BLOOD FEUD June 2016. Published by Oni Press, Inc. 1305 SE Martin Luther King Jr. Blvd., Suite A, Portland, OR 97214.

PRINTED IN CHINA.

LIBRARY OF CONGRESS CONTROL NUMBER: 2015959961

1 2 3 4 5 6 7 8 9 10

CHAPTER 1

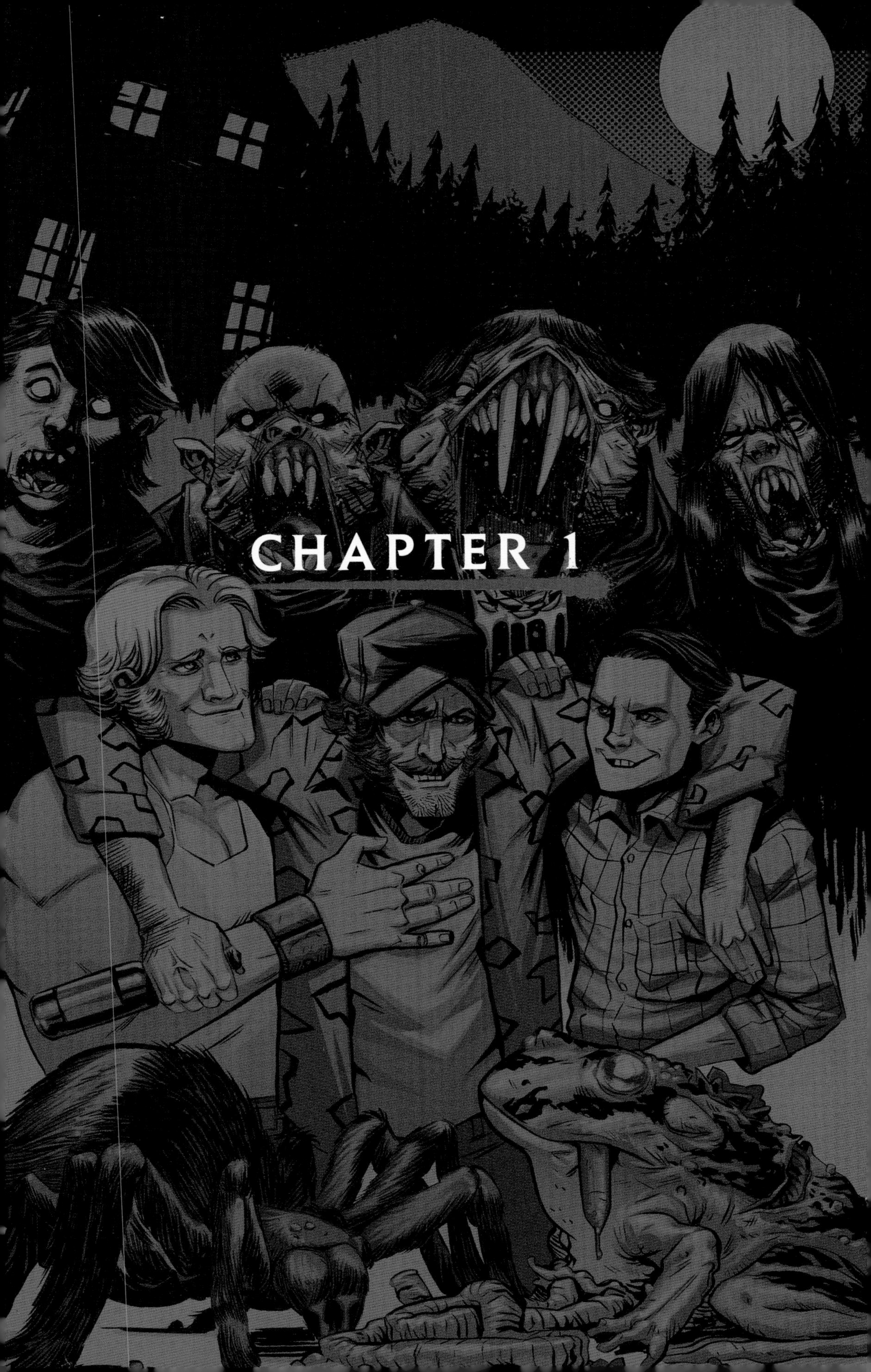

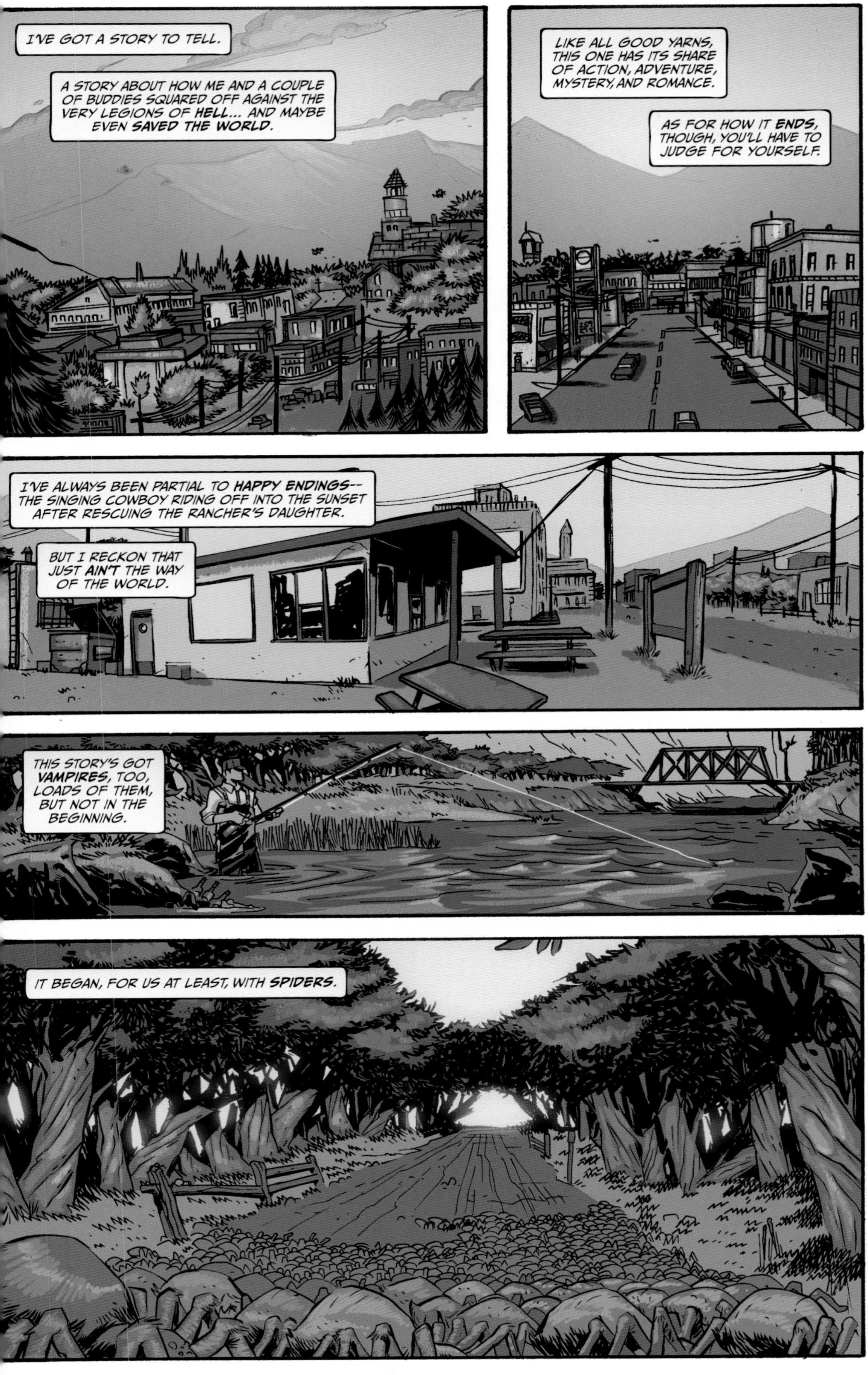
I'VE GOT A STORY TO TELL.
A STORY ABOUT HOW ME AND A COUPLE OF BUDDIES SQUARED OFF AGAINST THE VERY LEGIONS OF HELL... AND MAYBE EVEN SAVED THE WORLD.
LIKE ALL GOOD YARNS, THIS ONE HAS ITS SHARE OF ACTION, ADVENTURE, MYSTERY, AND ROMANCE.
AS FOR HOW IT ENDS, THOUGH, YOU'LL HAVE TO JUDGE FOR YOURSELF.
I'VE ALWAYS BEEN PARTIAL TO HAPPY ENDINGS-- THE SINGING COWBOY RIDING OFF INTO THE SUNSET AFTER RESCUING THE RANCHER'S DAUGHTER.
BUT I RECKON THAT JUST AIN'T THE WAY OF THE WORLD.
THIS STORY'S GOT VAMPIRES, TOO, LOADS OF THEM, BUT NOT IN THE BEGINNING.
IT BEGAN, FOR US AT LEAST, WITH SPIDERS.

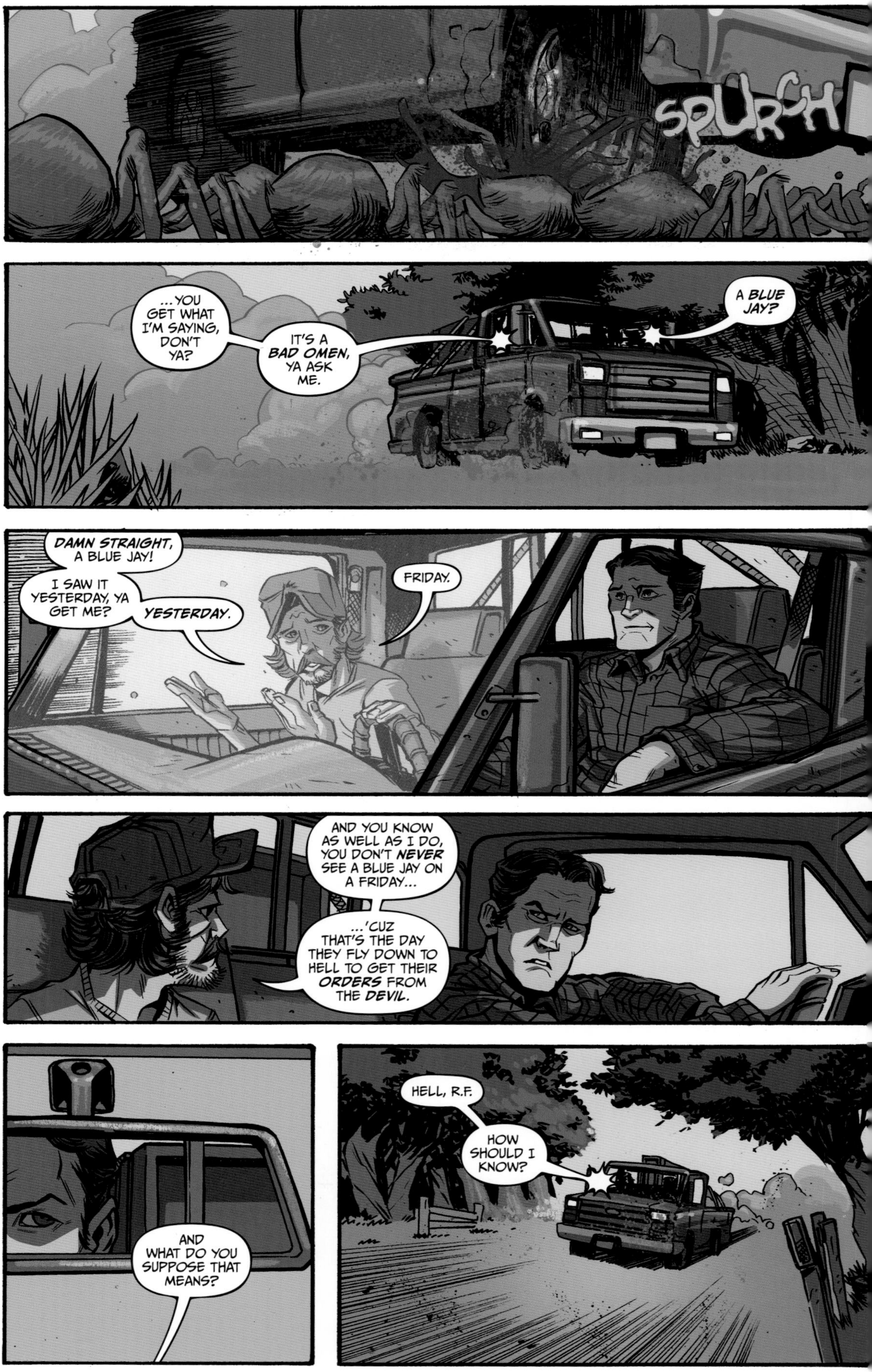
SPURCH
...YOU GET WHAT I'M SAYING, DON'T YA?
IT'S A BAD OMEN, YA ASK ME.
A BLUE JAY?
DAMN STRAIGHT, A BLUE JAY!
I SAW IT YESTERDAY, YA GET ME?
YESTERDAY.
FRIDAY.
AND YOU KNOW AS WELL AS I DO, YOU DON'T NEVER SEE A BLUE JAY ON A FRIDAY...
...'CUZ THAT'S THE DAY THEY FLY DOWN TO HELL TO GET THEIR ORDERS FROM THE DEVIL.
AND WHAT DO YOU SUPPOSE THAT MEANS?
HELL, R.F.
HOW SHOULD I KNOW?

I AIN'T NO EXPERT IN *OMENS* AND *PORTENTS* AND THE LIKE, BUT I KNOW ONE WHEN I SEE--

LOOK OUT!

SKREEKKKKK

DON'T KNOW IF YOU *REALIZE* IT, MA'AM...

...BUT STANDING IN THE MIDDLE OF THE ROAD LIKE THAT IS A GOOD WAY TO GET YOURSELF KILLED.

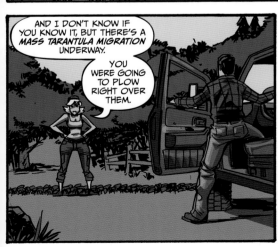

AND I DON'T KNOW IF YOU KNOW IT, BUT THERE'S A *MASS TARANTULA MIGRATION* UNDERWAY.

YOU WERE GOING TO PLOW RIGHT OVER THEM.

LIVED HERE ALL MY LIFE. SPIDERS AIN'T NOTHING NEW.

THEY'LL BE RUNNING AGAIN THIS TIME NEXT YEAR.

YOU'D THINK THAT IF YOU'RE ACCUSTOMED TO THE SPIDERS...

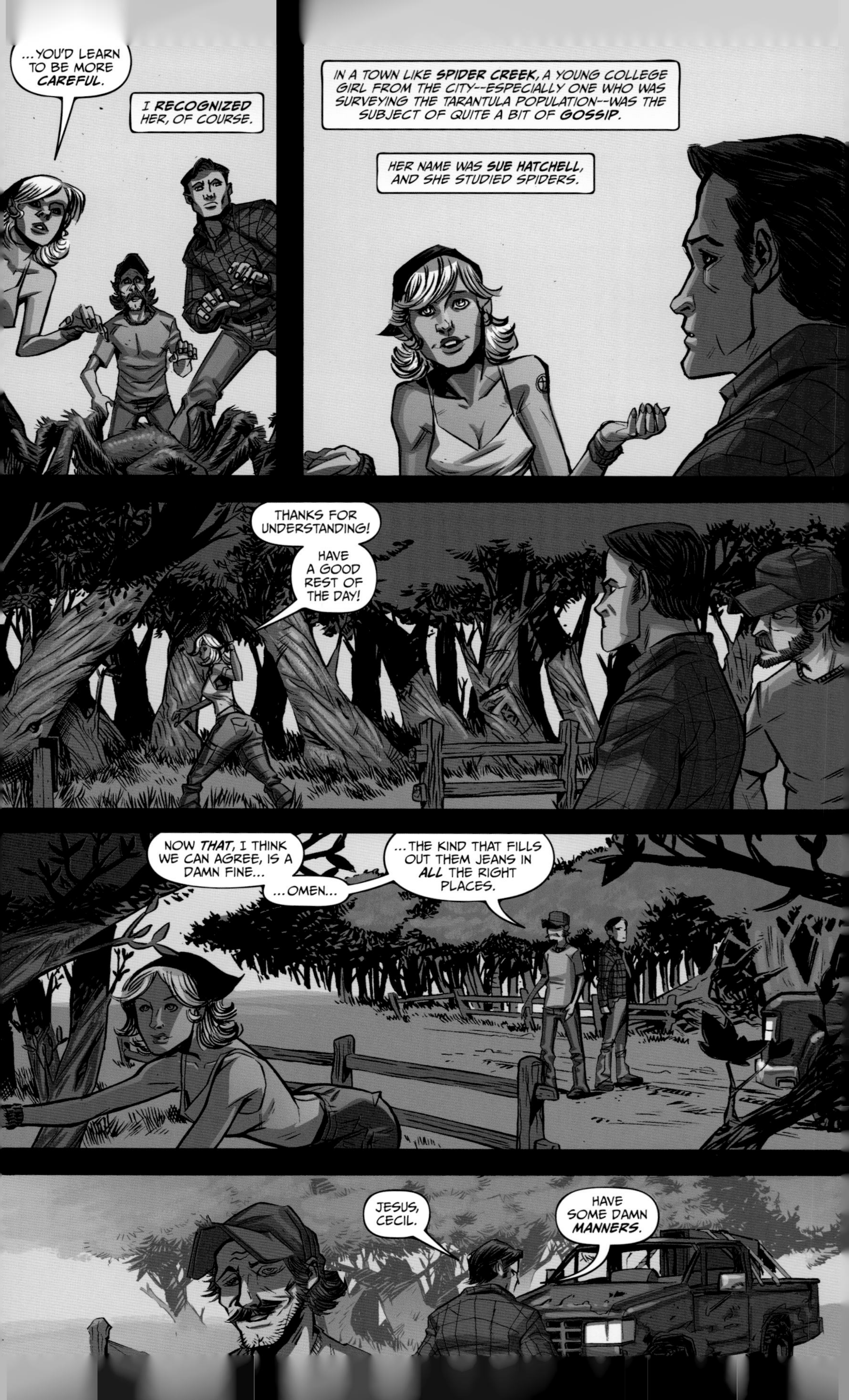
...YOU'D LEARN TO BE MORE CAREFUL.
I RECOGNIZED HER, OF COURSE.
IN A TOWN LIKE SPIDER CREEK, A YOUNG COLLEGE GIRL FROM THE CITY--ESPECIALLY ONE WHO WAS SURVEYING THE TARANTULA POPULATION--WAS THE SUBJECT OF QUITE A BIT OF GOSSIP.
HER NAME WAS SUE HATCHELL, AND SHE STUDIED SPIDERS.
THANKS FOR UNDERSTANDING!
HAVE A GOOD REST OF THE DAY!
NOW THAT, I THINK WE CAN AGREE, IS A DAMN FINE...
...OMEN...
...THE KIND THAT FILLS OUT THEM JEANS IN ALL THE RIGHT PLACES.
JESUS, CECIL.
HAVE SOME DAMN MANNERS.

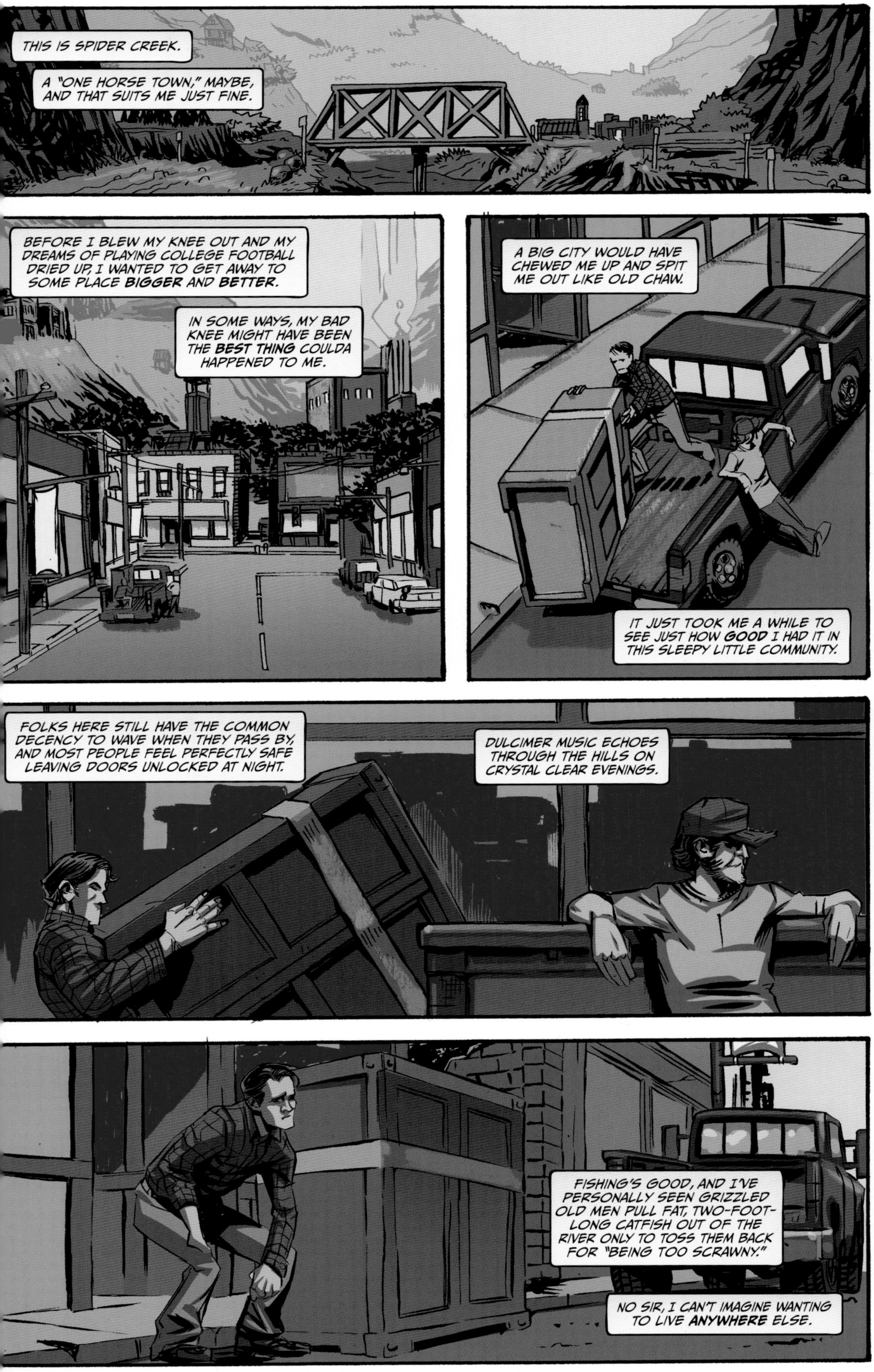

THIS IS SPIDER CREEK.
A "ONE HORSE TOWN," MAYBE, AND THAT SUITS ME JUST FINE.
BEFORE I BLEW MY KNEE OUT AND MY DREAMS OF PLAYING COLLEGE FOOTBALL DRIED UP, I WANTED TO GET AWAY TO SOME PLACE **BIGGER** AND **BETTER**.
IN SOME WAYS, MY BAD KNEE MIGHT HAVE BEEN THE **BEST THING** COULDA HAPPENED TO ME.
A BIG CITY WOULD HAVE CHEWED ME UP AND SPIT ME OUT LIKE OLD CHAW.
IT JUST TOOK ME A WHILE TO SEE JUST HOW **GOOD** I HAD IT IN THIS SLEEPY LITTLE COMMUNITY.
FOLKS HERE STILL HAVE THE COMMON DECENCY TO WAVE WHEN THEY PASS BY, AND MOST PEOPLE FEEL PERFECTLY SAFE LEAVING DOORS UNLOCKED AT NIGHT.
DULCIMER MUSIC ECHOES THROUGH THE HILLS ON CRYSTAL CLEAR EVENINGS.
FISHING'S GOOD, AND I'VE PERSONALLY SEEN GRIZZLED OLD MEN PULL FAT, TWO-FOOT-LONG CATFISH OUT OF THE RIVER ONLY TO TOSS THEM BACK FOR "BEING TOO SCRAWNY."
NO SIR, I CAN'T IMAGINE WANTING TO LIVE **ANYWHERE** ELSE.

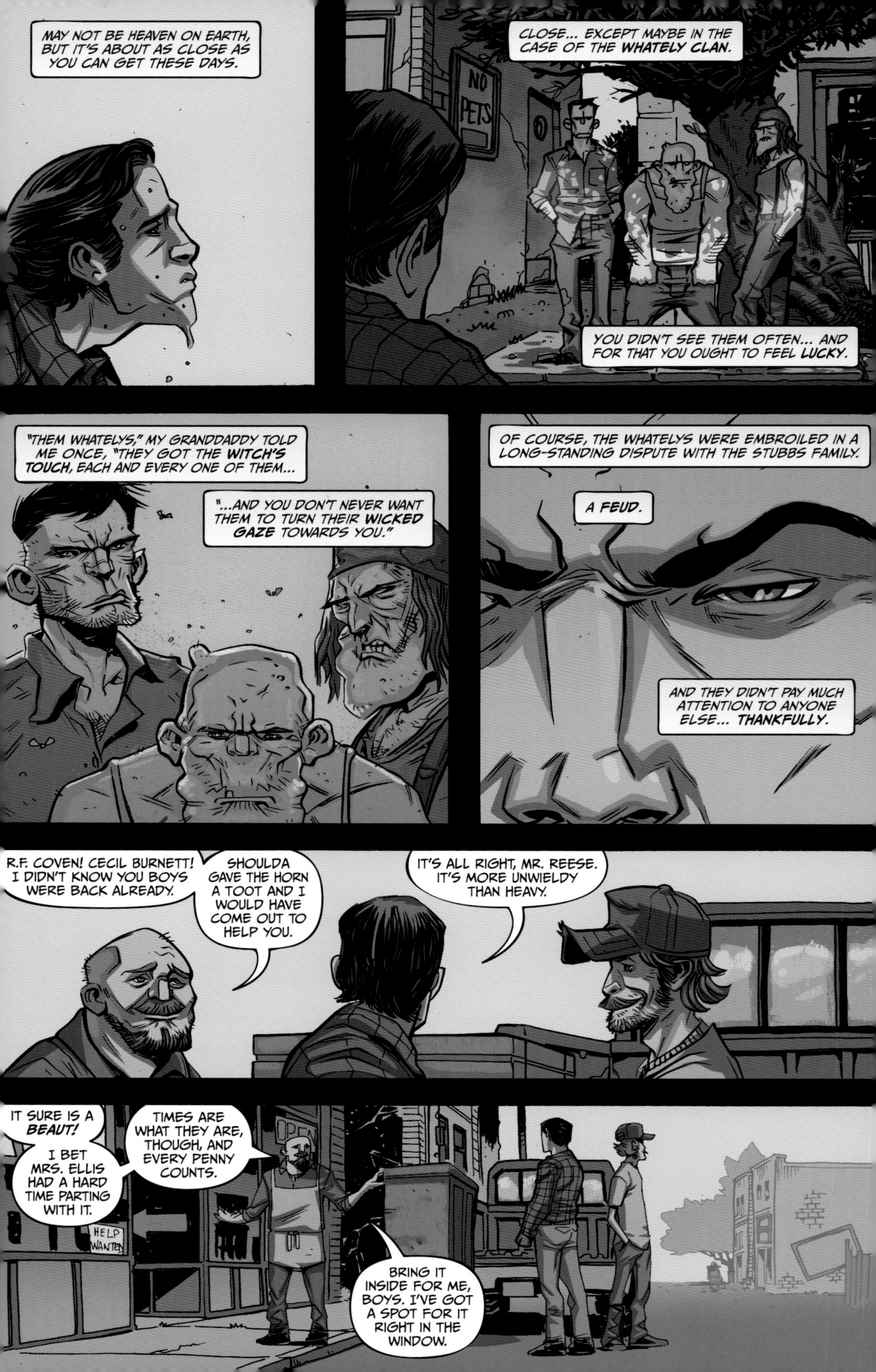
MAY NOT BE HEAVEN ON EARTH, BUT IT'S ABOUT AS CLOSE AS YOU CAN GET THESE DAYS.
CLOSE... EXCEPT MAYBE IN THE CASE OF THE WHATELY CLAN.
NO PETS
YOU DIDN'T SEE THEM OFTEN... AND FOR THAT YOU OUGHT TO FEEL LUCKY.
"THEM WHATELYS," MY GRANDDADDY TOLD ME ONCE, "THEY GOT THE WITCH'S TOUCH, EACH AND EVERY ONE OF THEM...
"...AND YOU DON'T NEVER WANT THEM TO TURN THEIR WICKED GAZE TOWARDS YOU."
OF COURSE, THE WHATELYS WERE EMBROILED IN A LONG-STANDING DISPUTE WITH THE STUBBS FAMILY.
A FEUD.
AND THEY DIDN'T PAY MUCH ATTENTION TO ANYONE ELSE... THANKFULLY.
R.F. COVEN! CECIL BURNETT! I DIDN'T KNOW YOU BOYS WERE BACK ALREADY.
SHOULDA GAVE THE HORN A TOOT AND I WOULD HAVE COME OUT TO HELP YOU.
IT'S ALL RIGHT, MR. REESE. IT'S MORE UNWIELDY THAN HEAVY.
IT SURE IS A BEAUT!
I BET MRS. ELLIS HAD A HARD TIME PARTING WITH IT.
TIMES ARE WHAT THEY ARE, THOUGH, AND EVERY PENNY COUNTS.
OPEN
HELP WANTED
BRING IT INSIDE FOR ME, BOYS. I'VE GOT A SPOT FOR IT RIGHT IN THE WINDOW.

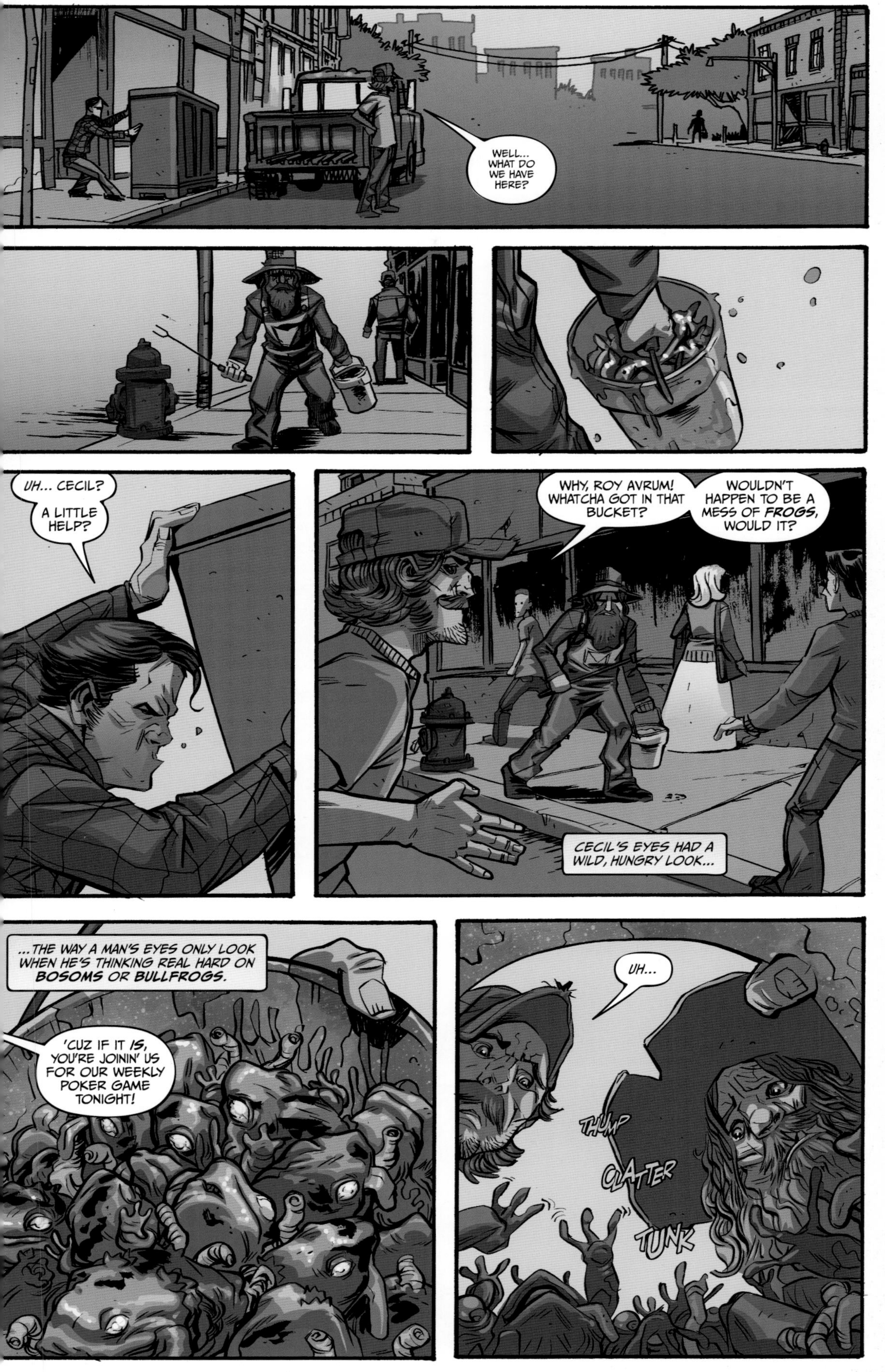
WELL... WHAT DO WE HAVE HERE?
UH... CECIL? A LITTLE HELP?
WHY, ROY AVRUM! WHATCHA GOT IN THAT BUCKET?
WOULDN'T HAPPEN TO BE A MESS OF FROGS, WOULD IT?
CECIL'S EYES HAD A WILD, HUNGRY LOOK...
...THE WAY A MAN'S EYES ONLY LOOK WHEN HE'S THINKING REAL HARD ON BOSOMS OR BULLFROGS.
'CUZ IF IT IS, YOU'RE JOININ' US FOR OUR WEEKLY POKER GAME TONIGHT!
UH...
THUMP
CLATTER
TUNK

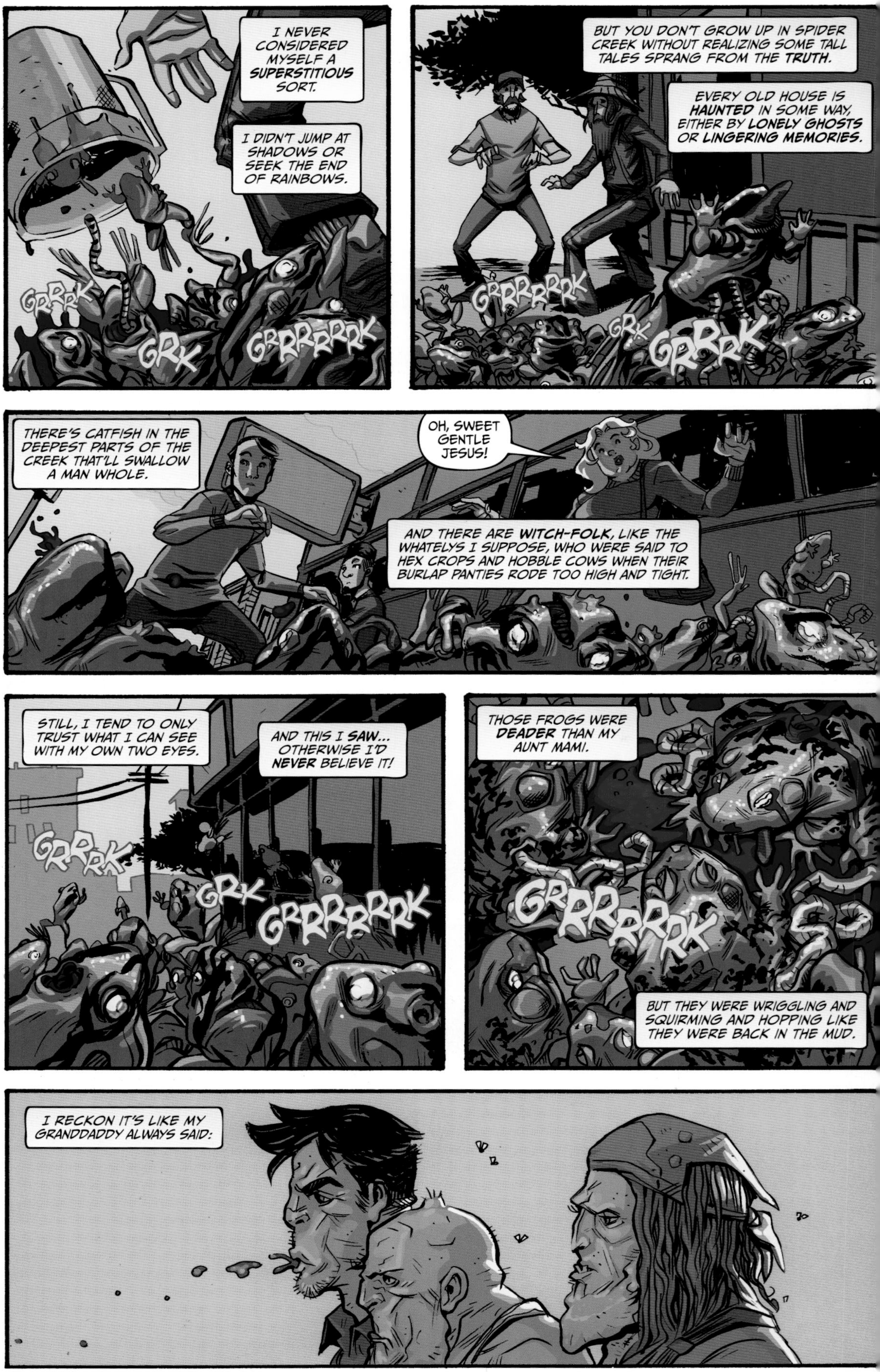
I NEVER CONSIDERED MYSELF A SUPERSTITIOUS SORT.
I DIDN'T JUMP AT SHADOWS OR SEEK THE END OF RAINBOWS.
GRRRK
GRK
GRRRRRRK
BUT YOU DON'T GROW UP IN SPIDER CREEK WITHOUT REALIZING SOME TALL TALES SPRANG FROM THE TRUTH.
EVERY OLD HOUSE IS HAUNTED IN SOME WAY, EITHER BY LONELY GHOSTS OR LINGERING MEMORIES.
GRRRRRRK
GRK
GRRRK
THERE'S CATFISH IN THE DEEPEST PARTS OF THE CREEK THAT'LL SWALLOW A MAN WHOLE.
OH, SWEET GENTLE JESUS!
AND THERE ARE WITCH-FOLK, LIKE THE WHATELYS I SUPPOSE, WHO WERE SAID TO HEX CROPS AND HOBBLE COWS WHEN THEIR BURLAP PANTIES RODE TOO HIGH AND TIGHT.
STILL, I TEND TO ONLY TRUST WHAT I CAN SEE WITH MY OWN TWO EYES.
AND THIS I SAW... OTHERWISE I'D NEVER BELIEVE IT!
GRRRK
GRK
GRRRRRRK
THOSE FROGS WERE DEADER THAN MY AUNT MAMI.
GRRRRRRK
BUT THEY WERE WRIGGLING AND SQUIRMING AND HOPPING LIKE THEY WERE BACK IN THE MUD.
I RECKON IT'S LIKE MY GRANDDADDY ALWAYS SAID:

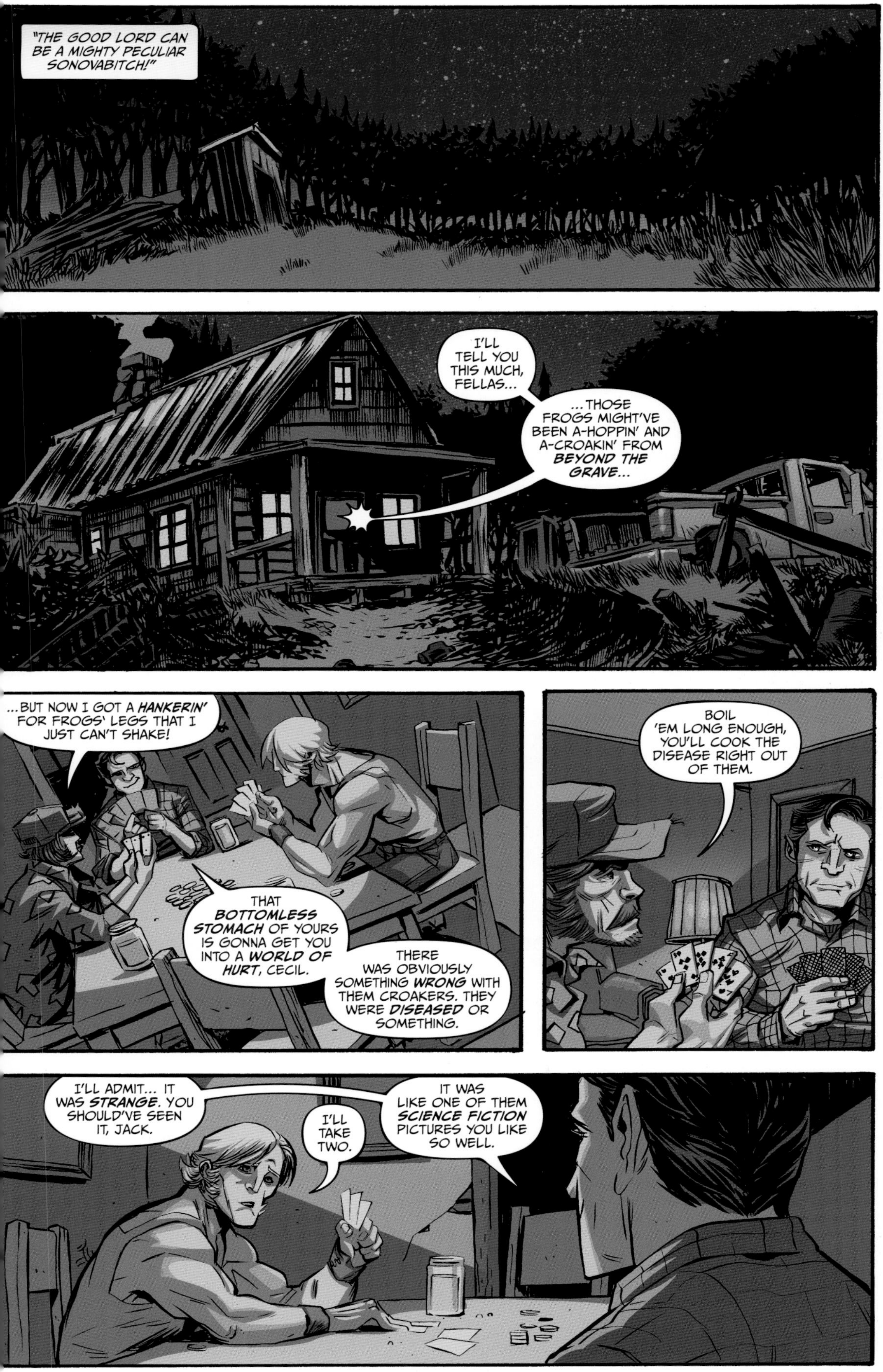
"THE GOOD LORD CAN BE A MIGHTY PECULIAR SONOVABITCH!"
I'LL TELL YOU THIS MUCH, FELLAS...
...THOSE FROGS MIGHT'VE BEEN A-HOPPIN' AND A-CROAKIN' FROM BEYOND THE GRAVE...
...BUT NOW I GOT A HANKERIN' FOR FROGS' LEGS THAT I JUST CAN'T SHAKE!
THAT BOTTOMLESS STOMACH OF YOURS IS GONNA GET YOU INTO A WORLD OF HURT, CECIL.
THERE WAS OBVIOUSLY SOMETHING WRONG WITH THEM CROAKERS. THEY WERE DISEASED OR SOMETHING.
BOIL 'EM LONG ENOUGH, YOU'LL COOK THE DISEASE RIGHT OUT OF THEM.
I'LL ADMIT... IT WAS STRANGE. YOU SHOULD'VE SEEN IT, JACK.
IT WAS LIKE ONE OF THEM SCIENCE FICTION PICTURES YOU LIKE SO WELL.
I'LL TAKE TWO.

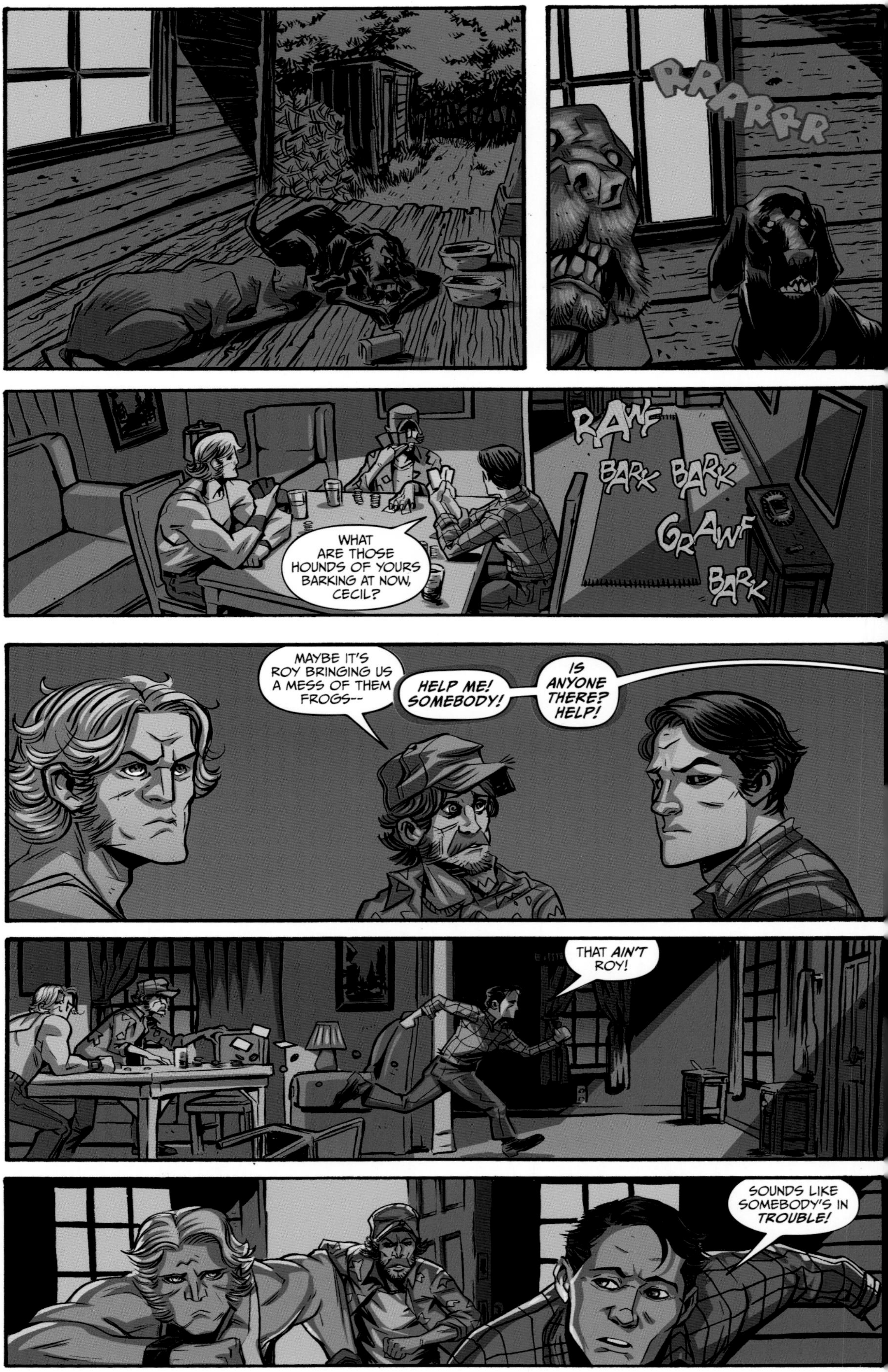
RRRRRRR
RAWF
BARK BARK
GRAWF
BARK
WHAT ARE THOSE HOUNDS OF YOURS BARKING AT NOW, CECIL?
MAYBE IT'S ROY BRINGING US A MESS OF THEM FROGS--
HELP ME! SOMEBODY!
IS ANYONE THERE? HELP!
THAT AIN'T ROY!
SOUNDS LIKE SOMEBODY'S IN TROUBLE!

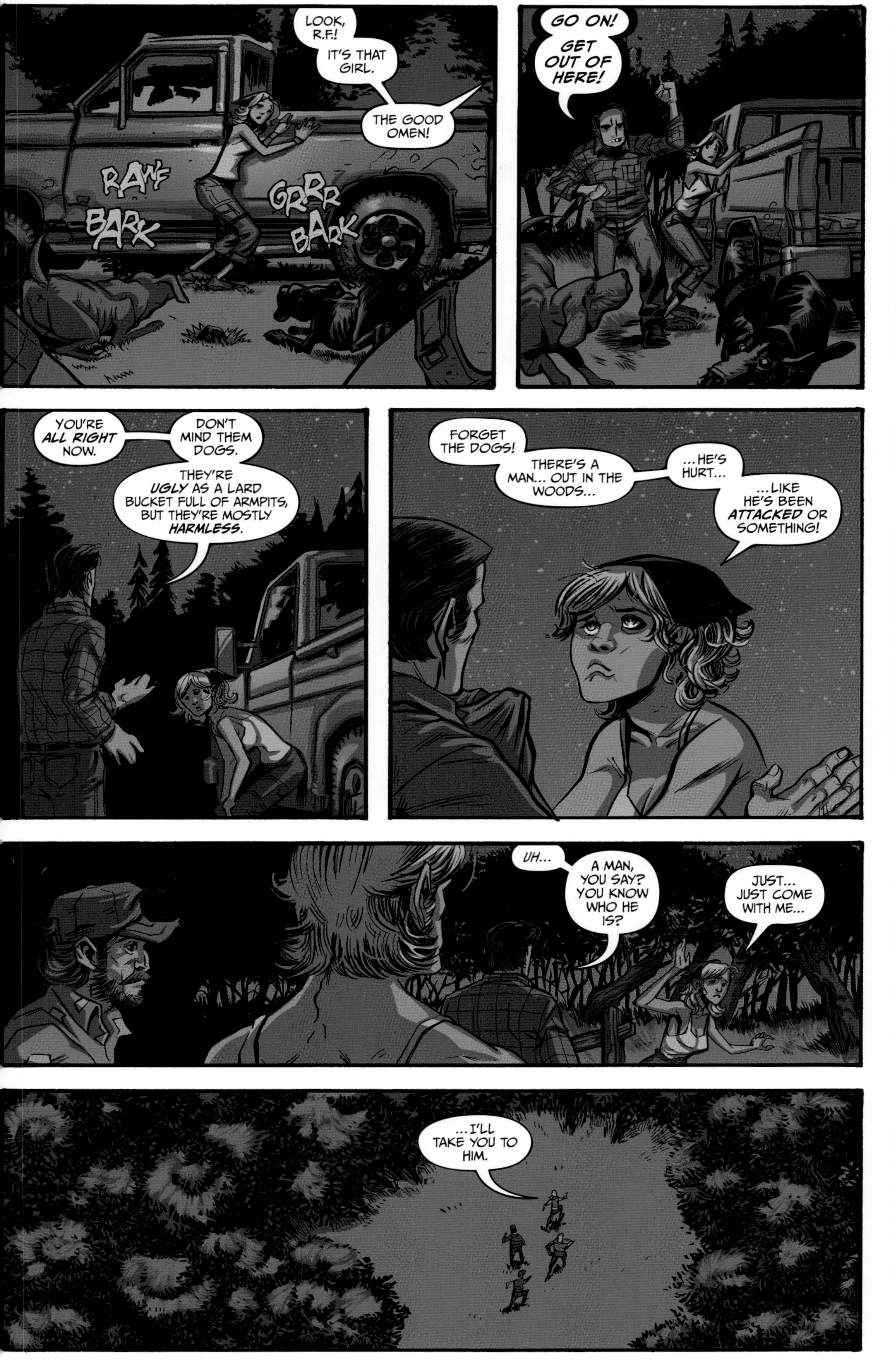
LOOK, R.F.!
IT'S THAT GIRL.
THE GOOD OMEN!
RAWF
BARK
GRRR
BARK
GO ON!
GET OUT OF HERE!
YOU'RE ALL RIGHT NOW.
DON'T MIND THEM DOGS.
THEY'RE UGLY AS A LARD BUCKET FULL OF ARMPITS, BUT THEY'RE MOSTLY HARMLESS.
FORGET THE DOGS!
THERE'S A MAN... OUT IN THE WOODS...
...HE'S HURT...
...LIKE HE'S BEEN ATTACKED OR SOMETHING!
UH...
A MAN, YOU SAY? YOU KNOW WHO HE IS?
JUST... JUST COME WITH ME...
...I'LL TAKE YOU TO HIM.

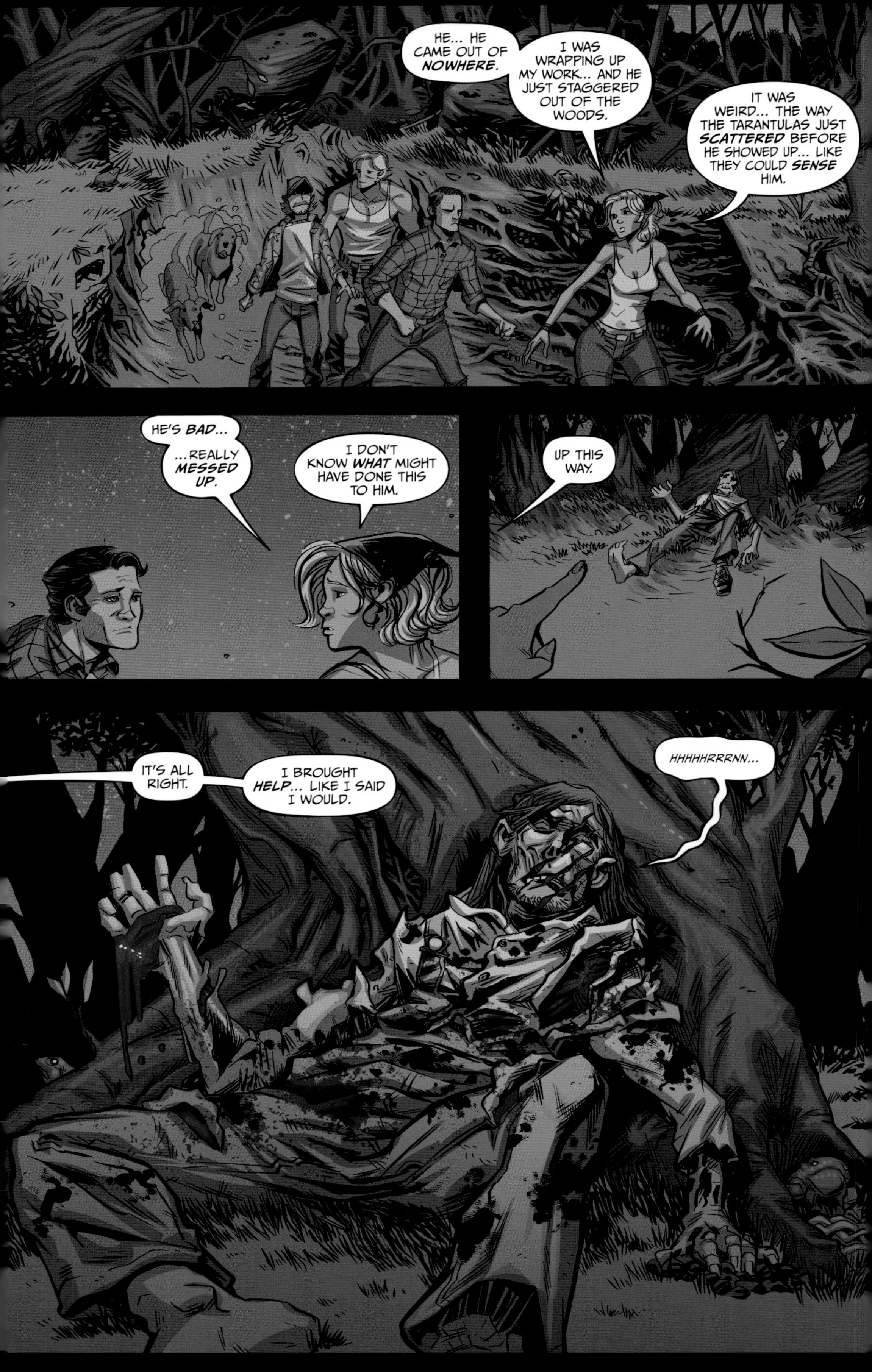
HE... HE CAME OUT OF NOWHERE.
I WAS WRAPPING UP MY WORK... AND HE JUST STAGGERED OUT OF THE WOODS.
IT WAS WEIRD... THE WAY THE TARANTULAS JUST SCATTERED BEFORE HE SHOWED UP... LIKE THEY COULD SENSE HIM.
HE'S BAD...
...REALLY MESSED UP.
I DON'T KNOW WHAT MIGHT HAVE DONE THIS TO HIM.
UP THIS WAY.
IT'S ALL RIGHT.
I BROUGHT HELP... LIKE I SAID I WOULD.
HHHHHHRRRNN...

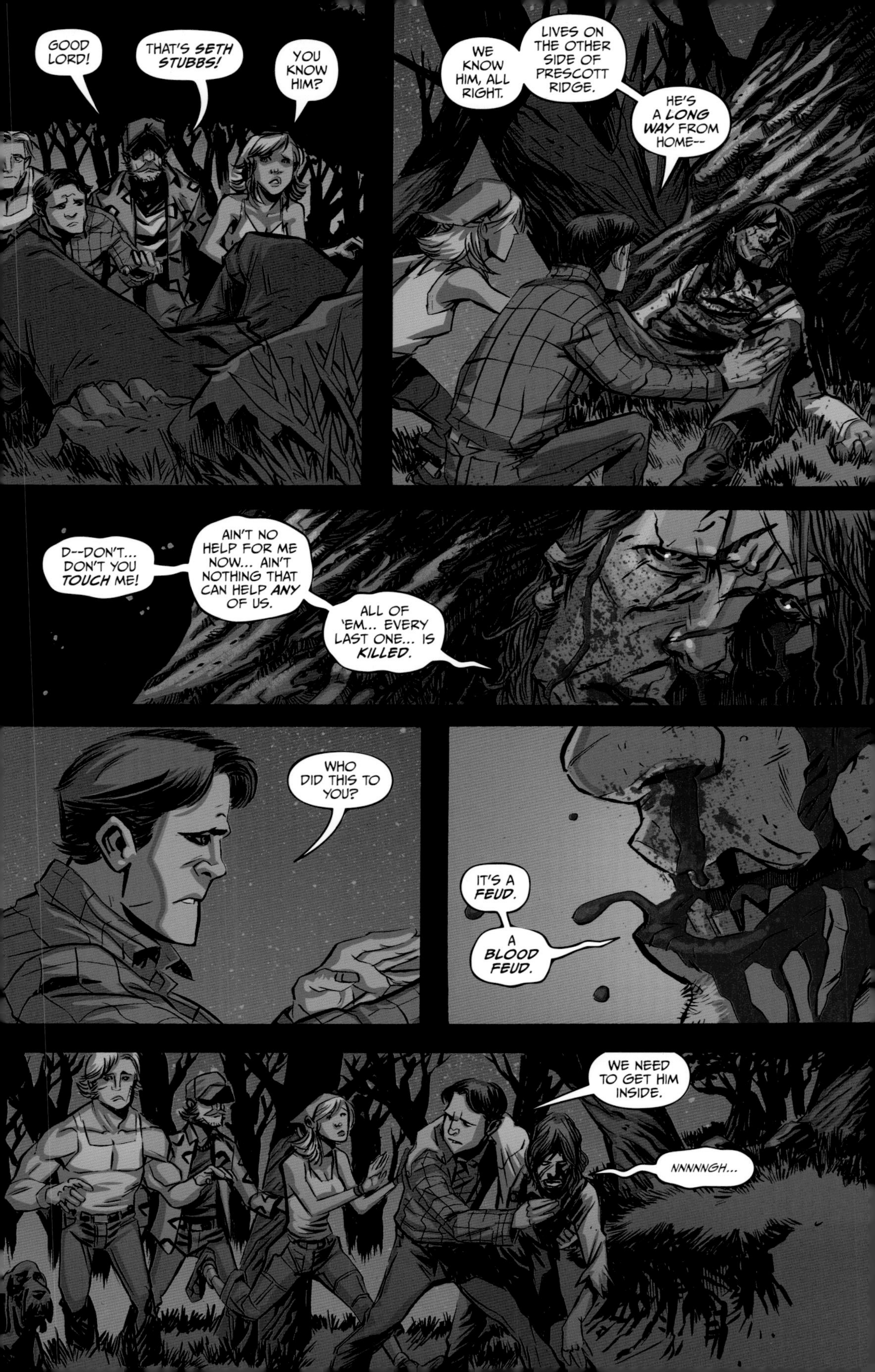
GOOD LORD!
THAT'S SETH STUBBS!
YOU KNOW HIM?
WE KNOW HIM, ALL RIGHT.
LIVES ON THE OTHER SIDE OF PRESCOTT RIDGE.
HE'S A LONG WAY FROM HOME--
D--DON'T... DON'T YOU TOUCH ME!
AIN'T NO HELP FOR ME NOW... AIN'T NOTHING THAT CAN HELP ANY OF US.
ALL OF 'EM... EVERY LAST ONE... IS KILLED.
WHO DID THIS TO YOU?
IT'S A FEUD.
A BLOOD FEUD.
WE NEED TO GET HIM INSIDE.
NNNNNGH...

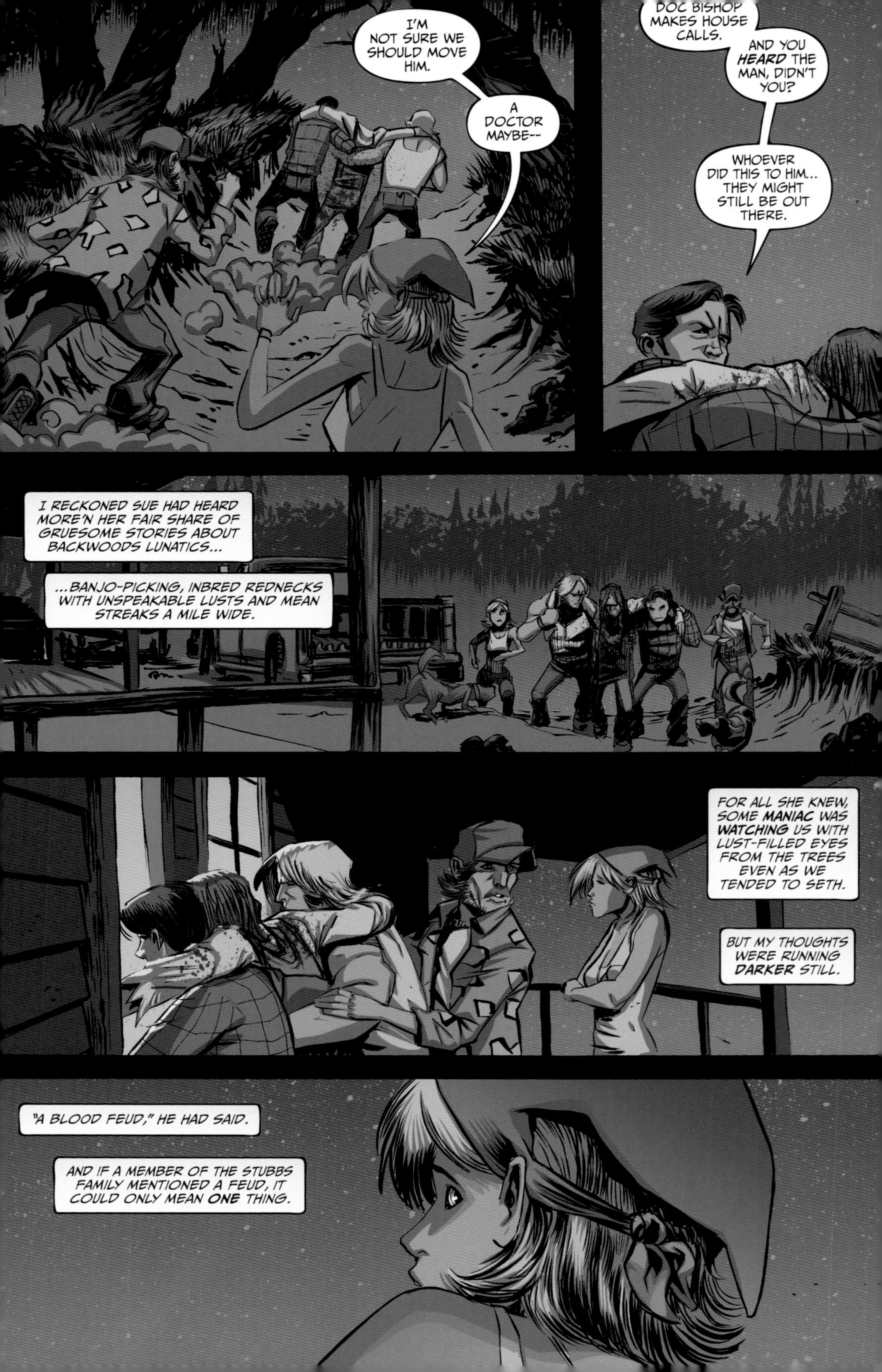

I'M NOT SURE WE SHOULD MOVE HIM.
A DOCTOR MAYBE--
DOC BISHOP MAKES HOUSE CALLS.
AND YOU HEARD THE MAN, DIDN'T YOU?
WHOEVER DID THIS TO HIM.. THEY MIGHT STILL BE OUT THERE.
I RECKONED SUE HAD HEARD MORE'N HER FAIR SHARE OF GRUESOME STORIES ABOUT BACKWOODS LUNATICS...
...BANJO-PICKING, INBRED REDNECKS WITH UNSPEAKABLE LUSTS AND MEAN STREAKS A MILE WIDE.
FOR ALL SHE KNEW, SOME MANIAC WAS WATCHING US WITH LUST-FILLED EYES FROM THE TREES EVEN AS WE TENDED TO SETH.
BUT MY THOUGHTS WERE RUNNING DARKER STILL.
"A BLOOD FEUD," HE HAD SAID.
AND IF A MEMBER OF THE STUBBS FAMILY MENTIONED A FEUD, IT COULD ONLY MEAN ONE THING.

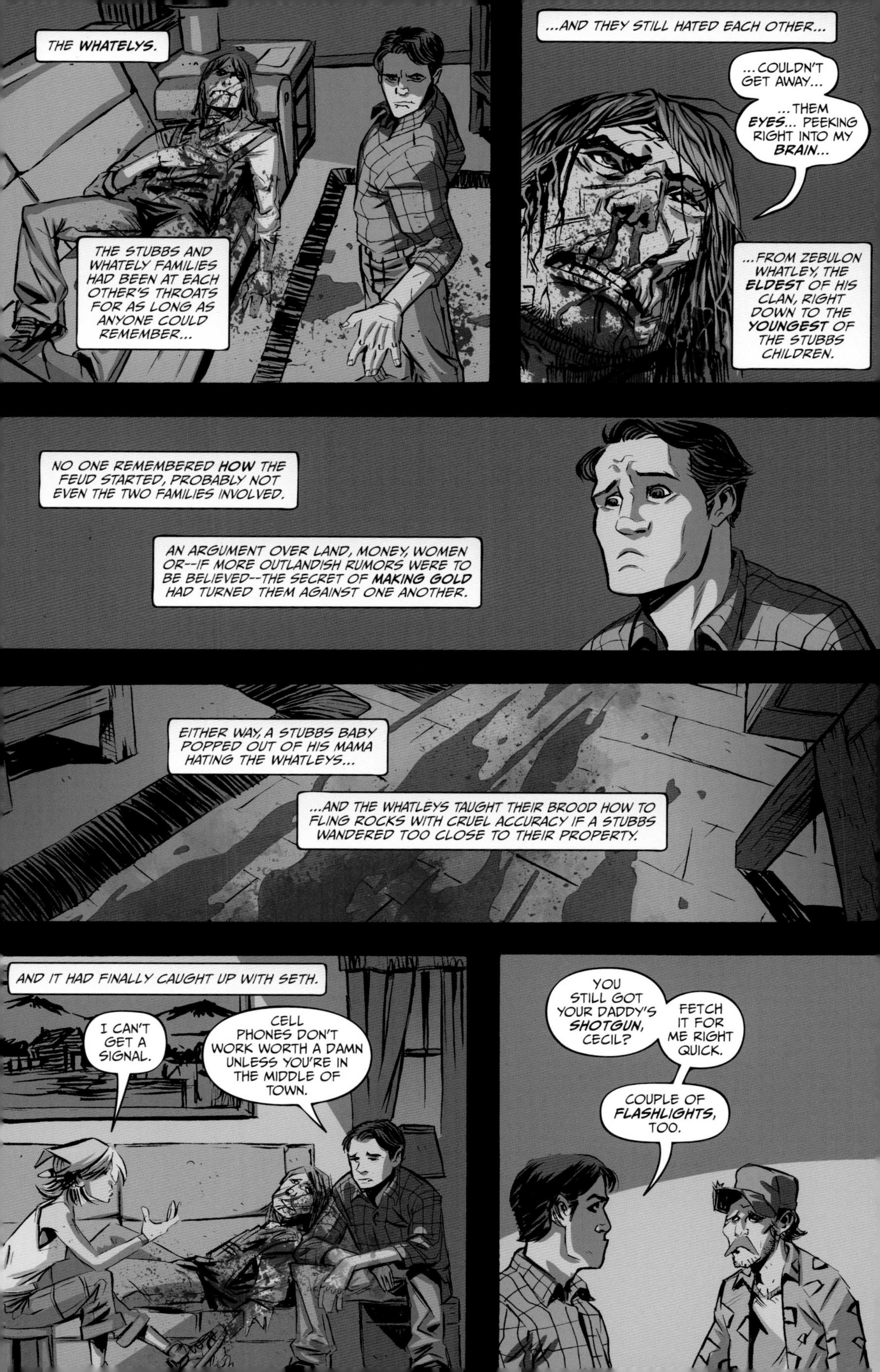
THE WHATELYS.
THE STUBBS AND WHATELY FAMILIES HAD BEEN AT EACH OTHER'S THROATS FOR AS LONG AS ANYONE COULD REMEMBER...
...AND THEY STILL HATED EACH OTHER...
...COULDN'T GET AWAY...
...THEM EYES... PEEKING RIGHT INTO MY BRAIN...
...FROM ZEBULON WHATLEY, THE ELDEST OF HIS CLAN, RIGHT DOWN TO THE YOUNGEST OF THE STUBBS CHILDREN.
NO ONE REMEMBERED HOW THE FEUD STARTED, PROBABLY NOT EVEN THE TWO FAMILIES INVOLVED.
AN ARGUMENT OVER LAND, MONEY, WOMEN OR--IF MORE OUTLANDISH RUMORS WERE TO BE BELIEVED--THE SECRET OF MAKING GOLD HAD TURNED THEM AGAINST ONE ANOTHER.
EITHER WAY, A STUBBS BABY POPPED OUT OF HIS MAMA HATING THE WHATLEYS...
...AND THE WHATLEYS TAUGHT THEIR BROOD HOW TO FLING ROCKS WITH CRUEL ACCURACY IF A STUBBS WANDERED TOO CLOSE TO THEIR PROPERTY.
AND IT HAD FINALLY CAUGHT UP WITH SETH.
I CAN'T GET A SIGNAL.
CELL PHONES DON'T WORK WORTH A DAMN UNLESS YOU'RE IN THE MIDDLE OF TOWN.
YOU STILL GOT YOUR DADDY'S SHOTGUN, CECIL?
FETCH IT FOR ME RIGHT QUICK.
COUPLE OF FLASHLIGHTS, TOO.

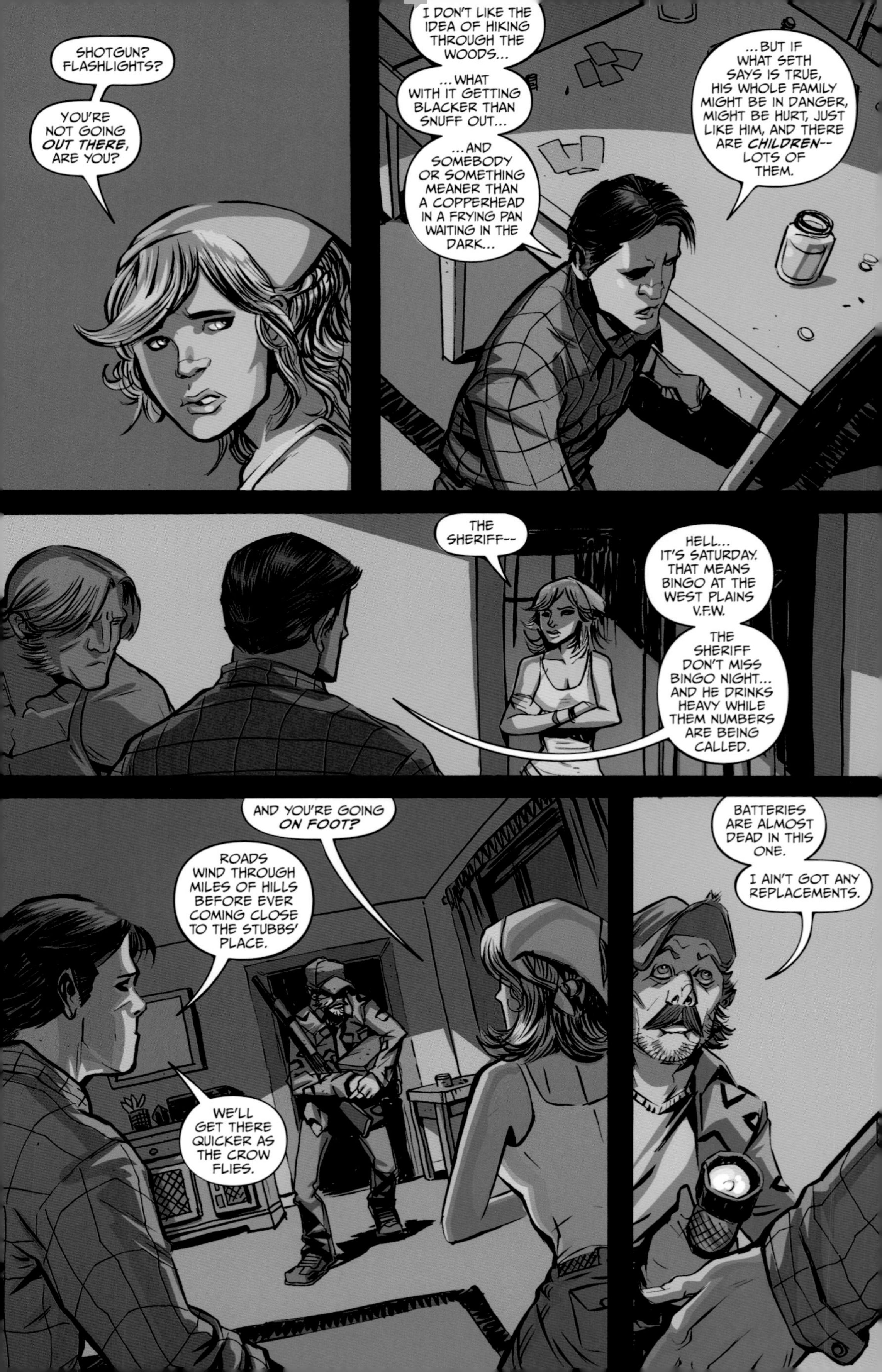

SHOTGUN? FLASHLIGHTS?
YOU'RE NOT GOING *OUT THERE*, ARE YOU?
I DON'T LIKE THE IDEA OF HIKING THROUGH THE WOODS...
...WHAT WITH IT GETTING BLACKER THAN SNUFF OUT...
...AND SOMEBODY OR SOMETHING MEANER THAN A COPPERHEAD IN A FRYING PAN WAITING IN THE DARK...
...BUT IF WHAT SETH SAYS IS TRUE, HIS WHOLE FAMILY MIGHT BE IN DANGER, MIGHT BE HURT, JUST LIKE HIM, AND THERE ARE *CHILDREN*-- LOTS OF THEM.
THE SHERIFF--
HELL... IT'S SATURDAY. THAT MEANS BINGO AT THE WEST PLAINS V.F.W.
THE SHERIFF DON'T MISS BINGO NIGHT... AND HE DRINKS HEAVY WHILE THEM NUMBERS ARE BEING CALLED.
AND YOU'RE GOING *ON FOOT?*
ROADS WIND THROUGH MILES OF HILLS BEFORE EVER COMING CLOSE TO THE STUBBS' PLACE.
WE'LL GET THERE QUICKER AS THE CROW FLIES.
BATTERIES ARE ALMOST DEAD IN THIS ONE.
I AIN'T GOT ANY REPLACEMENTS.

YOU OUGHT TO TAKE THIS, TOO.

THAT WHAT I THINK IT IS?

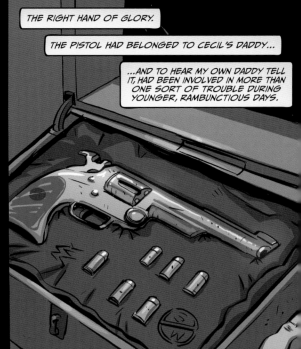

THE RIGHT HAND OF GLORY.

THE PISTOL HAD BELONGED TO CECIL'S DADDY...

...AND TO HEAR MY OWN DADDY TELL IT, HAD BEEN INVOLVED IN MORE THAN ONE SORT OF TROUBLE DURING YOUNGER, RAMBUNCTIOUS DAYS.

JACK AND ME WILL BE BACK AS SOON AS WE CAN.

IN THE MEANTIME, TEND TO SETH AS BEST YOU CAN.

CECIL, YOU GET THE DOC OUT HERE RIGHT QUICK.

AND YOU MIGHT AS WELL TRY TO RAISE THE SHERIFF, TOO, FOR ALL THE GOOD IT WILL DO YOU.

SIT TIGHT.

IF ALL'S WELL, WE'LL BRING SOME OF SETH'S FOLKS BACK WITH US.

CHANCES ARE DOC BISHOP WILL BE HERE AND HAVE EVERYTHING UNDER CONTROL BY THE TIME WE GET BACK.

LOOKS LIKE WE'RE THE CAVALRY.

WELL... WHAT ELSE IS NEW?

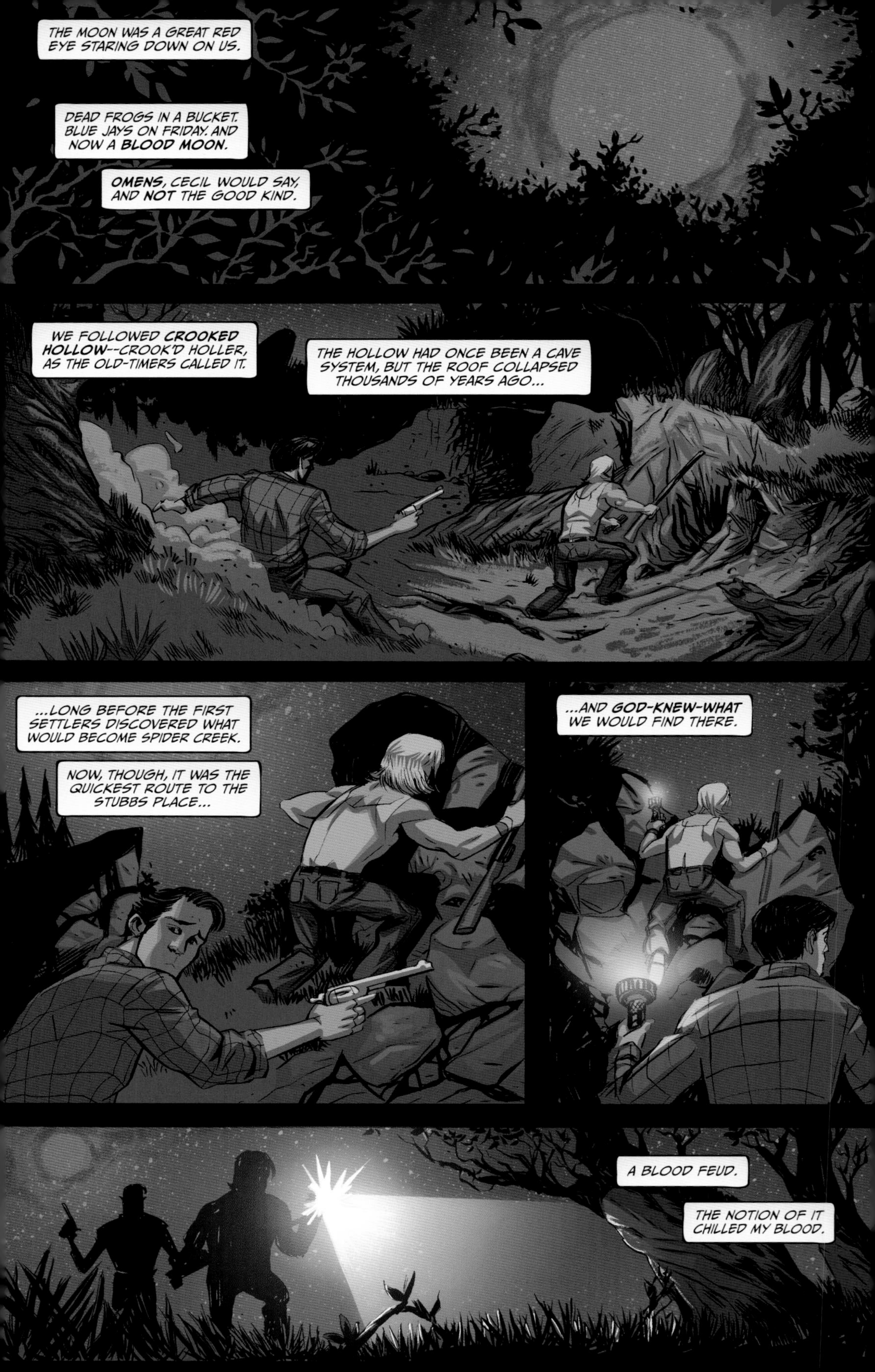
THE MOON WAS A GREAT RED EYE STARING DOWN ON US.
DEAD FROGS IN A BUCKET. BLUE JAYS ON FRIDAY. AND NOW A **BLOOD MOON**.
OMENS, CECIL WOULD SAY, AND **NOT** THE GOOD KIND.
WE FOLLOWED **CROOKED HOLLOW**--CROOK'D HOLLER, AS THE OLD-TIMERS CALLED IT.
THE HOLLOW HAD ONCE BEEN A CAVE SYSTEM, BUT THE ROOF COLLAPSED THOUSANDS OF YEARS AGO...
...LONG BEFORE THE FIRST SETTLERS DISCOVERED WHAT WOULD BECOME SPIDER CREEK.
NOW, THOUGH, IT WAS THE QUICKEST ROUTE TO THE STUBBS PLACE...
...AND **GOD-KNEW-WHAT** WE WOULD FIND THERE.
A BLOOD FEUD.
THE NOTION OF IT CHILLED MY BLOOD.

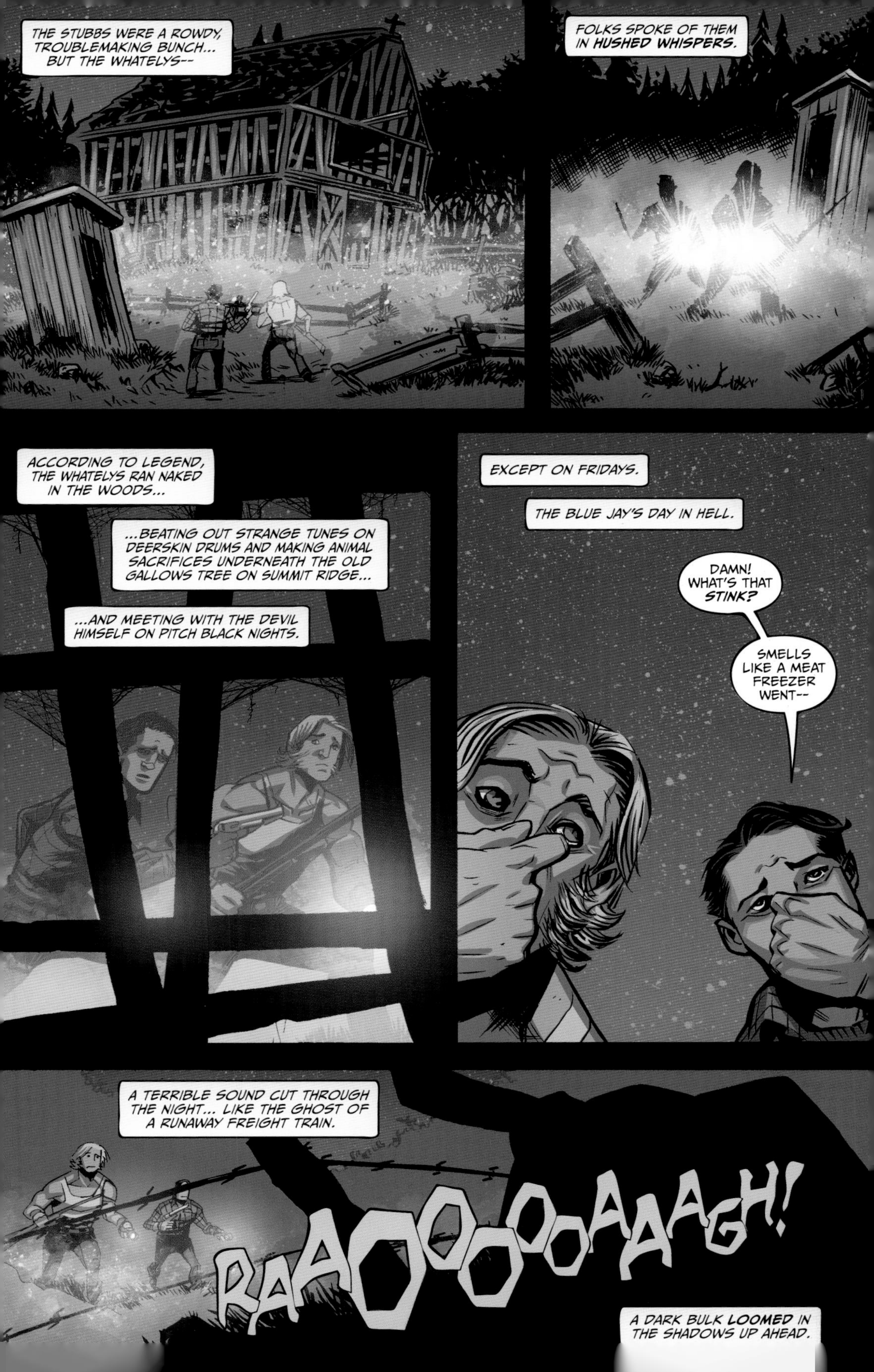
THE STUBBS WERE A ROWDY, TROUBLEMAKING BUNCH... BUT THE WHATELYS--
FOLKS SPOKE OF THEM IN HUSHED WHISPERS.
ACCORDING TO LEGEND, THE WHATELYS RAN NAKED IN THE WOODS...
...BEATING OUT STRANGE TUNES ON DEERSKIN DRUMS AND MAKING ANIMAL SACRIFICES UNDERNEATH THE OLD GALLOWS TREE ON SUMMIT RIDGE...
...AND MEETING WITH THE DEVIL HIMSELF ON PITCH BLACK NIGHTS.
EXCEPT ON FRIDAYS.
THE BLUE JAY'S DAY IN HELL.
DAMN! WHAT'S THAT STINK?
SMELLS LIKE A MEAT FREEZER WENT--
A TERRIBLE SOUND CUT THROUGH THE NIGHT... LIKE THE GHOST OF A RUNAWAY FREIGHT TRAIN.
RAAOOOOOAAAGH!
A DARK BULK LOOMED IN THE SHADOWS UP AHEAD.

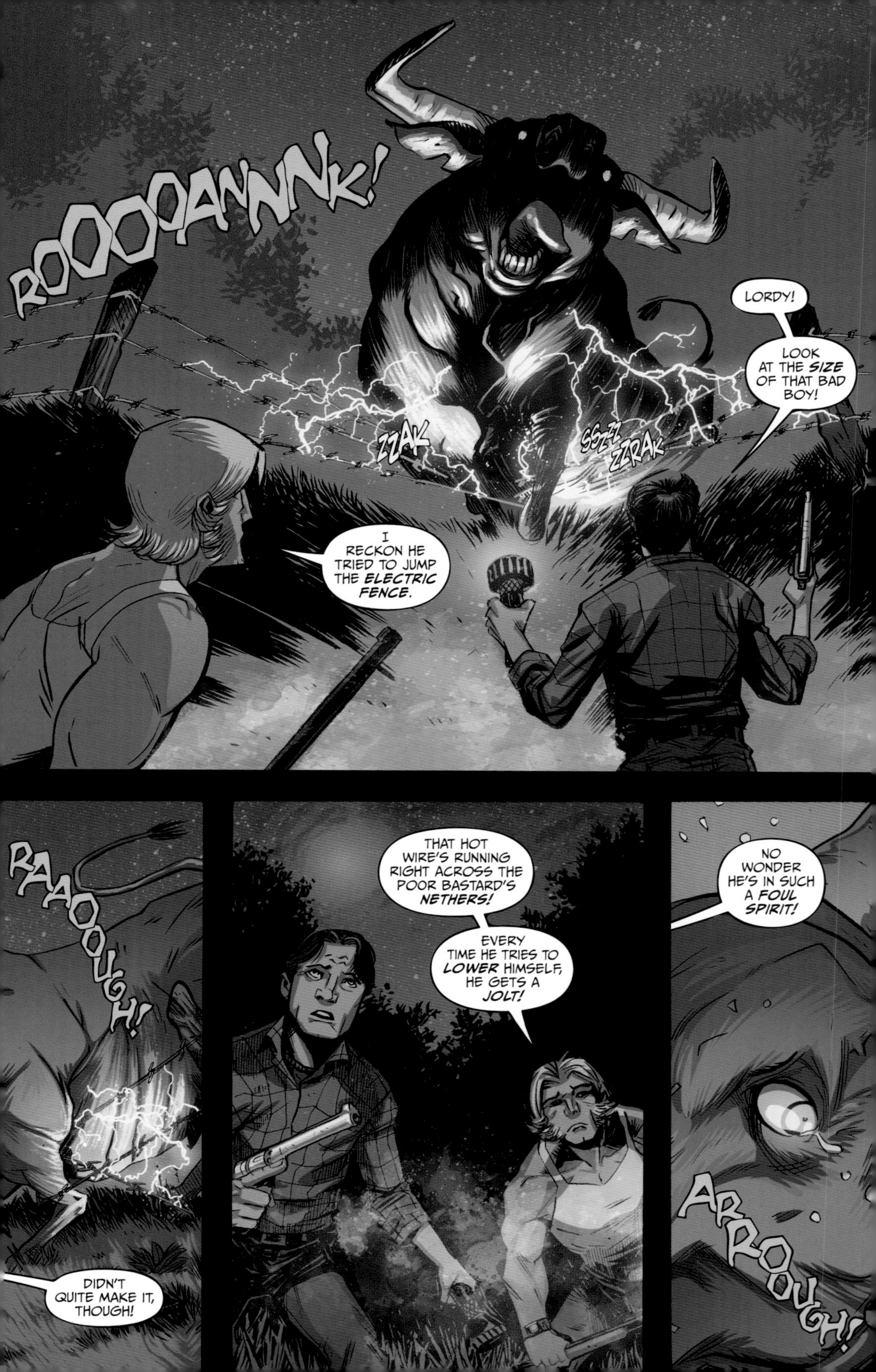
ROOOOANNNK!
LORDY!
LOOK AT THE SIZE OF THAT BAD BOY!
ZZAK
SSZZZ ZZRAK
I RECKON HE TRIED TO JUMP THE ELECTRIC FENCE.
RAAOOUGH!
DIDN'T QUITE MAKE IT, THOUGH!
THAT HOT WIRE'S RUNNING RIGHT ACROSS THE POOR BASTARD'S NETHERS!
EVERY TIME HE TRIES TO LOWER HIMSELF, HE GETS A JOLT!
NO WONDER HE'S IN SUCH A FOUL SPIRIT!
ARROUGH!

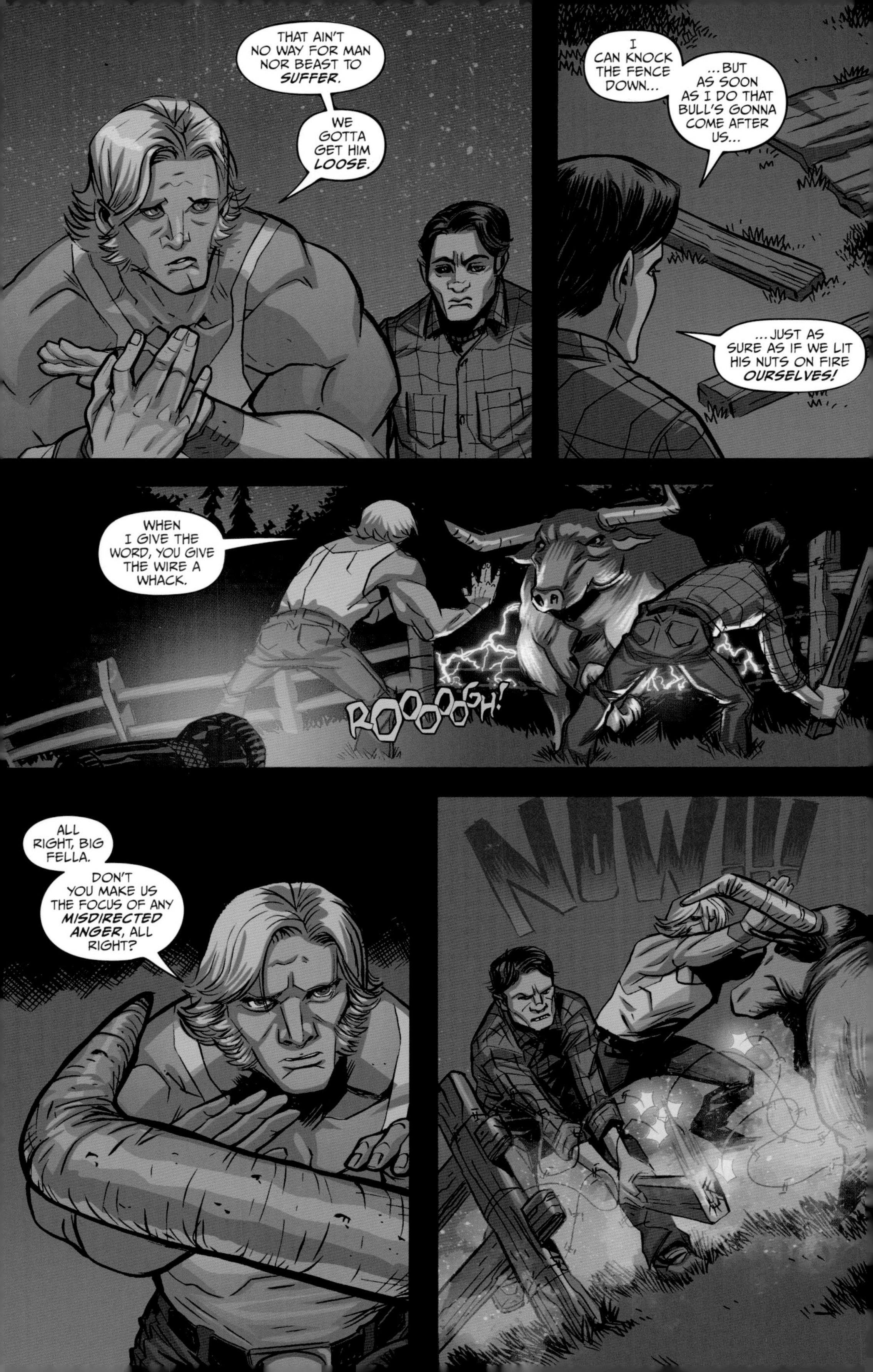
THAT AIN'T NO WAY FOR MAN NOR BEAST TO SUFFER.
WE GOTTA GET HIM LOOSE.
I CAN KNOCK THE FENCE DOWN...
...BUT AS SOON AS I DO THAT BULL'S GONNA COME AFTER US...
...JUST AS SURE AS IF WE LIT HIS NUTS ON FIRE OURSELVES!
WHEN I GIVE THE WORD, YOU GIVE THE WIRE A WHACK.
ROOOOOGH!
ALL RIGHT, BIG FELLA.
DON'T YOU MAKE US THE FOCUS OF ANY MISDIRECTED ANGER, ALL RIGHT?
NOW!!!

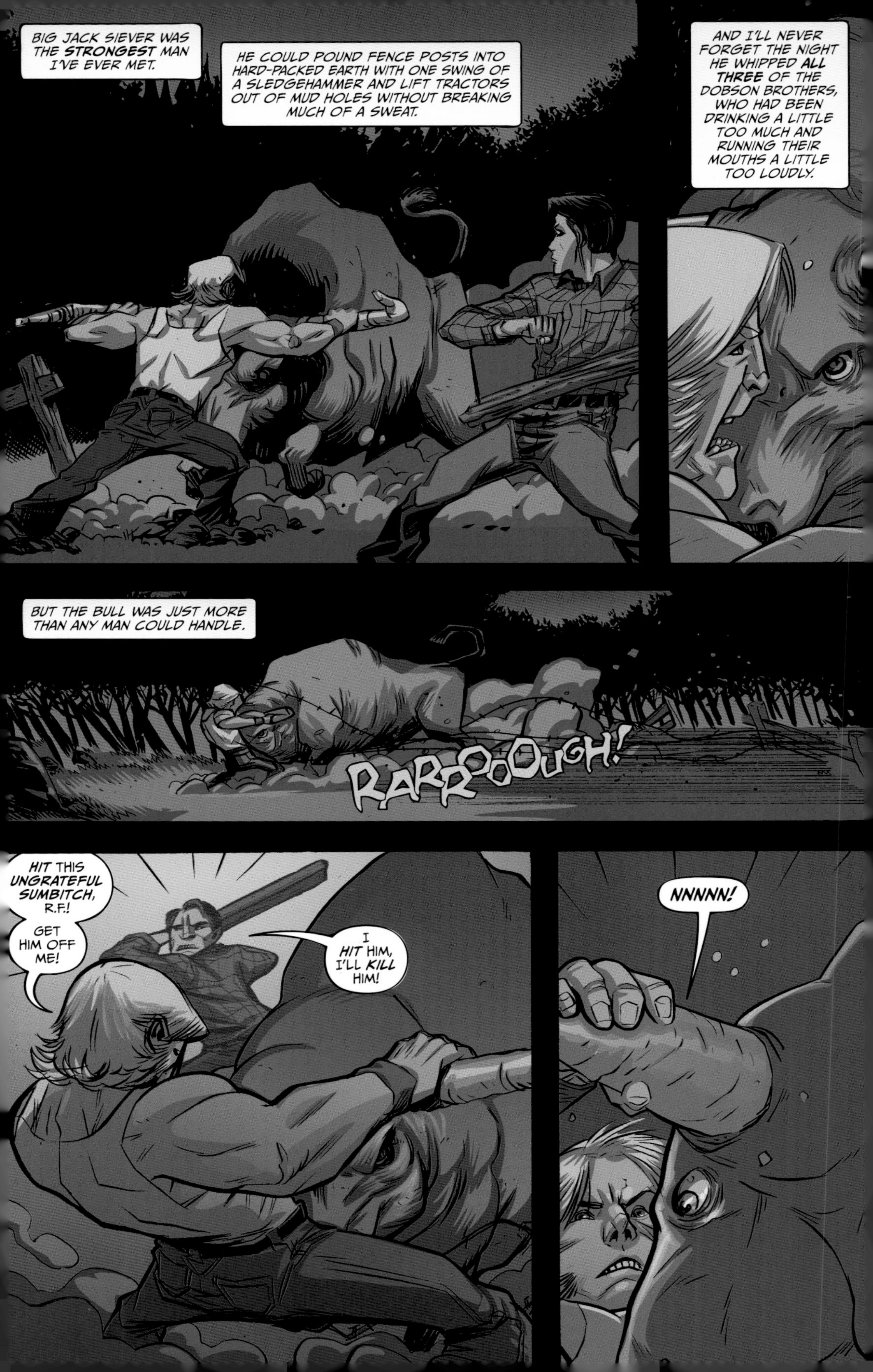
BIG JACK SIEVER WAS THE STRONGEST MAN I'VE EVER MET.
HE COULD POUND FENCE POSTS INTO HARD-PACKED EARTH WITH ONE SWING OF A SLEDGEHAMMER AND LIFT TRACTORS OUT OF MUD HOLES WITHOUT BREAKING MUCH OF A SWEAT.
AND I'LL NEVER FORGET THE NIGHT HE WHIPPED ALL THREE OF THE DOBSON BROTHERS, WHO HAD BEEN DRINKING A LITTLE TOO MUCH AND RUNNING THEIR MOUTHS A LITTLE TOO LOUDLY.
BUT THE BULL WAS JUST MORE THAN ANY MAN COULD HANDLE.
RARROOOUGH!
HIT THIS UNGRATEFUL SUMBITCH, R.F.!
GET HIM OFF ME!
I HIT HIM, I'LL KILL HIM!
NNNNN!

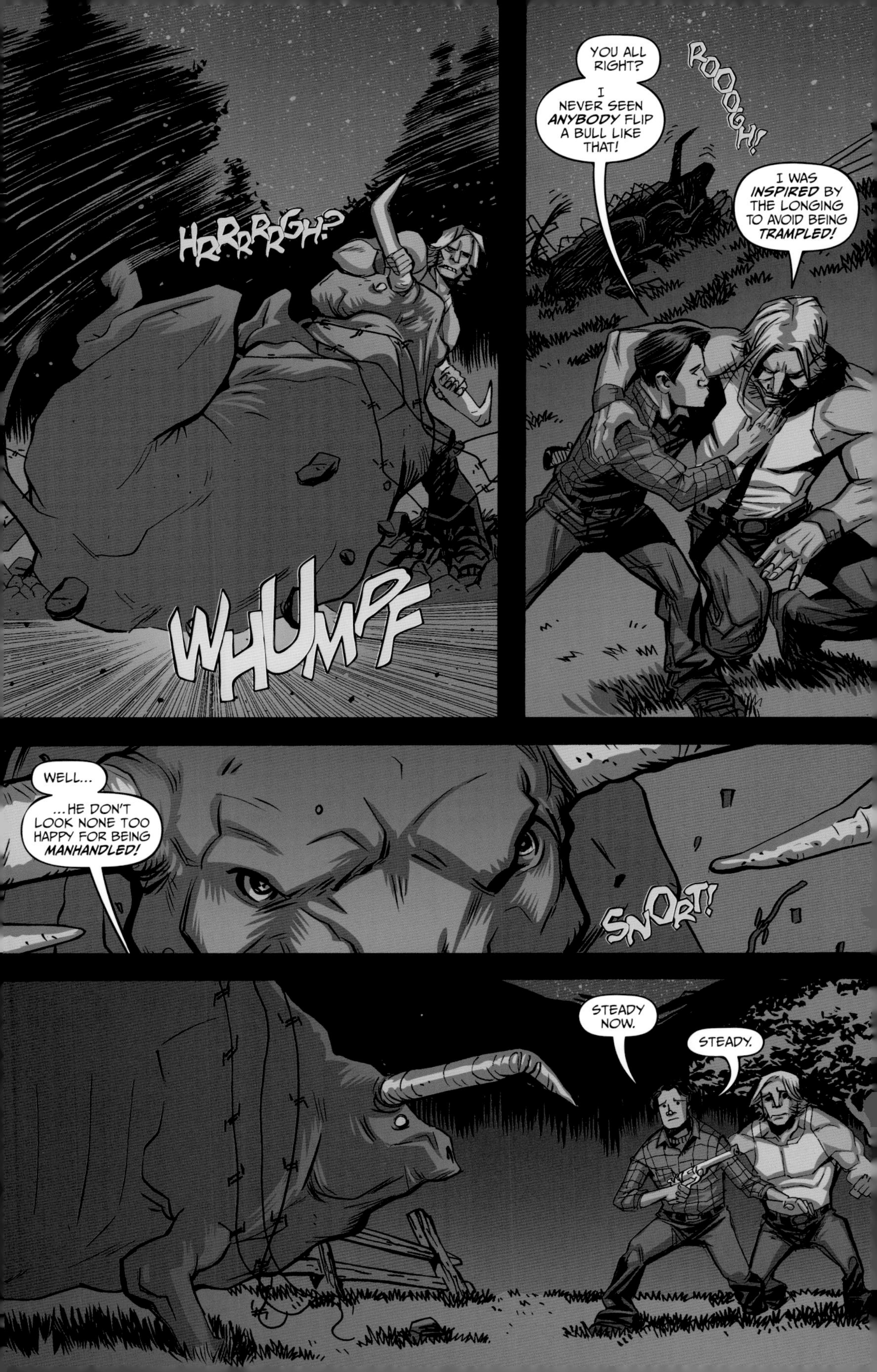
HRRRRGH?
WHUMPF
YOU ALL RIGHT?
I NEVER SEEN ANYBODY FLIP A BULL LIKE THAT!
ROOOGH!
I WAS INSPIRED BY THE LONGING TO AVOID BEING TRAMPLED!
WELL...
...HE DON'T LOOK NONE TOO HAPPY FOR BEING MANHANDLED!
SNORT!
STEADY NOW.
STEADY.

STEADY.

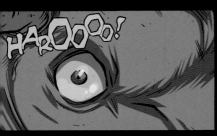

HARoOOOo!

WOULD YA LOOK AT THAT?

I THOUGHT FOR SURE HE WAS GONNA RUN US DOWN.

YOU MUST A SCARED THE HELL OUT OF HIM, THE WAY YOU THREW HIM OVER.

NAW. HE MIGHT'VE BEEN *SCARED*... BUT NOT OF *ME*.

"THERE'S SOMETHING *ELSE* OUT HERE THAT SPOOKED HIM...

"SOMETHING THAT MADE HIM JUMP THAT FENCE IN THE FIRST PLACE."

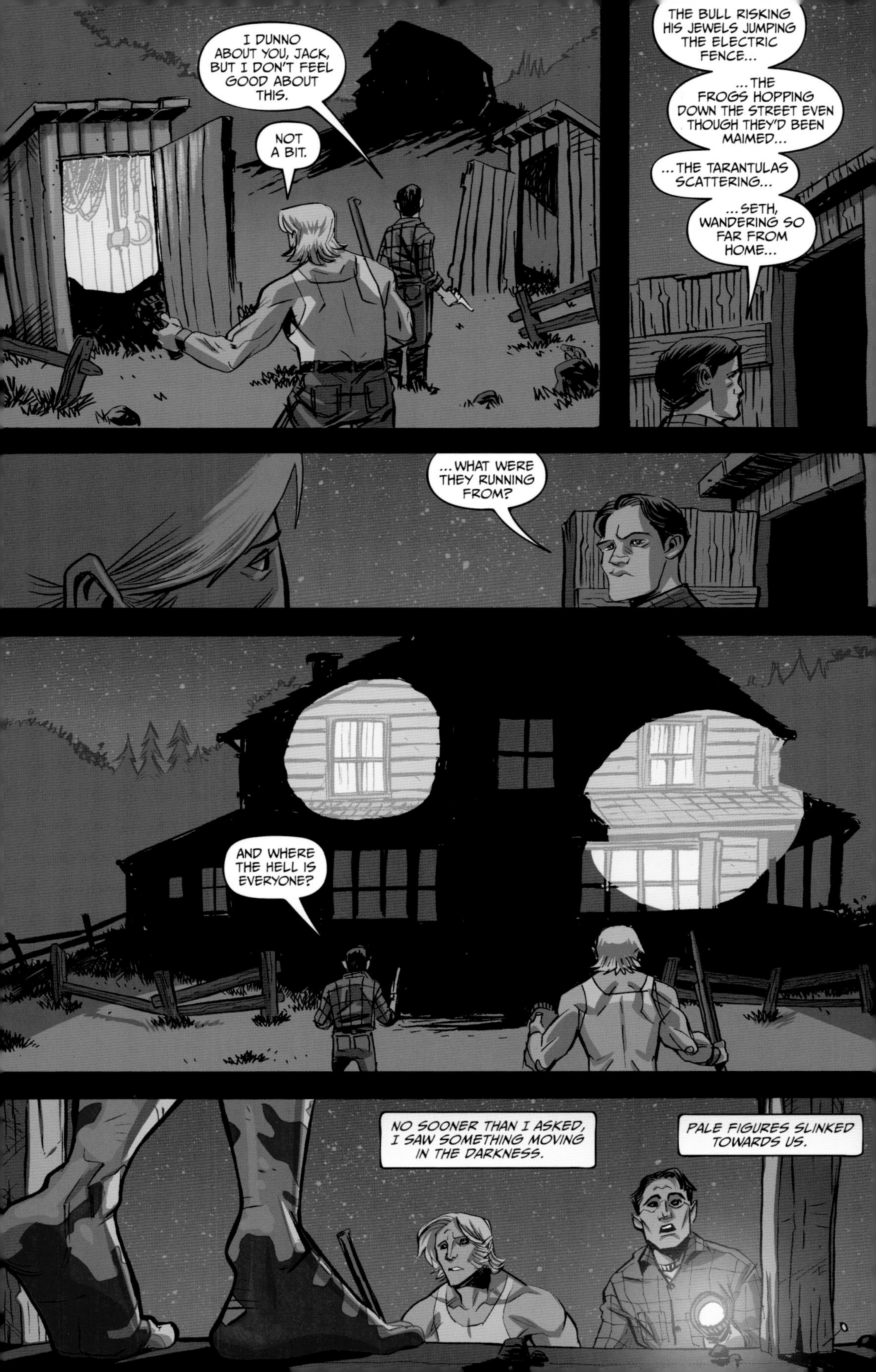
I DUNNO ABOUT YOU, JACK, BUT I DON'T FEEL GOOD ABOUT THIS.
NOT A BIT.
THE BULL RISKING HIS JEWELS JUMPING THE ELECTRIC FENCE...
...THE FROGS HOPPING DOWN THE STREET EVEN THOUGH THEY'D BEEN MAIMED...
...THE TARANTULAS SCATTERING...
...SETH, WANDERING SO FAR FROM HOME...
...WHAT WERE THEY RUNNING FROM?
AND WHERE THE HELL IS EVERYONE?
NO SOONER THAN I ASKED, I SAW SOMETHING MOVING IN THE DARKNESS.
PALE FIGURES SLINKED TOWARDS US.

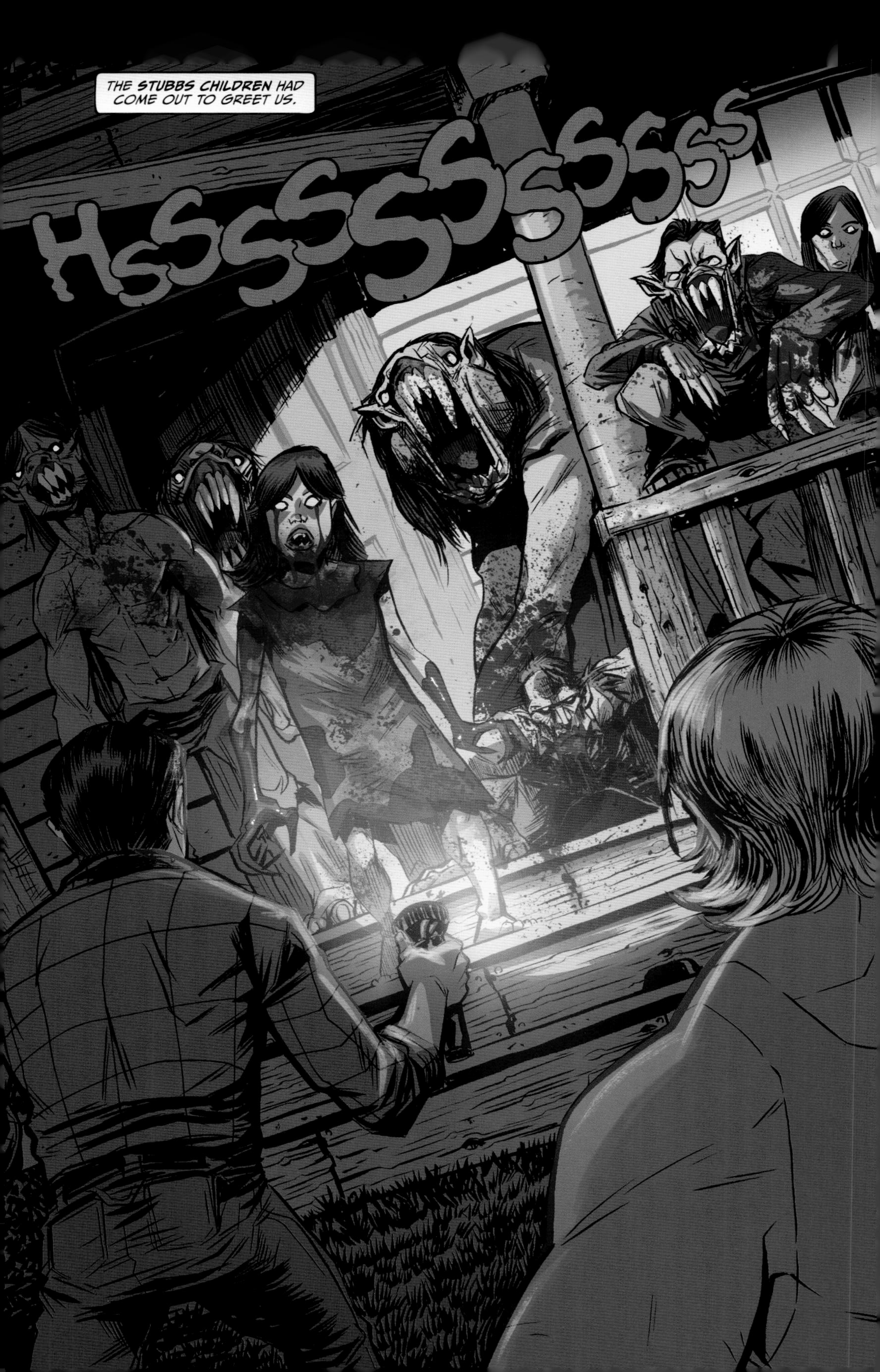
THE STUBBS CHILDREN HAD COME OUT TO GREET US.
HSSSSSSSSSSSS

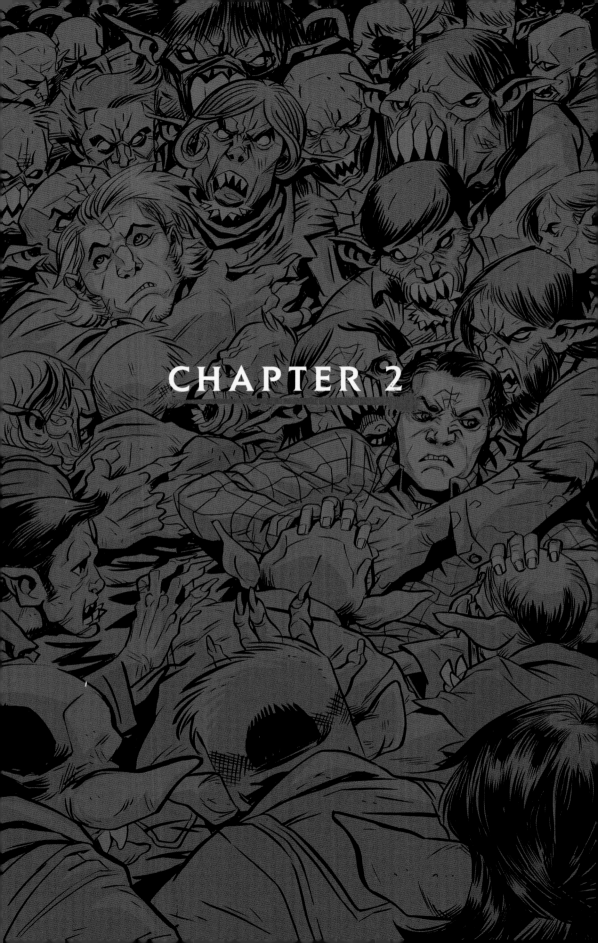

CHAPTER 2

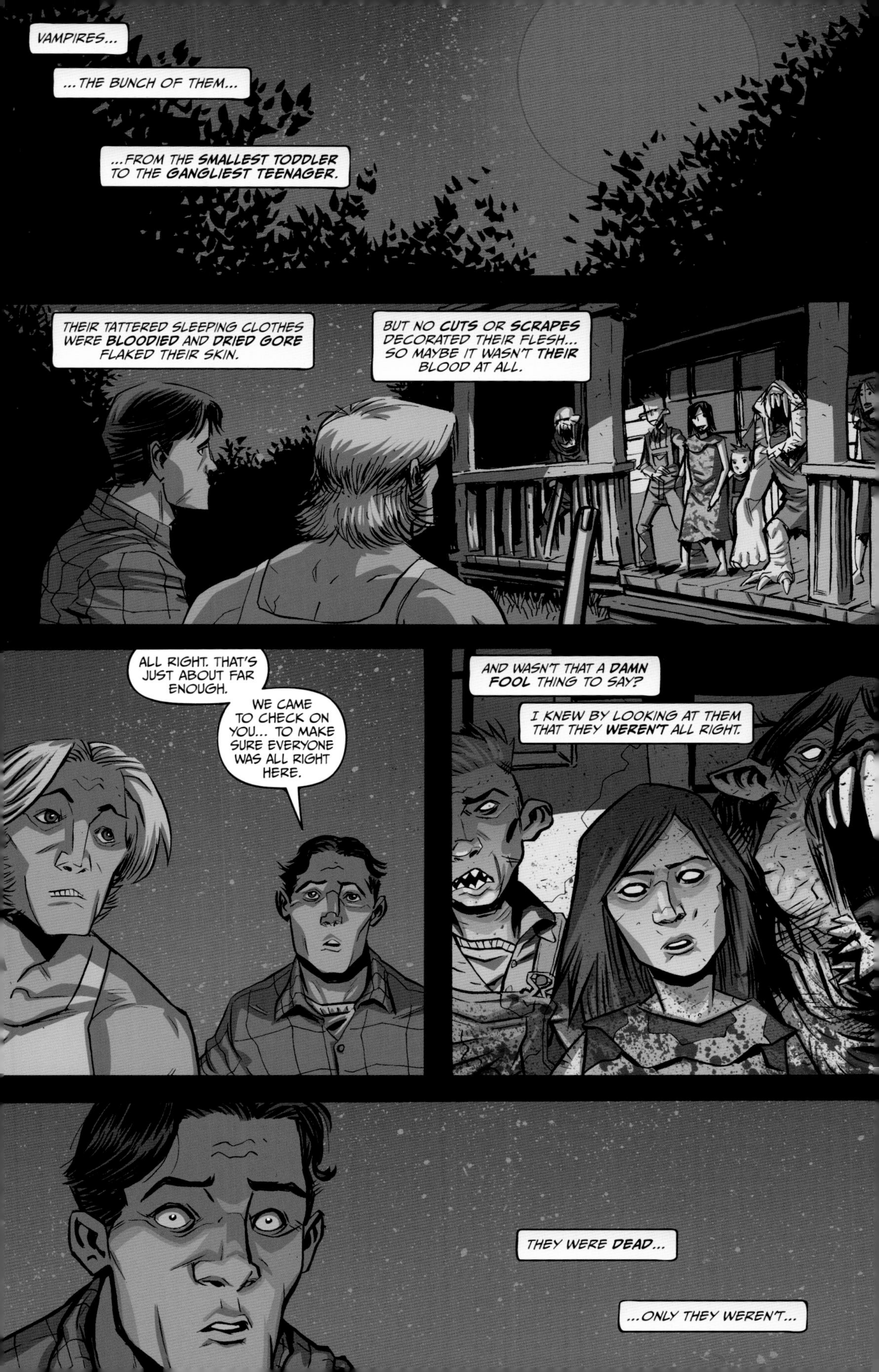
VAMPIRES...
...THE BUNCH OF THEM...
...FROM THE SMALLEST TODDLER TO THE GANGLIEST TEENAGER.
THEIR TATTERED SLEEPING CLOTHES WERE BLOODIED AND DRIED GORE FLAKED THEIR SKIN.
BUT NO CUTS OR SCRAPES DECORATED THEIR FLESH... SO MAYBE IT WASN'T THEIR BLOOD AT ALL.
ALL RIGHT. THAT'S JUST ABOUT FAR ENOUGH.
WE CAME TO CHECK ON YOU... TO MAKE SURE EVERYONE WAS ALL RIGHT HERE.
AND WASN'T THAT A DAMN FOOL THING TO SAY?
I KNEW BY LOOKING AT THEM THAT THEY WEREN'T ALL RIGHT.
THEY WERE DEAD...
...ONLY THEY WEREN'T...

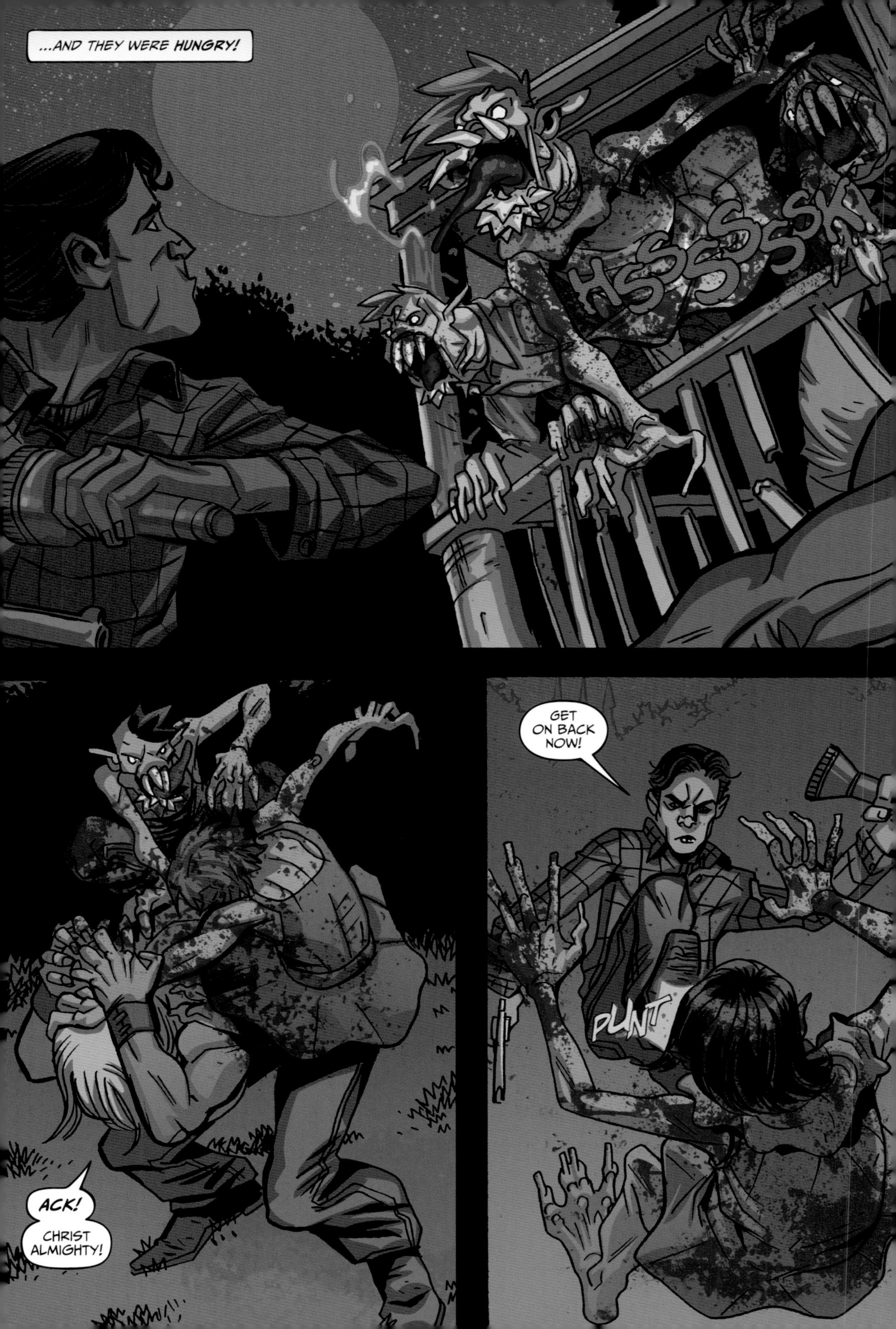
...AND THEY WERE HUNGRY!
HSSSSSK!
ACK!
CHRIST ALMIGHTY!
GET ON BACK NOW!
PUNT

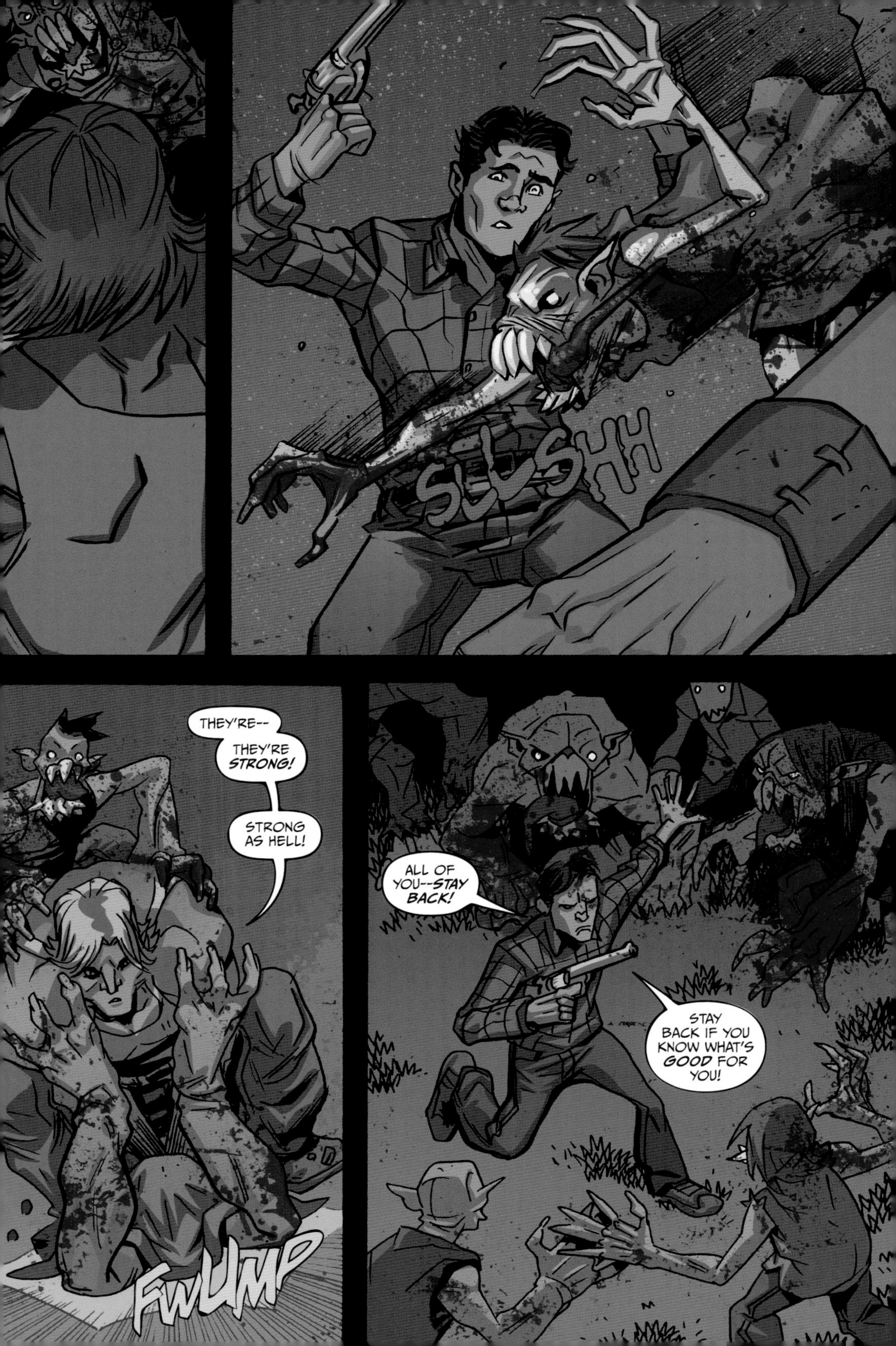
SLUSHH
THEY'RE--
THEY'RE STRONG!
STRONG AS HELL!
FWUMP
ALL OF YOU--STAY BACK!
STAY BACK IF YOU KNOW WHAT'S GOOD FOR YOU!

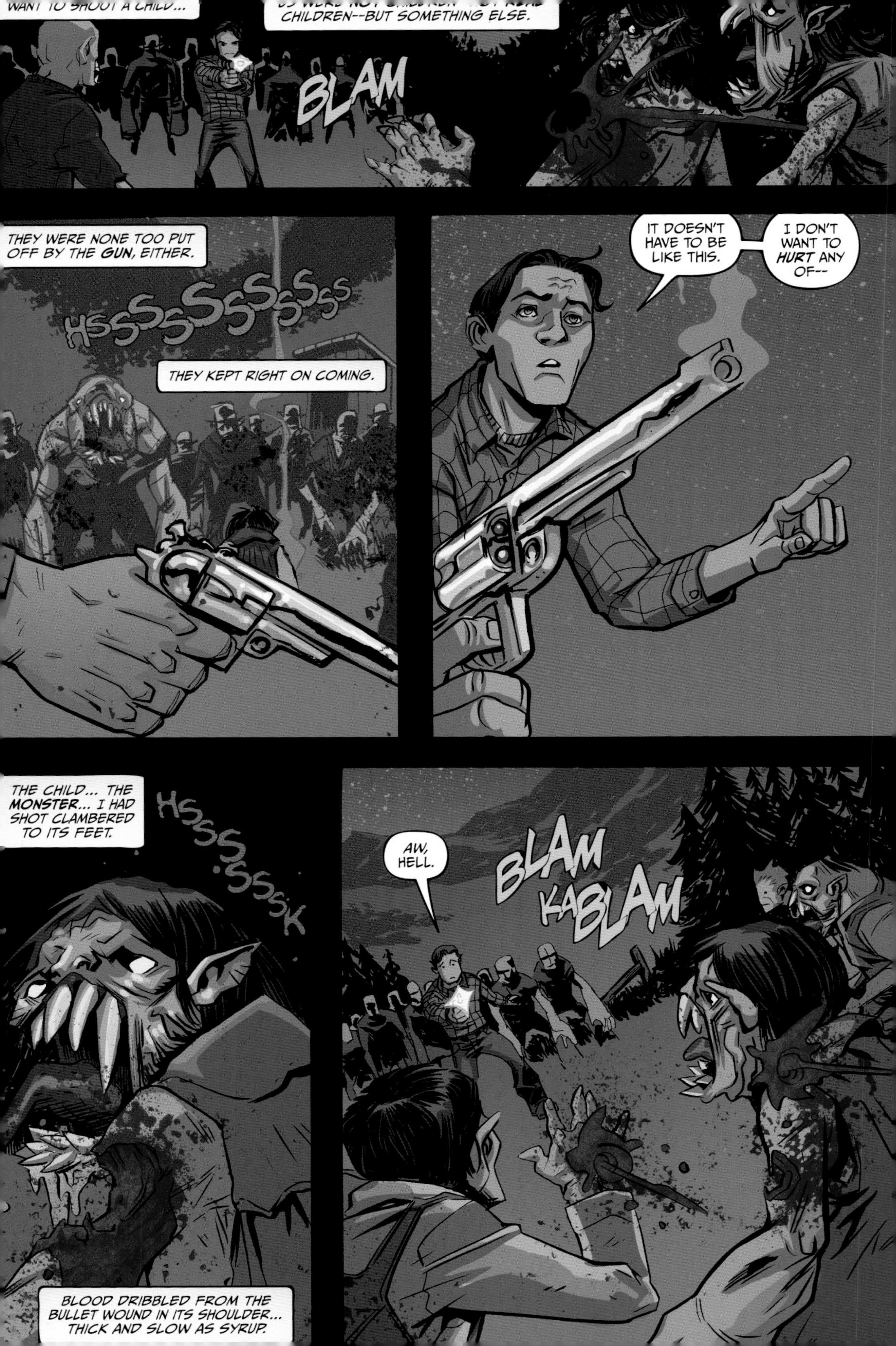
WANT TO SHOOT A CHILD...
CHILDREN--BUT SOMETHING ELSE.
BLAM
THEY WERE NONE TOO PUT OFF BY THE GUN, EITHER.
HSSSSSSSSSSSS
THEY KEPT RIGHT ON COMING.
IT DOESN'T HAVE TO BE LIKE THIS.
I DON'T WANT TO HURT ANY OF--
THE CHILD... THE MONSTER... I HAD SHOT CLAMBERED TO ITS FEET.
HSSSSSSSK
BLOOD DRIBBLED FROM THE BULLET WOUND IN ITS SHOULDER... THICK AND SLOW AS SYRUP.
AW, HELL.
BLAM
KABLAM

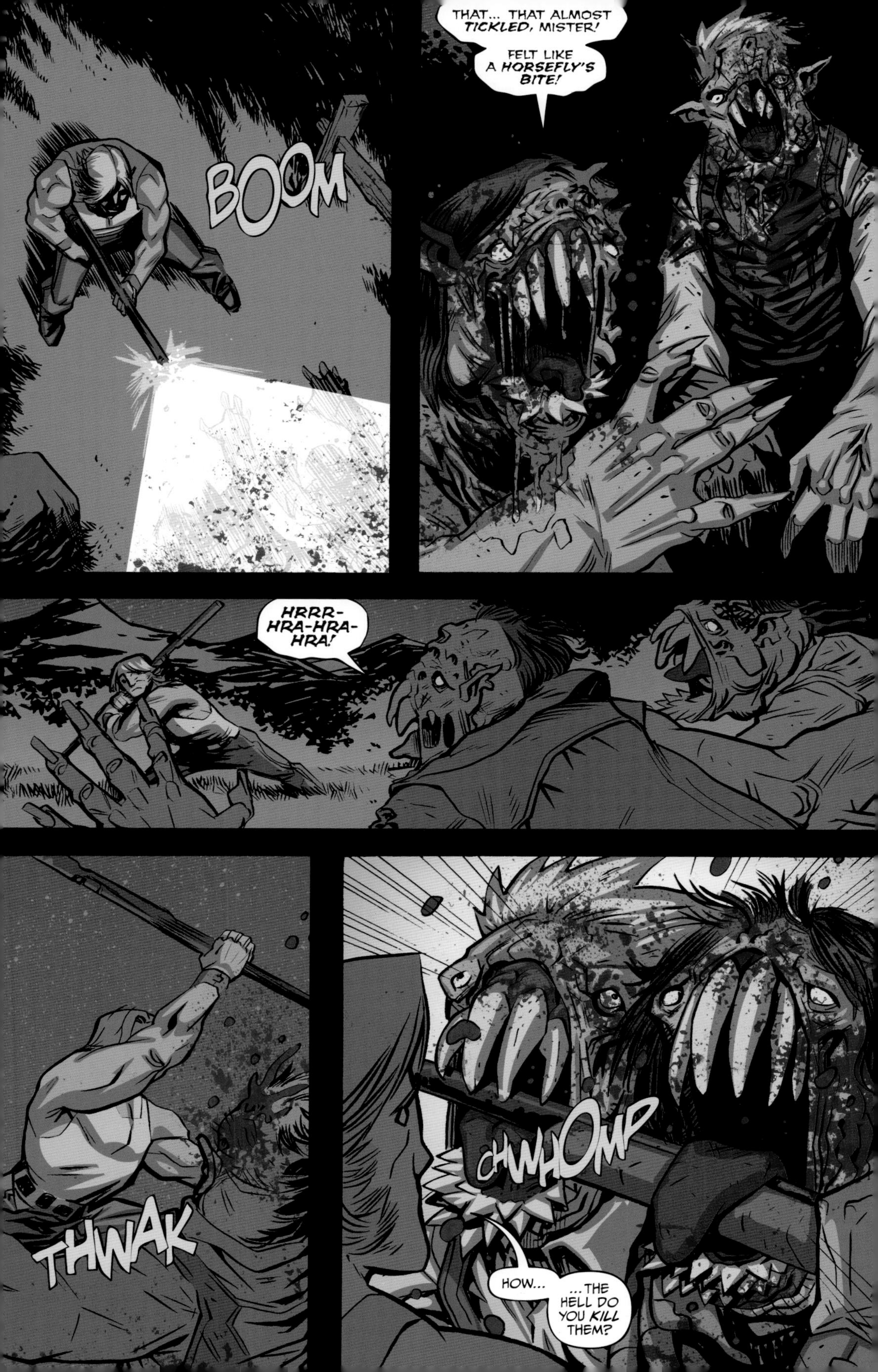
BOOM
THAT... THAT ALMOST TICKLED, MISTER!
FELT LIKE A HORSEFLY'S BITE!
HRRR-HRA-HRA-HRA!
THWAK
CHWHOMP
HOW...
...THE HELL DO YOU KILL THEM?

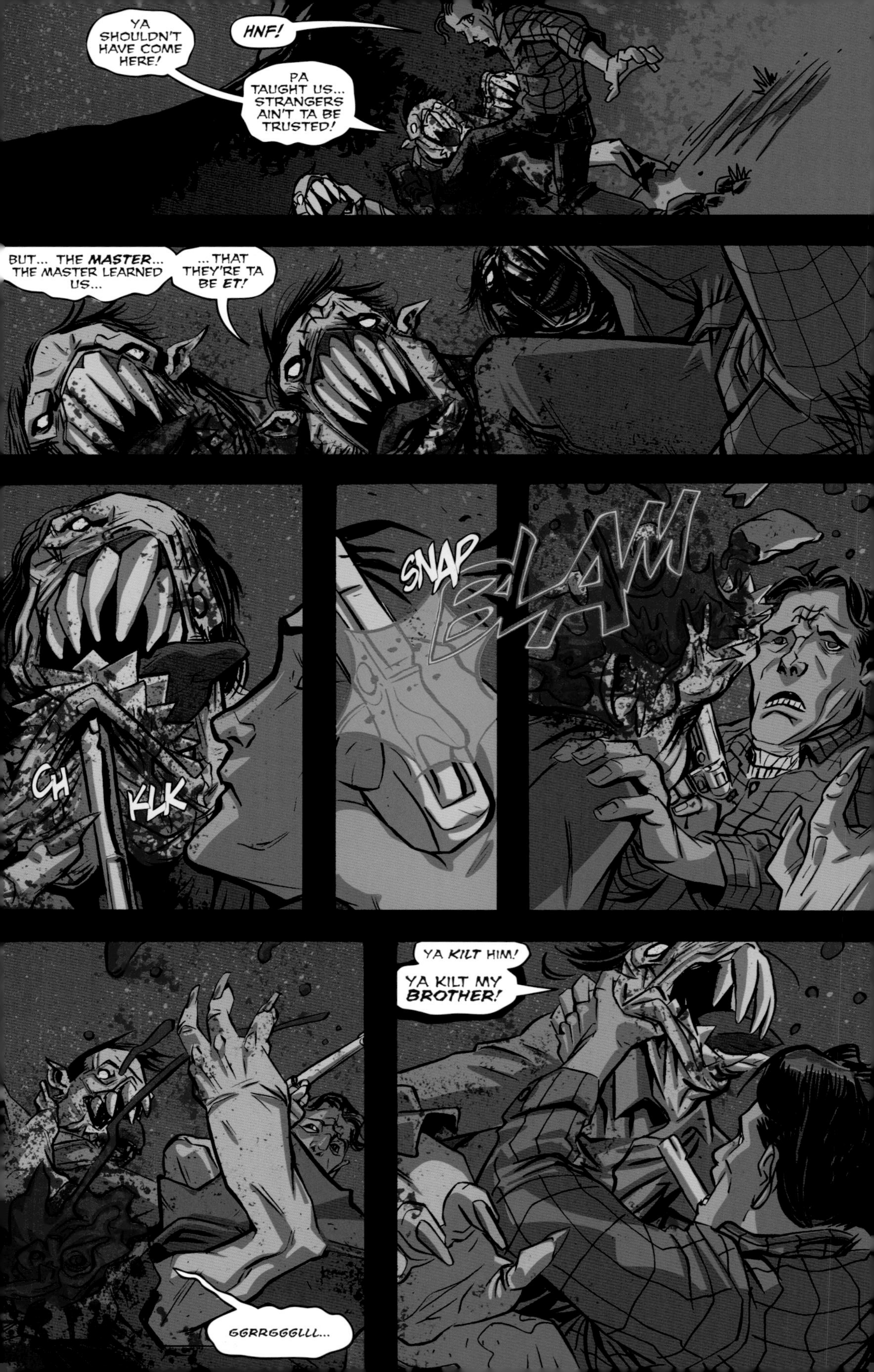
YA SHOULDN'T HAVE COME HERE!
HNF!
PA TAUGHT US... STRANGERS AIN'T TA BE TRUSTED!
BUT... THE MASTER... THE MASTER LEARNED US...
...THAT THEY'RE TA BE ET!
CH
KLK
SNAP
BLAM
YA KILT HIM!
YA KILT MY BROTHER!
GGRRGGGLLL...

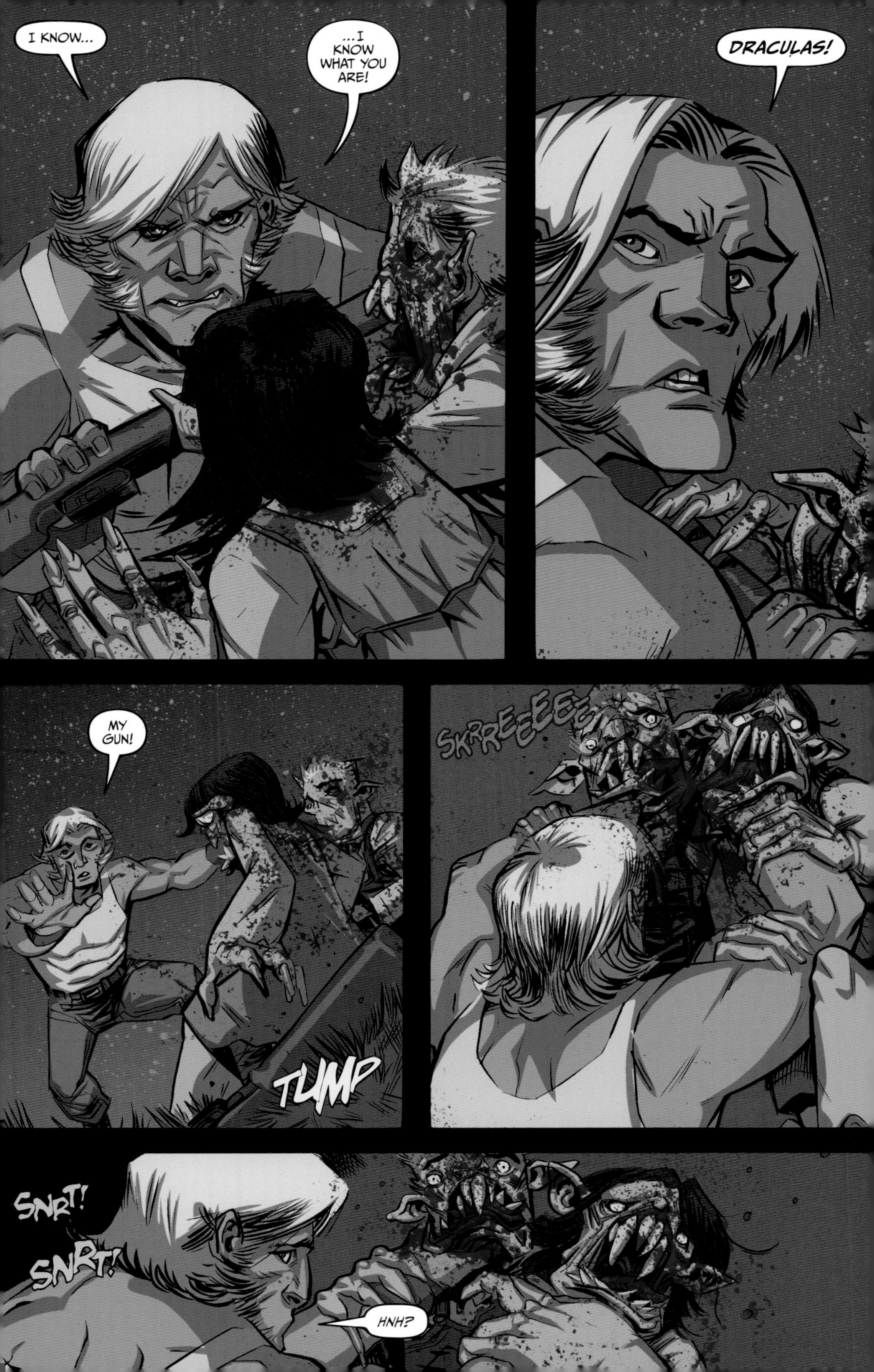
I KNOW...
...I KNOW WHAT YOU ARE!
DRACULAS!
MY GUN!
TUMP
SKRREEEEE
SNRT!
SNRT!
HNH?

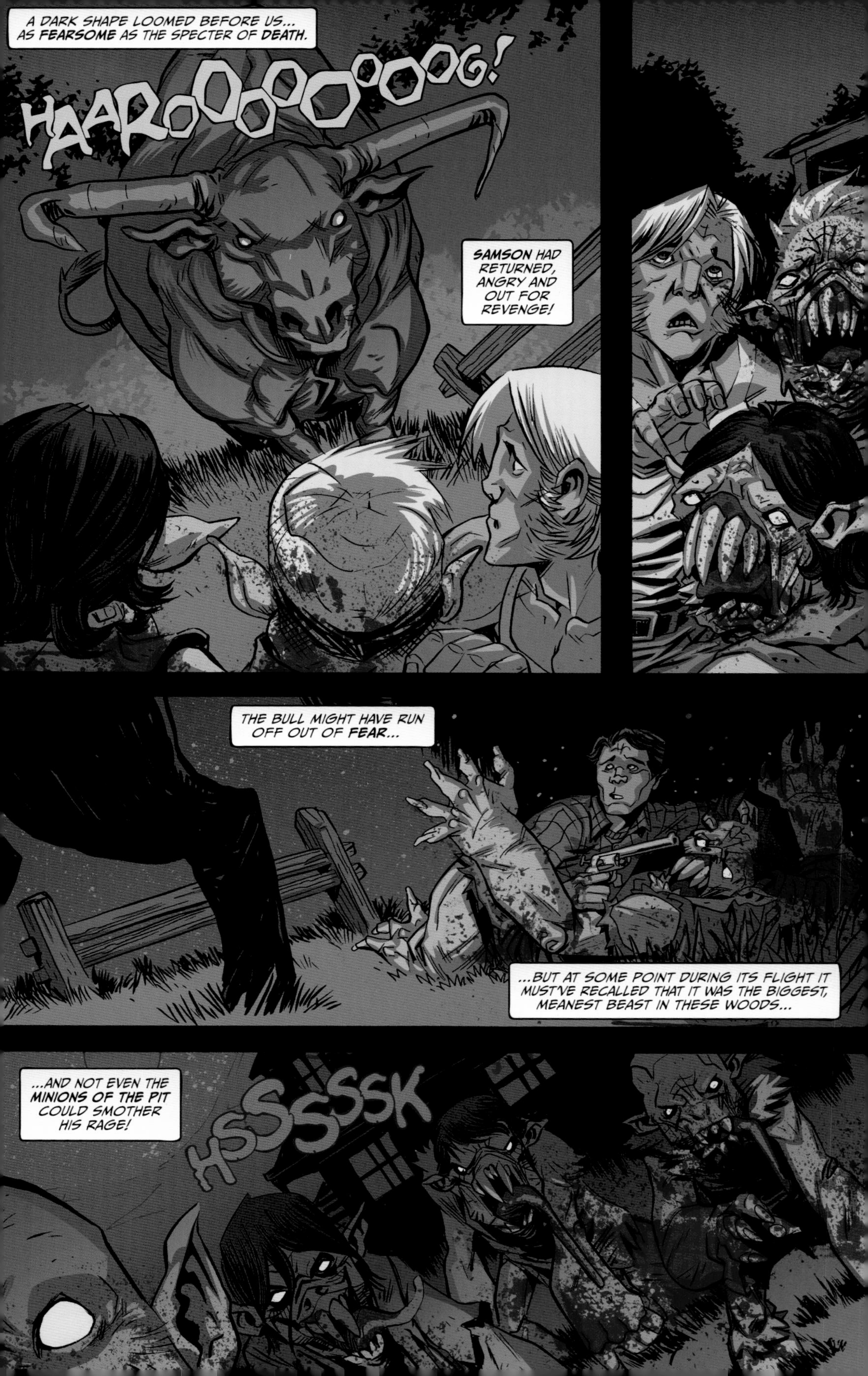
A DARK SHAPE LOOMED BEFORE US... AS FEARSOME AS THE SPECTER OF DEATH.
HAAROOOOOOOOG!
SAMSON HAD RETURNED, ANGRY AND OUT FOR REVENGE!
THE BULL MIGHT HAVE RUN OFF OUT OF FEAR...
...BUT AT SOME POINT DURING ITS FLIGHT IT MUST'VE RECALLED THAT IT WAS THE BIGGEST, MEANEST BEAST IN THESE WOODS...
...AND NOT EVEN THE MINIONS OF THE PIT COULD SMOTHER HIS RAGE!
HSSSSSSK

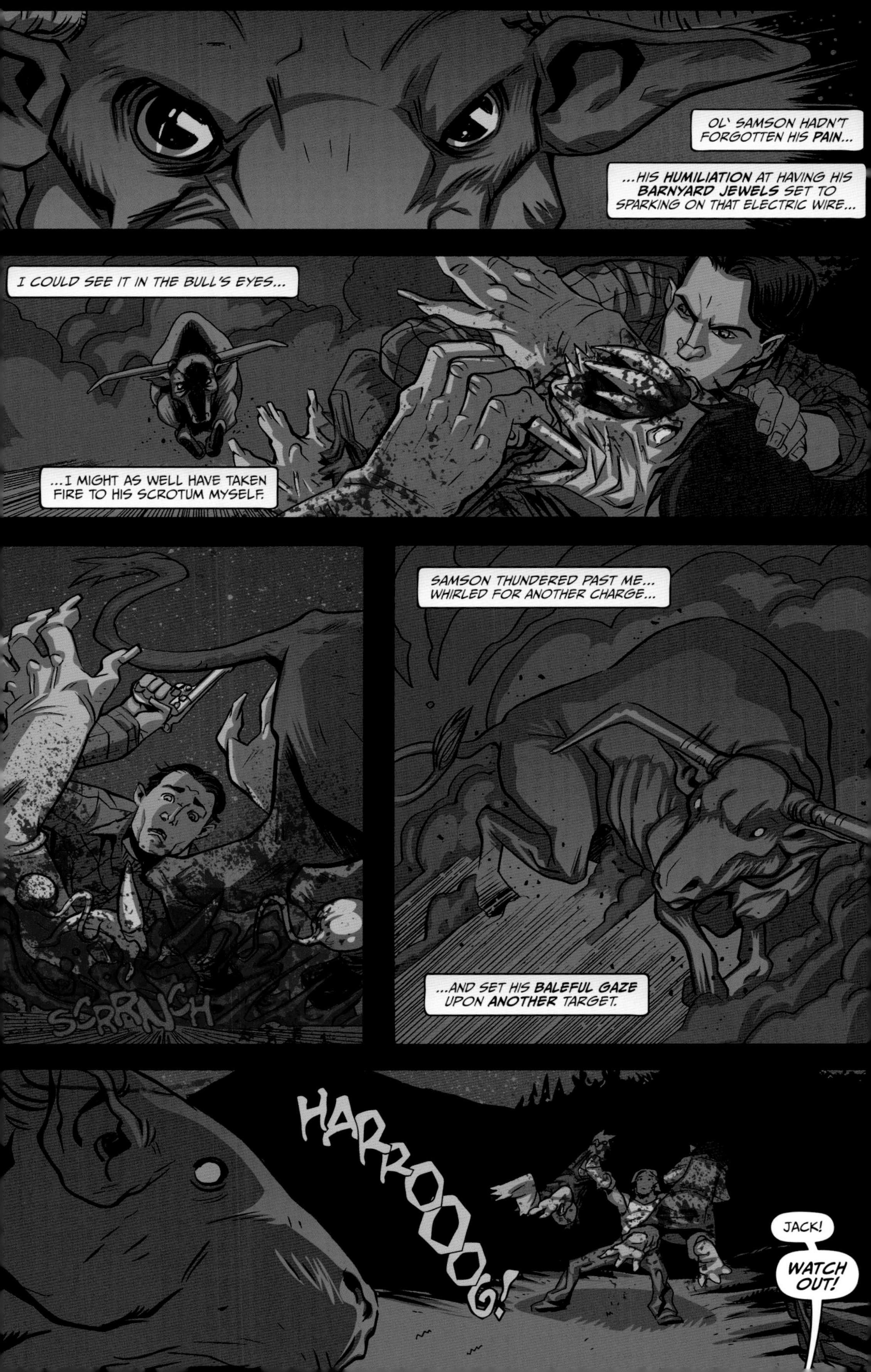
OL' SAMSON HADN'T FORGOTTEN HIS **PAIN**...
...HIS **HUMILIATION** AT HAVING HIS **BARNYARD JEWELS** SET TO SPARKING ON THAT ELECTRIC WIRE...
I COULD SEE IT IN THE BULL'S EYES...
...I MIGHT AS WELL HAVE TAKEN FIRE TO HIS SCROTUM MYSELF.
SCRRNCH
SAMSON THUNDERED PAST ME... WHIRLED FOR ANOTHER CHARGE...
...AND SET HIS **BALEFUL GAZE** UPON **ANOTHER** TARGET.
HARROOOOG!
JACK!
WATCH OUT!

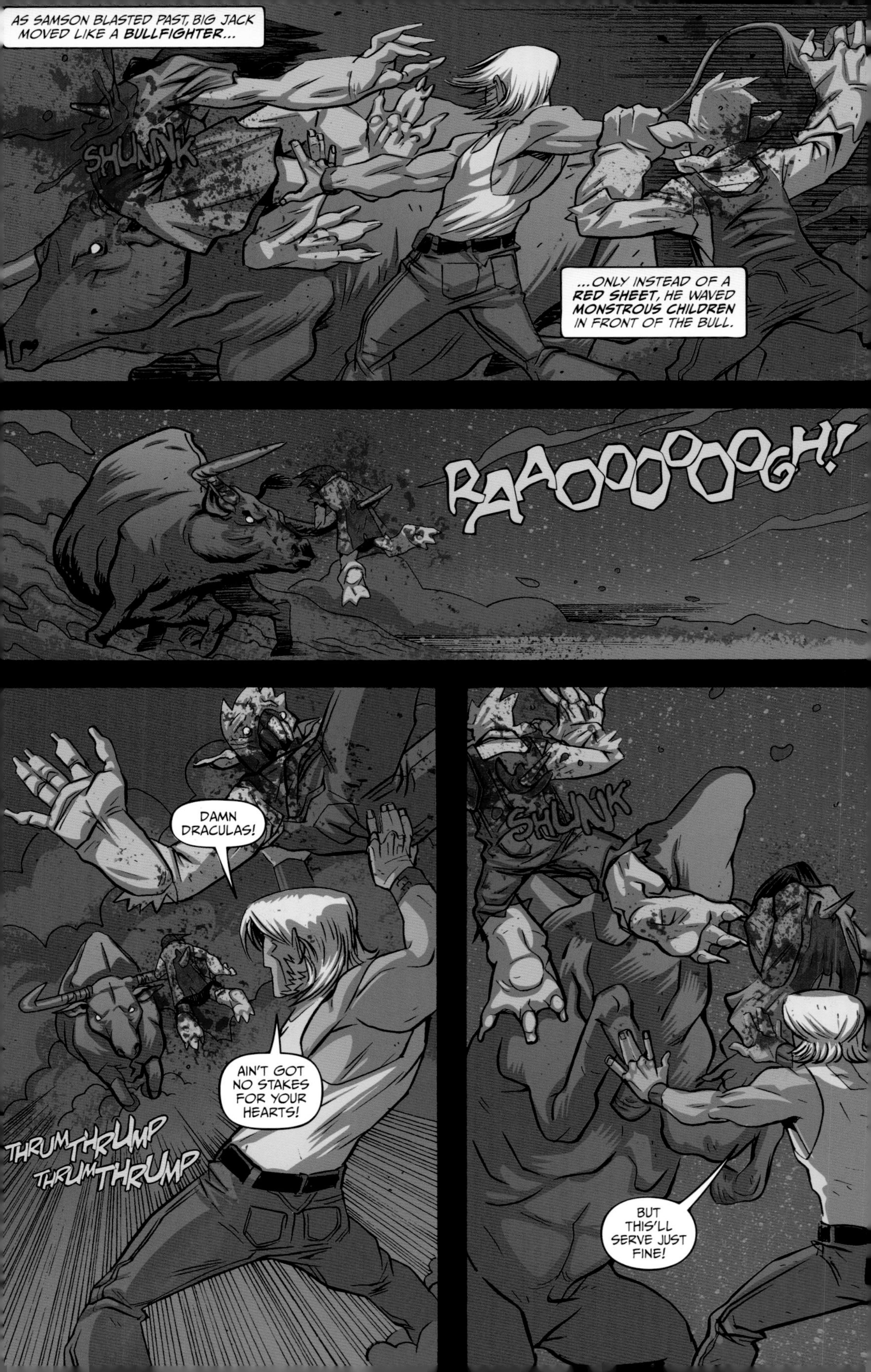
AS SAMSON BLASTED PAST, BIG JACK MOVED LIKE A **BULLFIGHTER**...
SHUNK
...ONLY INSTEAD OF A **RED SHEET**, HE WAVED **MONSTROUS CHILDREN** IN FRONT OF THE BULL.
RAAOOOOOOGH!
DAMN DRACULAS!
AIN'T GOT NO STAKES FOR YOUR HEARTS!
THRUM THRUMP THRUM THRUMP
SHUNK
BUT THIS'LL SERVE JUST FINE!

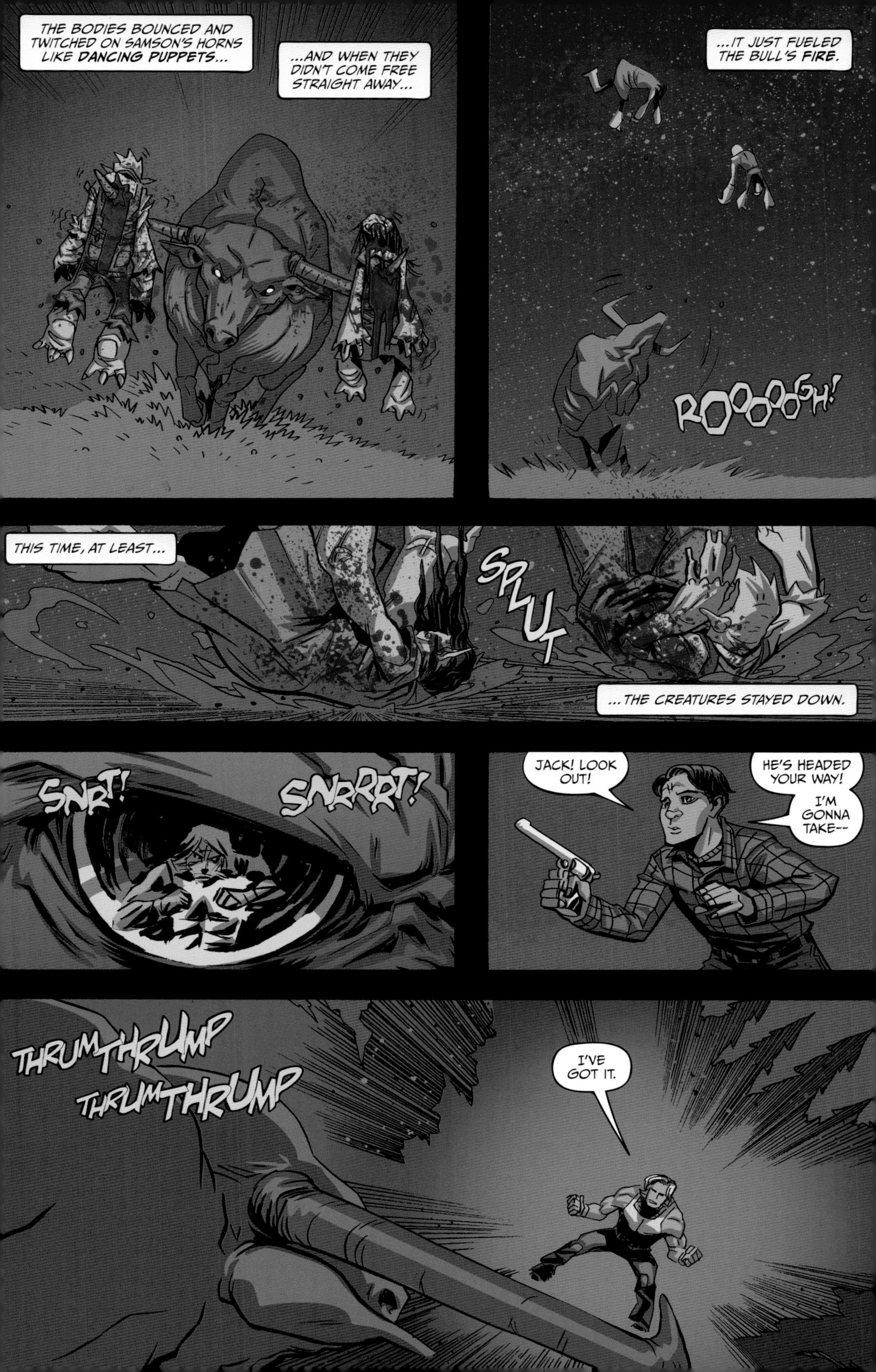
THE BODIES BOUNCED AND TWITCHED ON SAMSON'S HORNS LIKE DANCING PUPPETS...
...AND WHEN THEY DIDN'T COME FREE STRAIGHT AWAY...
...IT JUST FUELED THE BULL'S FIRE.
ROOOOOGH!
THIS TIME, AT LEAST...
SPLUT
...THE CREATURES STAYED DOWN.
SNRT!
SNRRRT!
JACK! LOOK OUT!
HE'S HEADED YOUR WAY!
I'M GONNA TAKE--
THRUMTHRUMP
THRUMTHRUMP
I'VE GOT IT.

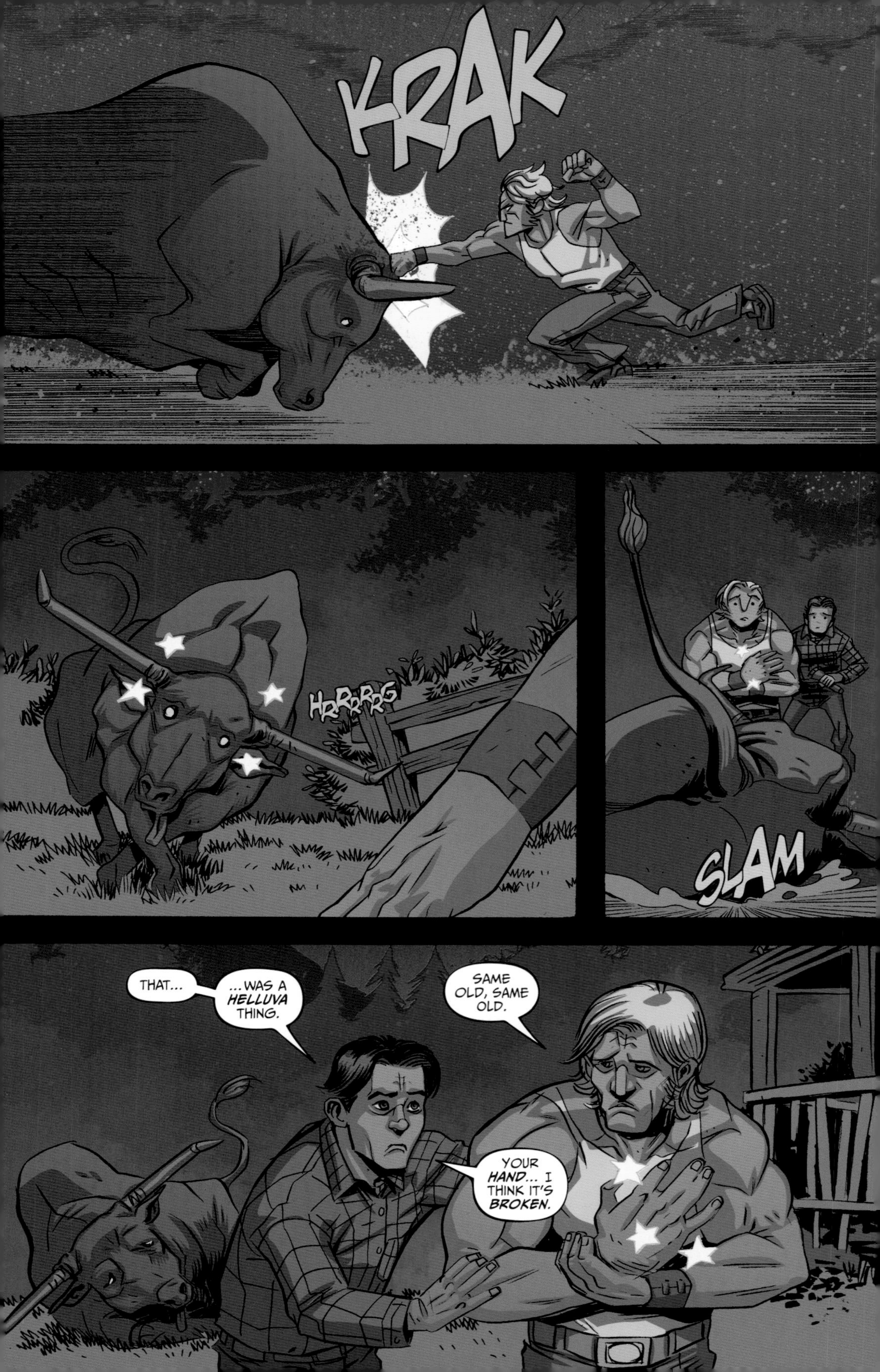
KRAK
HRRRRRG
SLAM
THAT...
...WAS A HELLUVA THING.
SAME OLD, SAME OLD.
YOUR HAND... I THINK IT'S BROKEN.

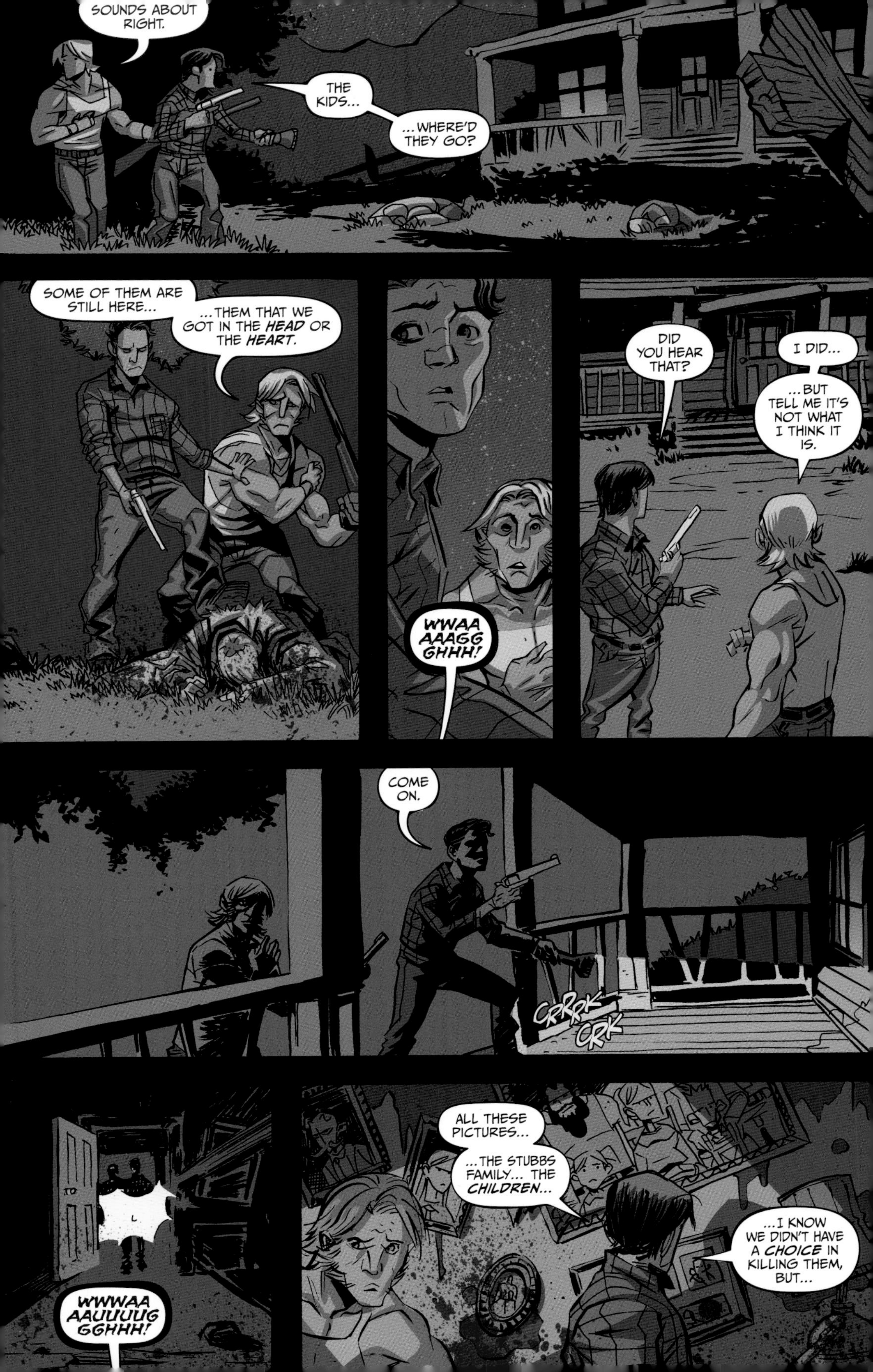
SOUNDS ABOUT RIGHT.
THE KIDS...
...WHERE'D THEY GO?
SOME OF THEM ARE STILL HERE...
...THEM THAT WE GOT IN THE HEAD OR THE HEART.
WWAA AAAGG GHHH!
DID YOU HEAR THAT?
I DID...
...BUT TELL ME IT'S NOT WHAT I THINK IT IS.
COME ON.
CRRRK
CRK
WWWAA AAUUUUG GGHHH!
ALL THESE PICTURES...
...THE STUBBS FAMILY... THE CHILDREN...
...I KNOW WE DIDN'T HAVE A CHOICE IN KILLING THEM, BUT...

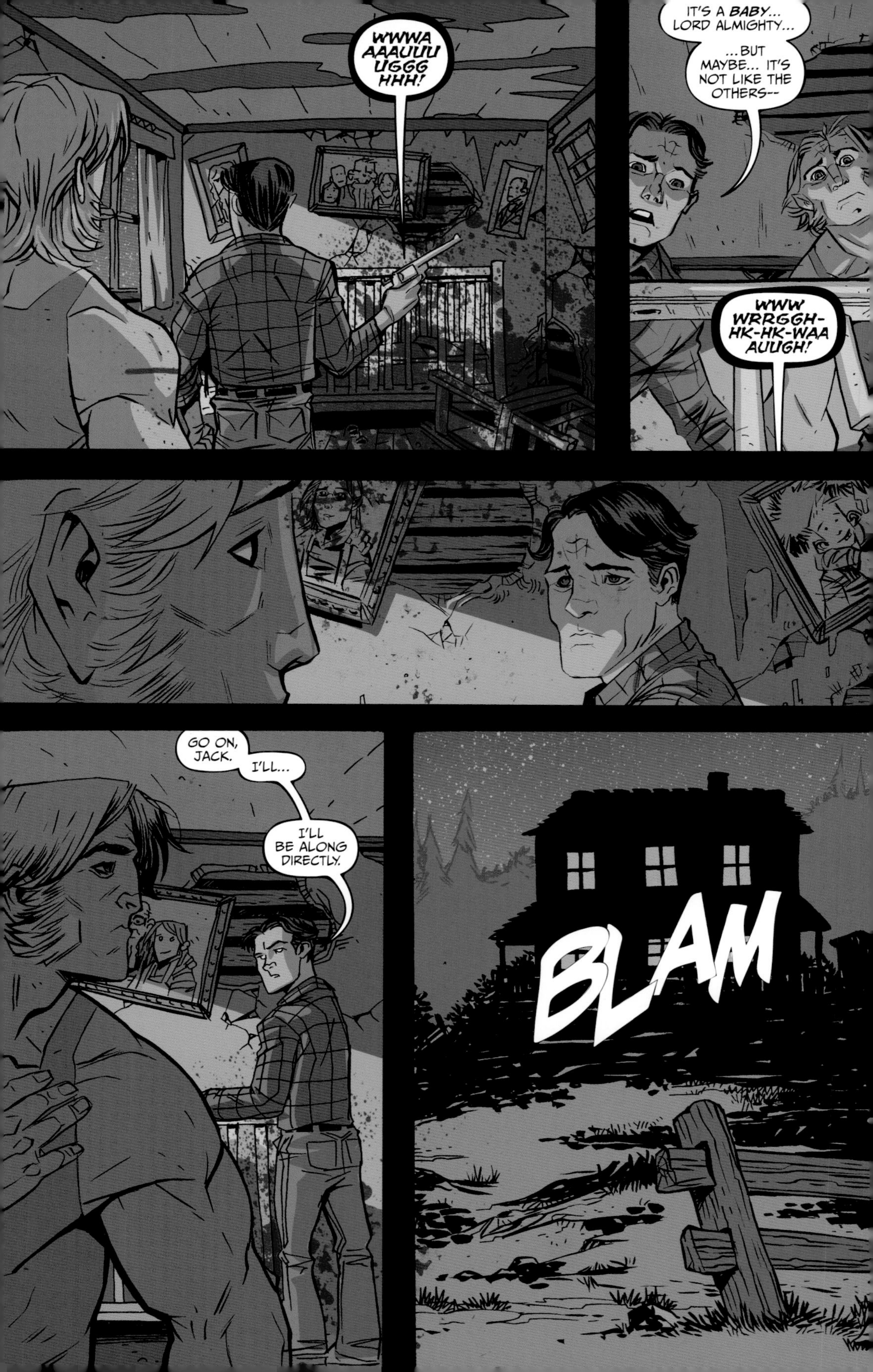
WWWA AAAUUU UGGG HHH!
IT'S A BABY... LORD ALMIGHTY...
...BUT MAYBE... IT'S NOT LIKE THE OTHERS--
WWW WRRGGH-HK-HK-WAA AUUGH!
GO ON, JACK.
I'LL...
I'LL BE ALONG DIRECTLY.
BLAM

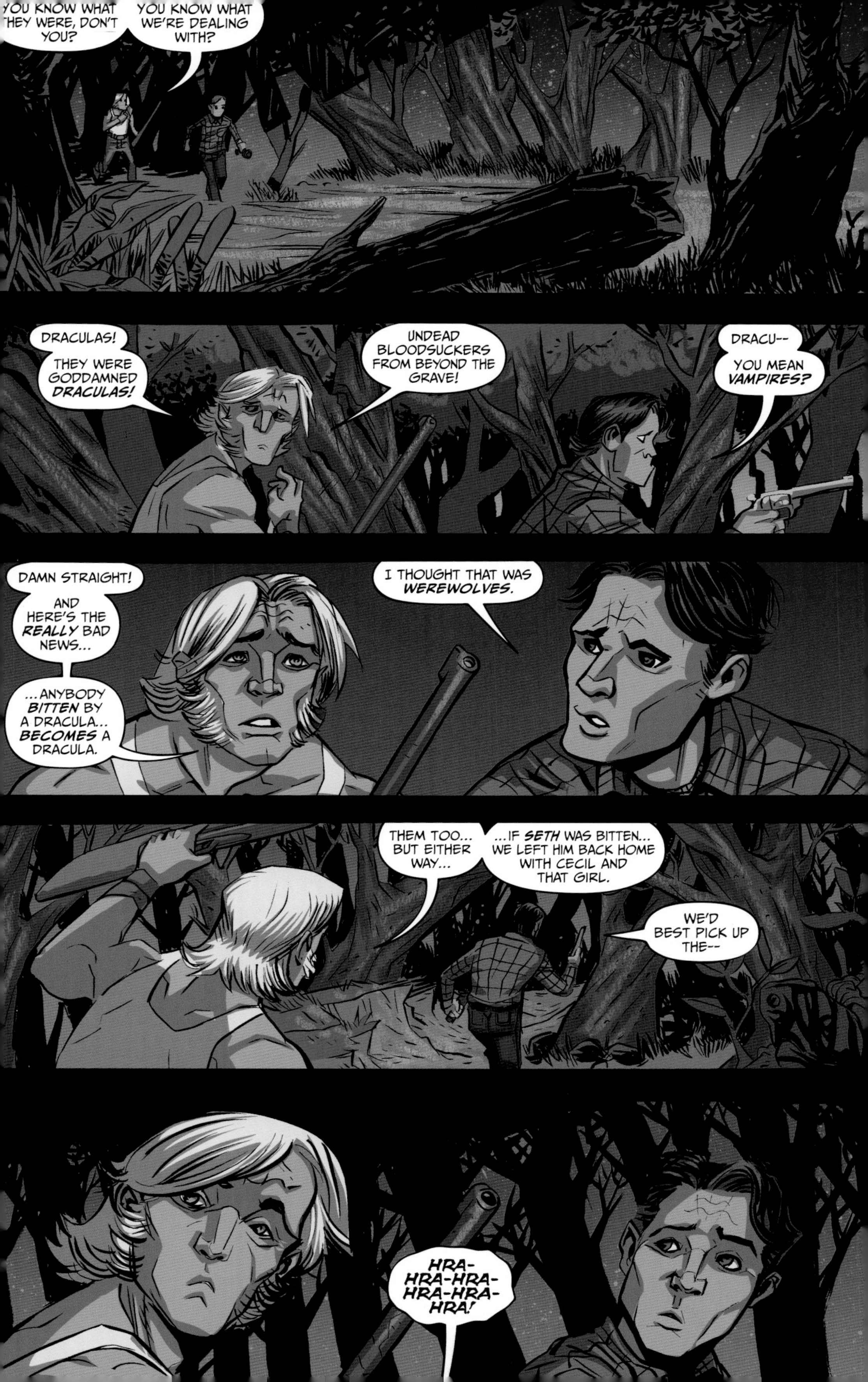
YOU KNOW WHAT THEY WERE, DON'T YOU?
YOU KNOW WHAT WE'RE DEALING WITH?
DRACULAS!
THEY WERE GODDAMNED *DRACULAS!*
UNDEAD BLOODSUCKERS FROM BEYOND THE GRAVE!
DRACU--
YOU MEAN *VAMPIRES?*
DAMN STRAIGHT!
AND HERE'S THE *REALLY* BAD NEWS...
...ANYBODY *BITTEN* BY A DRACULA... *BECOMES* A DRACULA.
I THOUGHT THAT WAS *WEREWOLVES.*
THEM TOO... BUT EITHER WAY...
...IF *SETH* WAS BITTEN... WE LEFT HIM BACK HOME WITH CECIL AND THAT GIRL.
WE'D BEST PICK UP THE--
HRA-HRA-HRA-HRA-HRA-HRA-HRA!

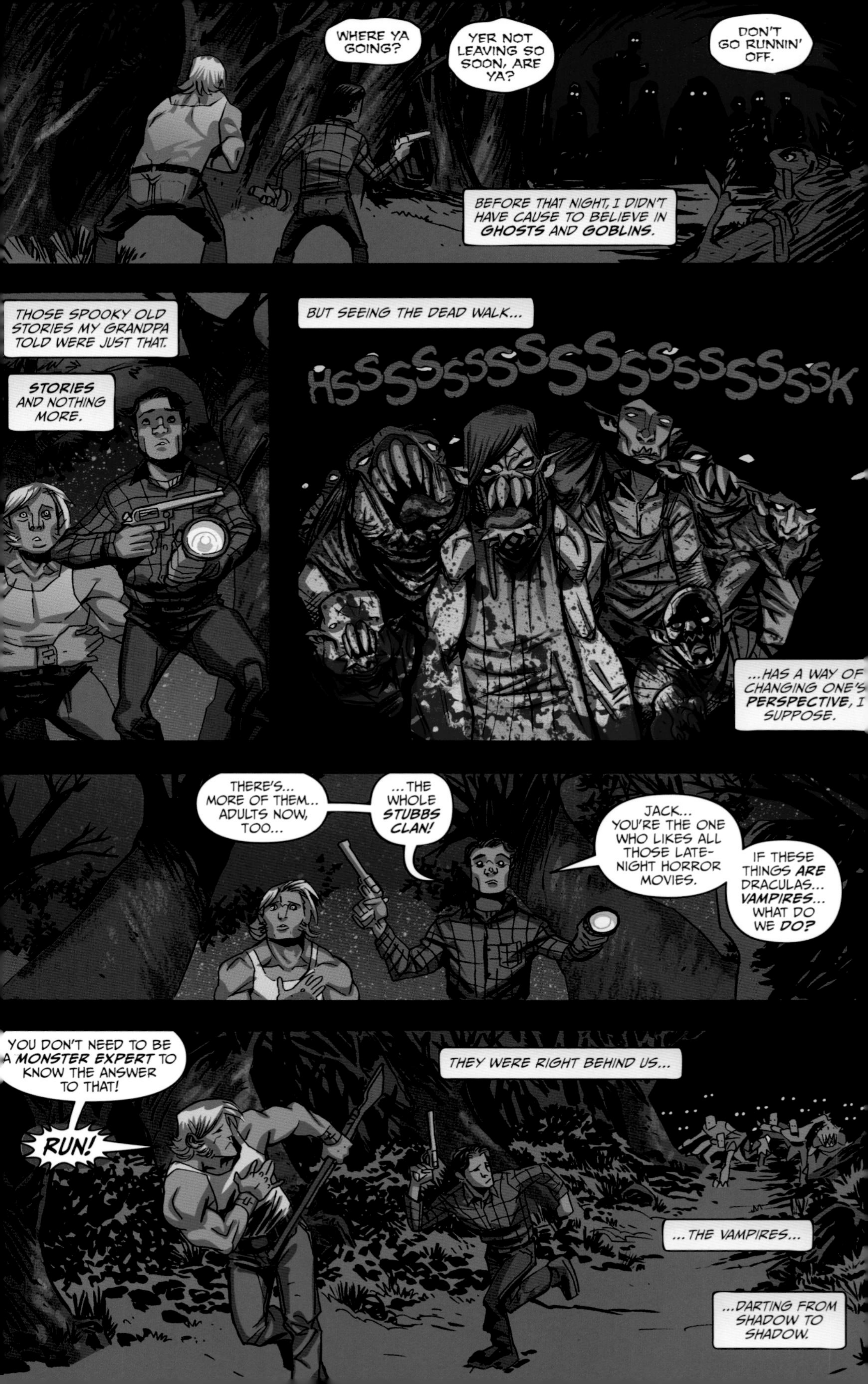
WHERE YA GOING?
YER NOT LEAVING SO SOON, ARE YA?
DON'T GO RUNNIN' OFF.
BEFORE THAT NIGHT, I DIDN'T HAVE CAUSE TO BELIEVE IN GHOSTS AND GOBLINS.
THOSE SPOOKY OLD STORIES MY GRANDPA TOLD WERE JUST THAT.
STORIES AND NOTHING MORE.
BUT SEEING THE DEAD WALK...
HSSSSSSSSSSSSSSSSSSSSK
...HAS A WAY OF CHANGING ONE'S PERSPECTIVE, I SUPPOSE.
THERE'S... MORE OF THEM... ADULTS NOW, TOO...
...THE WHOLE STUBBS CLAN!
JACK... YOU'RE THE ONE WHO LIKES ALL THOSE LATE-NIGHT HORROR MOVIES.
IF THESE THINGS ARE DRACULAS... VAMPIRES... WHAT DO WE DO?
YOU DON'T NEED TO BE A MONSTER EXPERT TO KNOW THE ANSWER TO THAT!
RUN!
THEY WERE RIGHT BEHIND US...
...THE VAMPIRES...
...DARTING FROM SHADOW TO SHADOW.

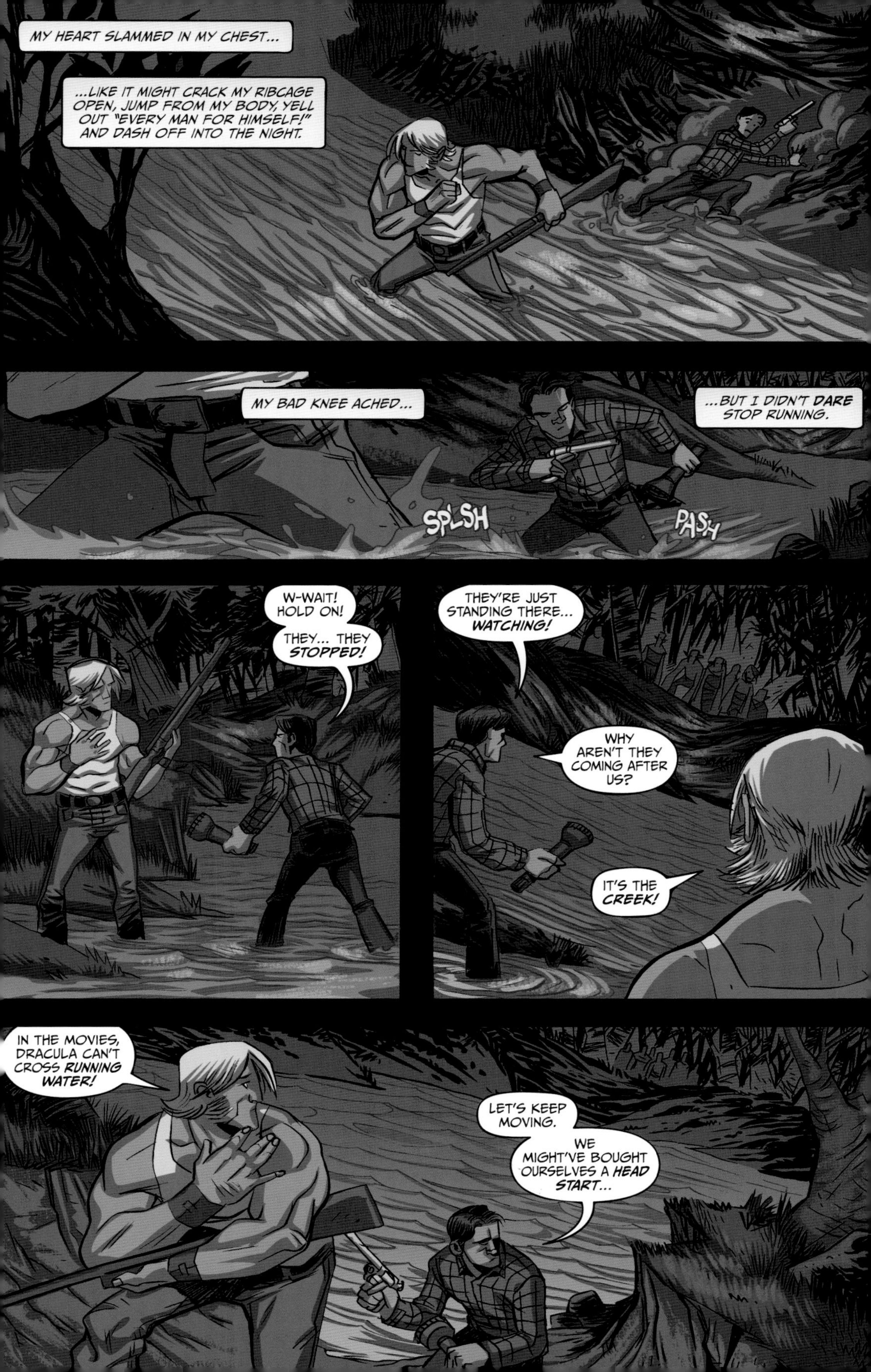
MY HEART SLAMMED IN MY CHEST...
...LIKE IT MIGHT CRACK MY RIBCAGE OPEN, JUMP FROM MY BODY, YELL OUT "EVERY MAN FOR HIMSELF!" AND DASH OFF INTO THE NIGHT.
MY BAD KNEE ACHED...
...BUT I DIDN'T DARE STOP RUNNING.
SPLSH
PASH
W-WAIT! HOLD ON!
THEY... THEY STOPPED!
THEY'RE JUST STANDING THERE... WATCHING!
WHY AREN'T THEY COMING AFTER US?
IT'S THE CREEK!
IN THE MOVIES, DRACULA CAN'T CROSS RUNNING WATER!
LET'S KEEP MOVING.
WE MIGHT'VE BOUGHT OURSELVES A HEAD START...

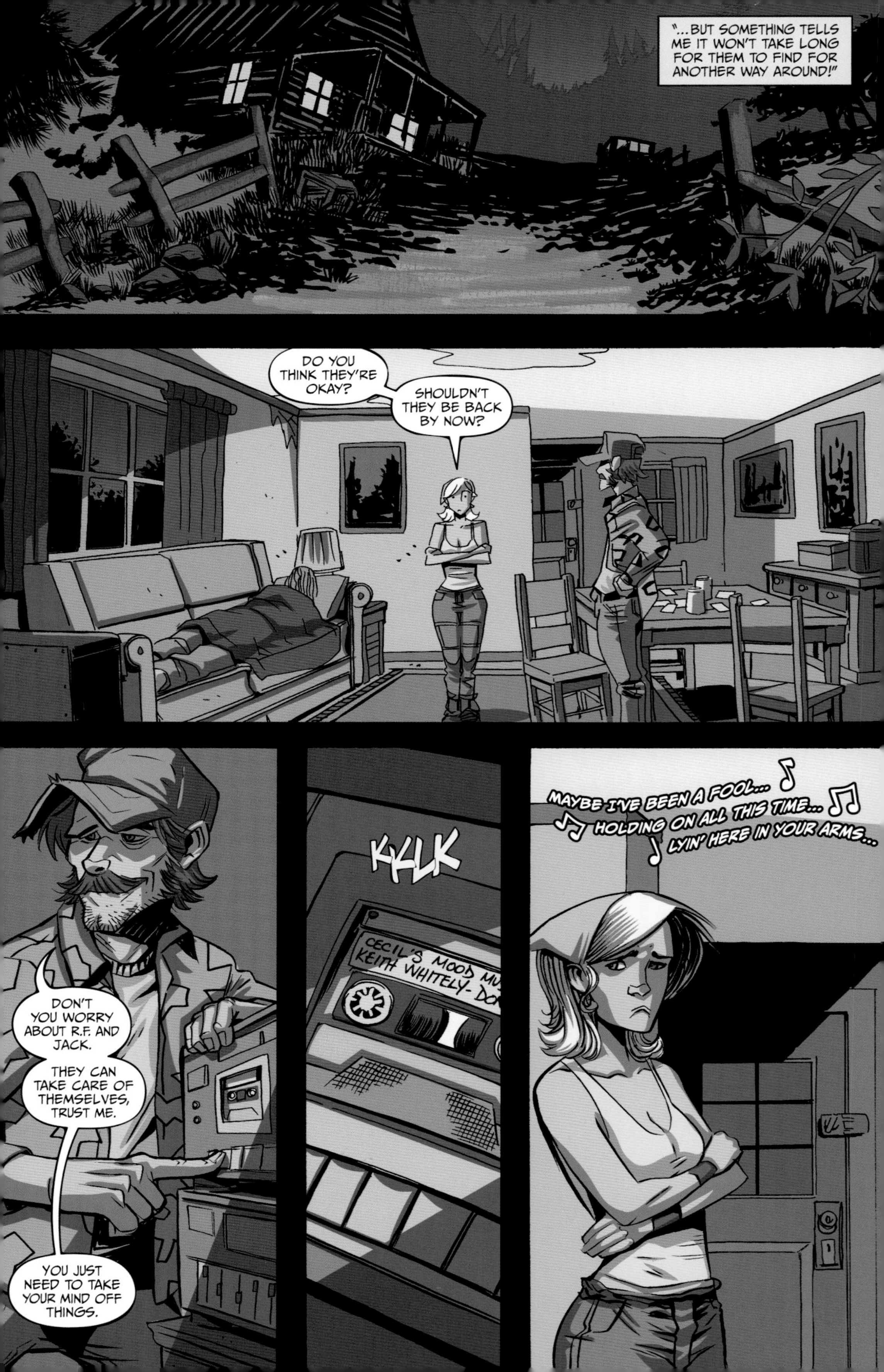
"...BUT SOMETHING TELLS ME IT WON'T TAKE LONG FOR THEM TO FIND FOR ANOTHER WAY AROUND!"
DO YOU THINK THEY'RE OKAY?
SHOULDN'T THEY BE BACK BY NOW?
DON'T YOU WORRY ABOUT R.F. AND JACK.
THEY CAN TAKE CARE OF THEMSELVES, TRUST ME.
YOU JUST NEED TO TAKE YOUR MIND OFF THINGS.
KKLK
CECIL'S MOOD MU
KEITH WHITELY- DO
MAYBE I'VE BEEN A FOOL...
HOLDING ON ALL THIS TIME...
LYIN' HERE IN YOUR ARMS...

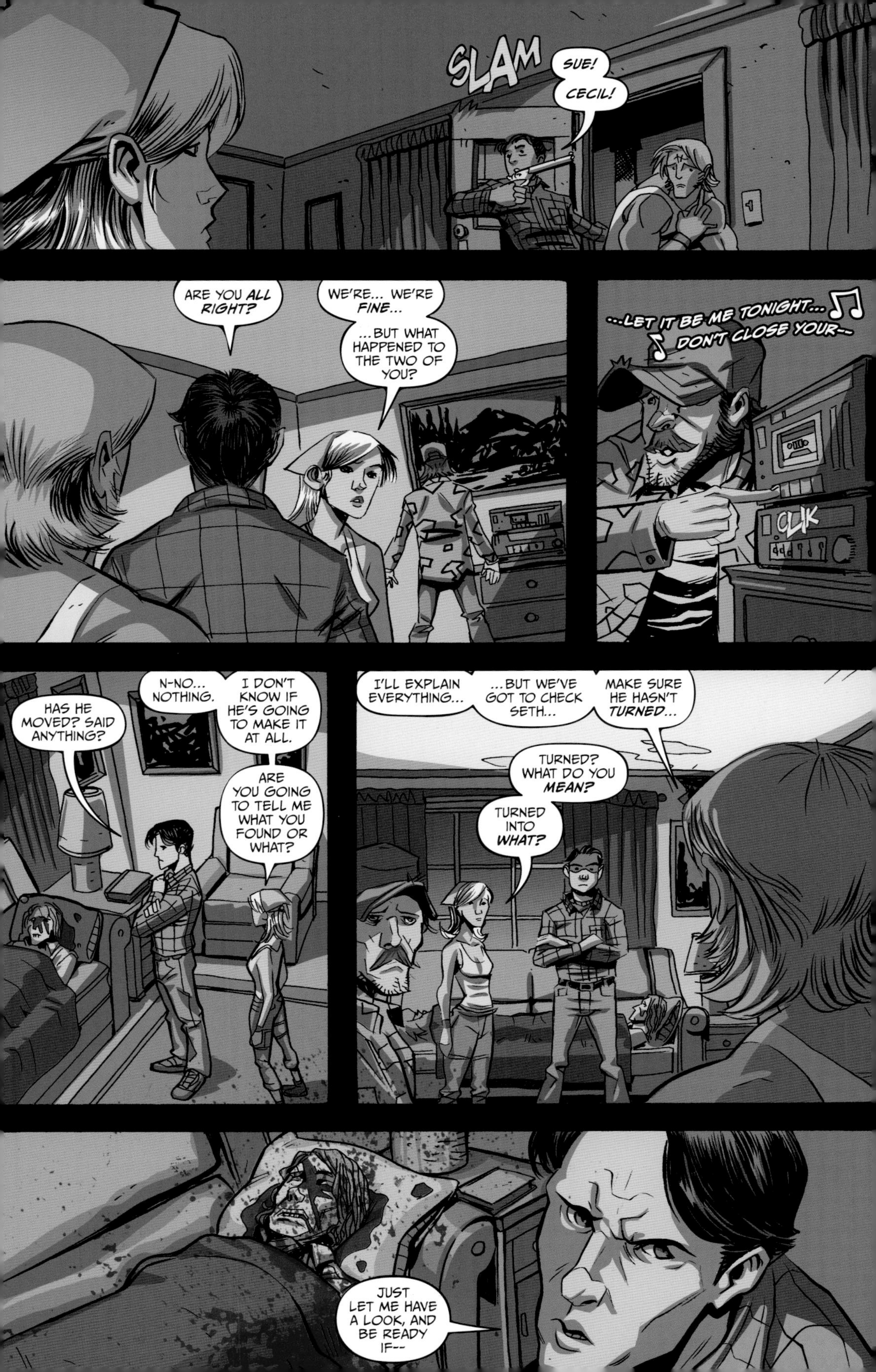
SLAM
SUE!
CECIL!
ARE YOU ALL RIGHT?
WE'RE... WE'RE FINE...
...BUT WHAT HAPPENED TO THE TWO OF YOU?
...LET IT BE ME TONIGHT...
DON'T CLOSE YOUR--
CLIK
HAS HE MOVED? SAID ANYTHING?
N-NO... NOTHING.
I DON'T KNOW IF HE'S GOING TO MAKE IT AT ALL.
ARE YOU GOING TO TELL ME WHAT YOU FOUND OR WHAT?
I'LL EXPLAIN EVERYTHING...
...BUT WE'VE GOT TO CHECK SETH...
MAKE SURE HE HASN'T TURNED...
TURNED? WHAT DO YOU MEAN?
TURNED INTO WHAT?
JUST LET ME HAVE A LOOK, AND BE READY IF--

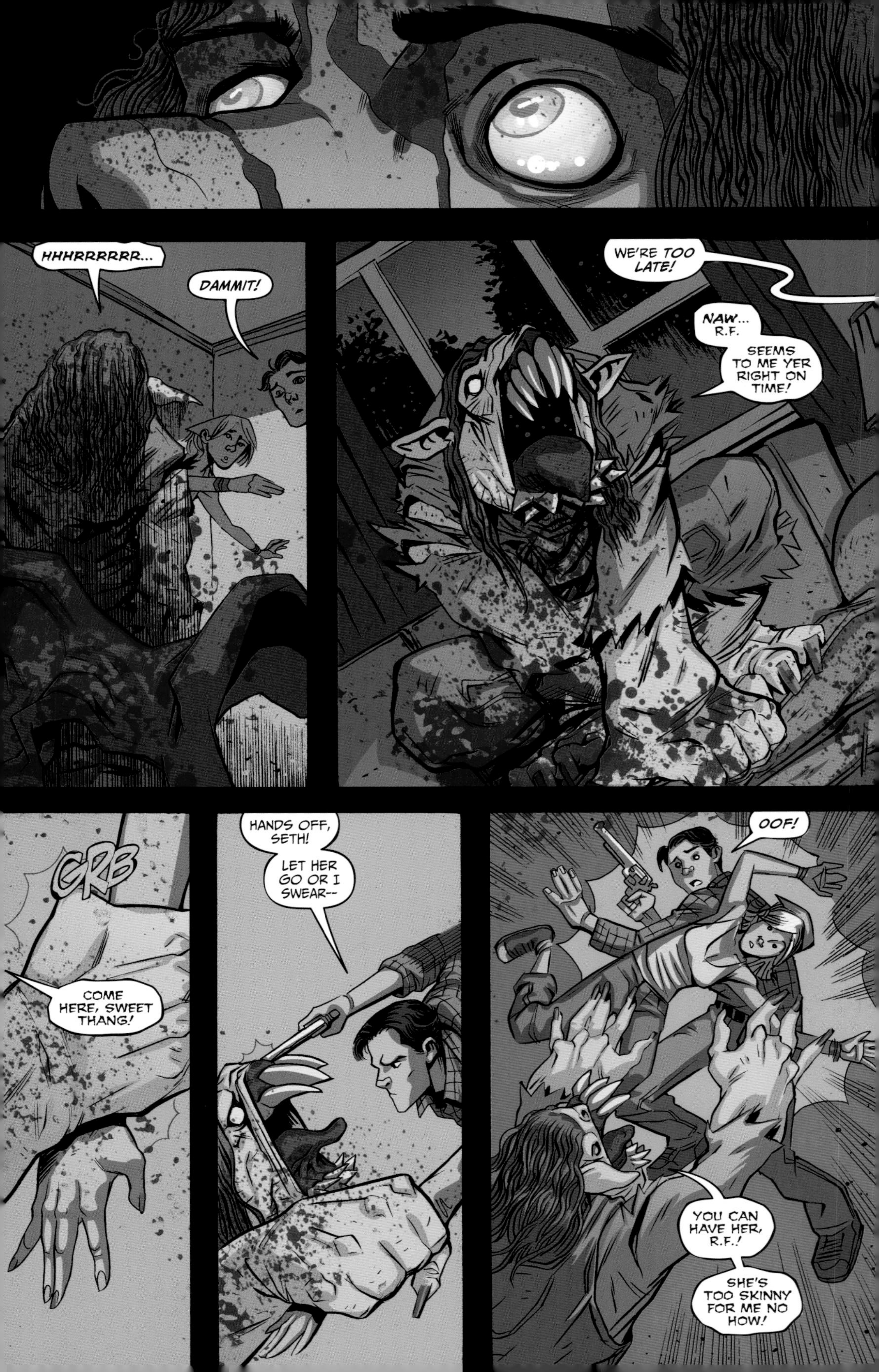
HHHRRRRRRR...
DAMMIT!
WE'RE TOO LATE!
NAW... R.F.
SEEMS TO ME YER RIGHT ON TIME!
GRB
COME HERE, SWEET THANG!
HANDS OFF, SETH!
LET HER GO OR I SWEAR--
OOF!
YOU CAN HAVE HER, R.F.!
SHE'S TOO SKINNY FOR ME NO HOW!

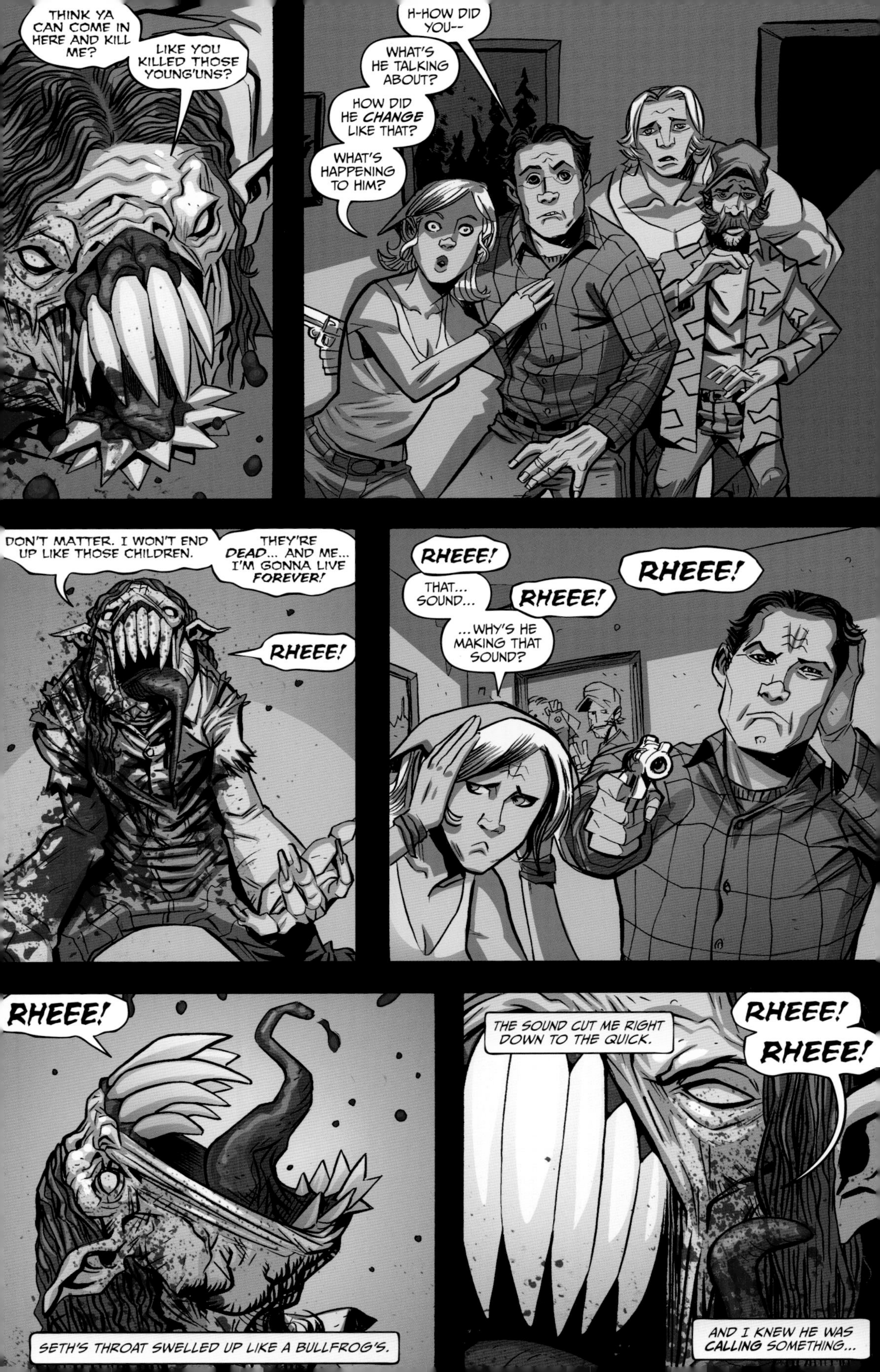
THINK YA CAN COME IN HERE AND KILL ME?
LIKE YOU KILLED THOSE YOUNG'UNS?
H-HOW DID YOU--
WHAT'S HE TALKING ABOUT?
HOW DID HE CHANGE LIKE THAT?
WHAT'S HAPPENING TO HIM?
DON'T MATTER. I WON'T END UP LIKE THOSE CHILDREN.
THEY'RE DEAD... AND ME... I'M GONNA LIVE FOREVER!
RHEEE!
RHEEE!
THAT... SOUND...
RHEEE!
RHEEE!
...WHY'S HE MAKING THAT SOUND?
RHEEE!
SETH'S THROAT SWELLED UP LIKE A BULLFROG'S.
THE SOUND CUT ME RIGHT DOWN TO THE QUICK.
RHEEE!
RHEEE!
AND I KNEW HE WAS CALLING SOMETHING...

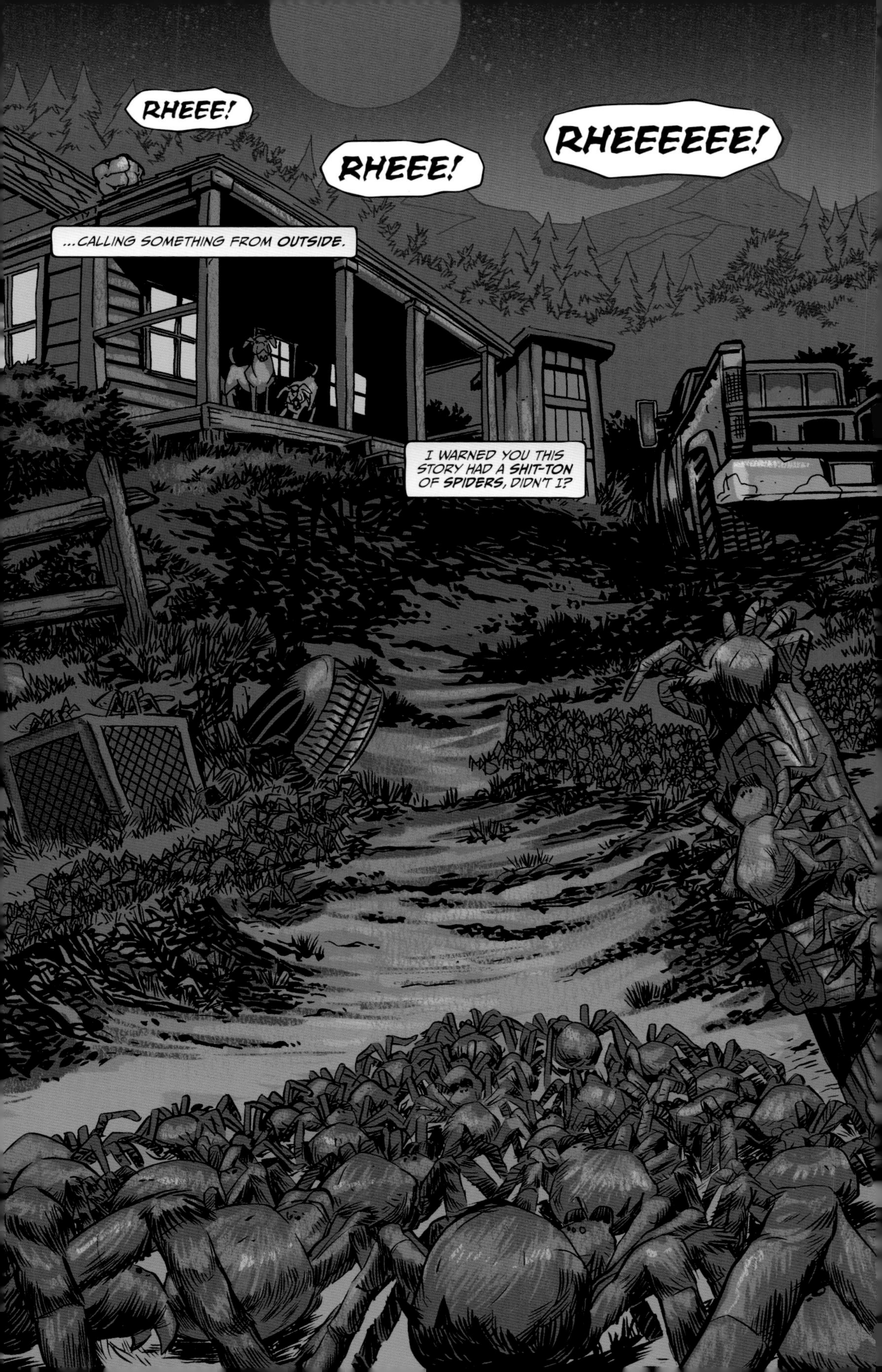
RHEEE!
RHEEE!
RHEEEEEEE!
...CALLING SOMETHING FROM OUTSIDE.
I WARNED YOU THIS STORY HAD A SHIT-TON OF SPIDERS, DIDN'T I?

CHAPTER 3

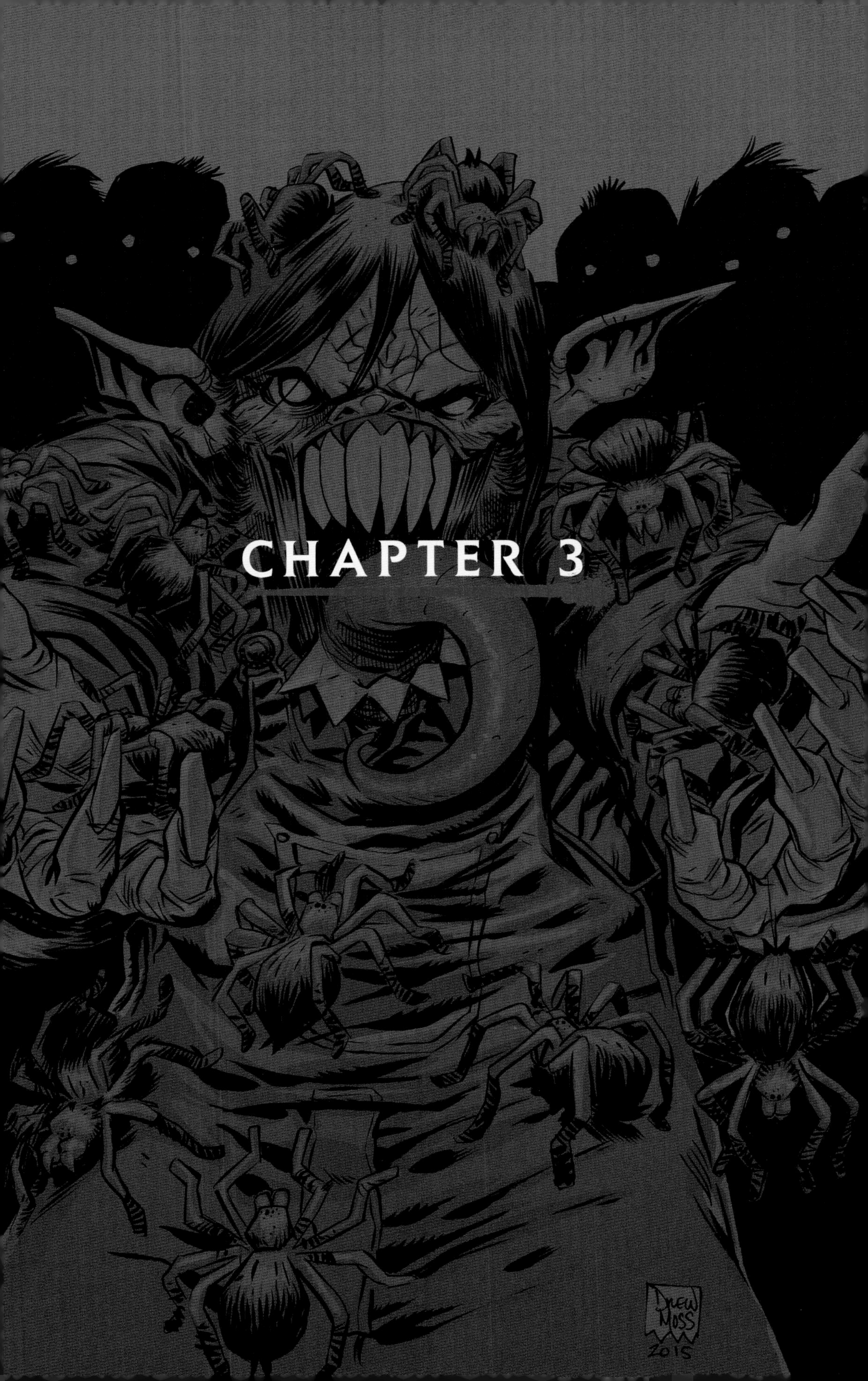
DREW MOSS
2015

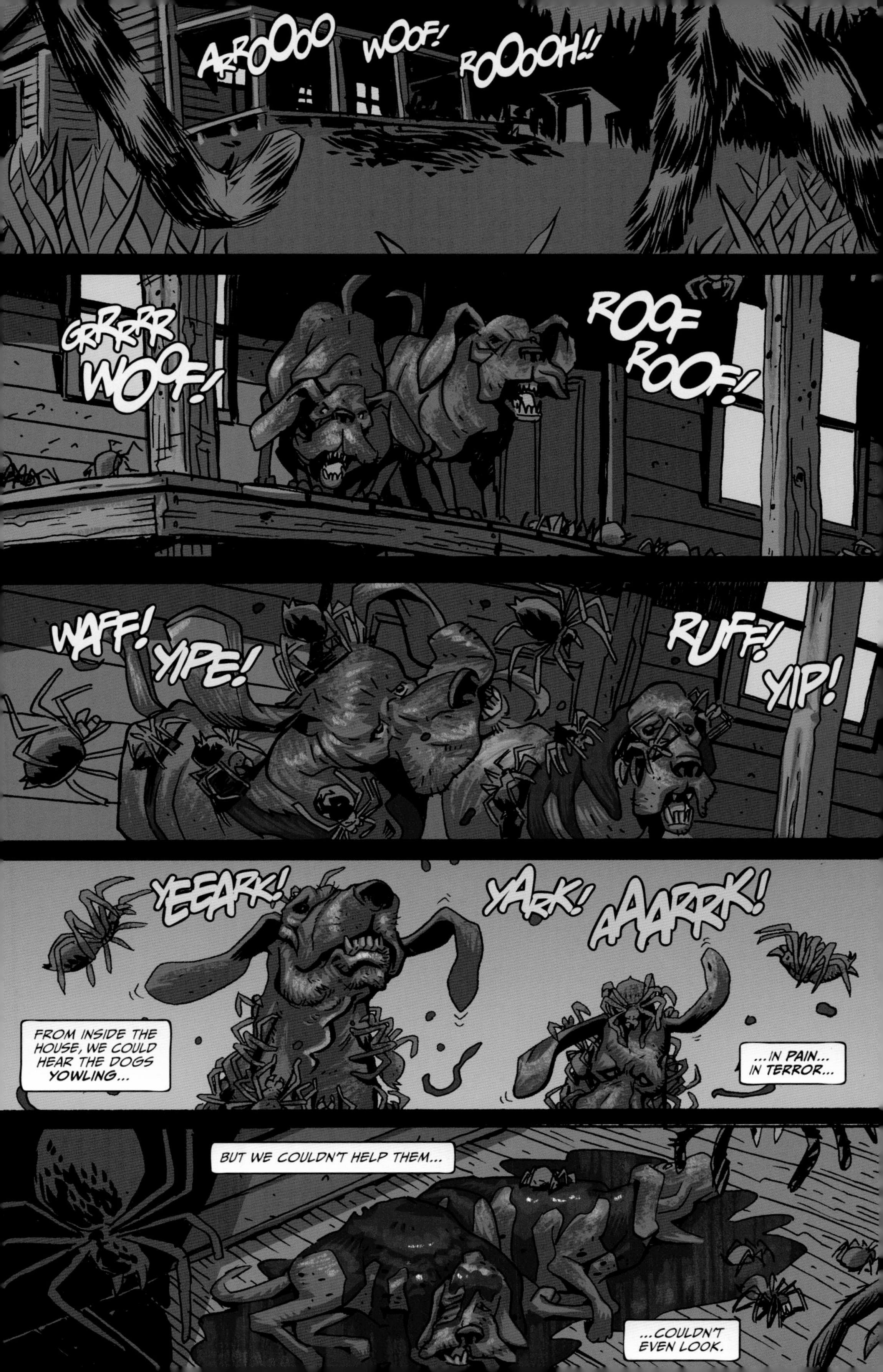
ARROOOO
WOOF!
ROOOOH!!
GRRRRR
WOOF!
ROOF
ROOF!
WAFF!
YIPE!
RUFF!
YIP!
YEEARK!
YARK!
AAARRK!
FROM INSIDE THE HOUSE, WE COULD HEAR THE DOGS YOWLING...
...IN PAIN... IN TERROR...
BUT WE COULDN'T HELP THEM...
...COULDN'T EVEN LOOK.

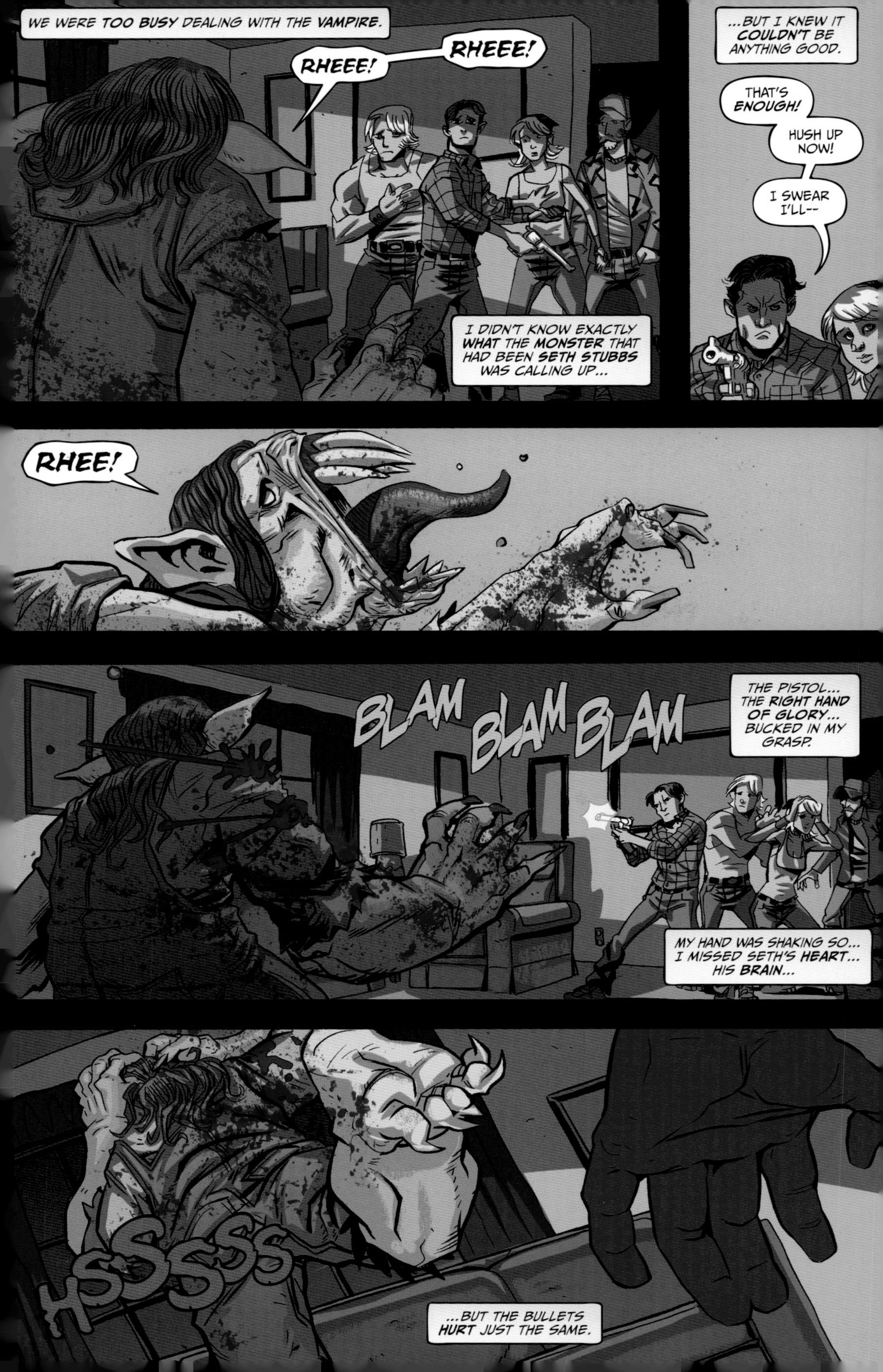
WE WERE TOO BUSY DEALING WITH THE VAMPIRE.
RHEEE!
RHEEE!
I DIDN'T KNOW EXACTLY WHAT THE MONSTER THAT HAD BEEN SETH STUBBS WAS CALLING UP...
...BUT I KNEW IT COULDN'T BE ANYTHING GOOD.
THAT'S ENOUGH!
HUSH UP NOW!
I SWEAR I'LL--
RHEE!
BLAM BLAM BLAM
THE PISTOL... THE RIGHT HAND OF GLORY... BUCKED IN MY GRASP.
MY HAND WAS SHAKING SO... I MISSED SETH'S HEART... HIS BRAIN...
HSSSSS
...BUT THE BULLETS HURT JUST THE SAME.

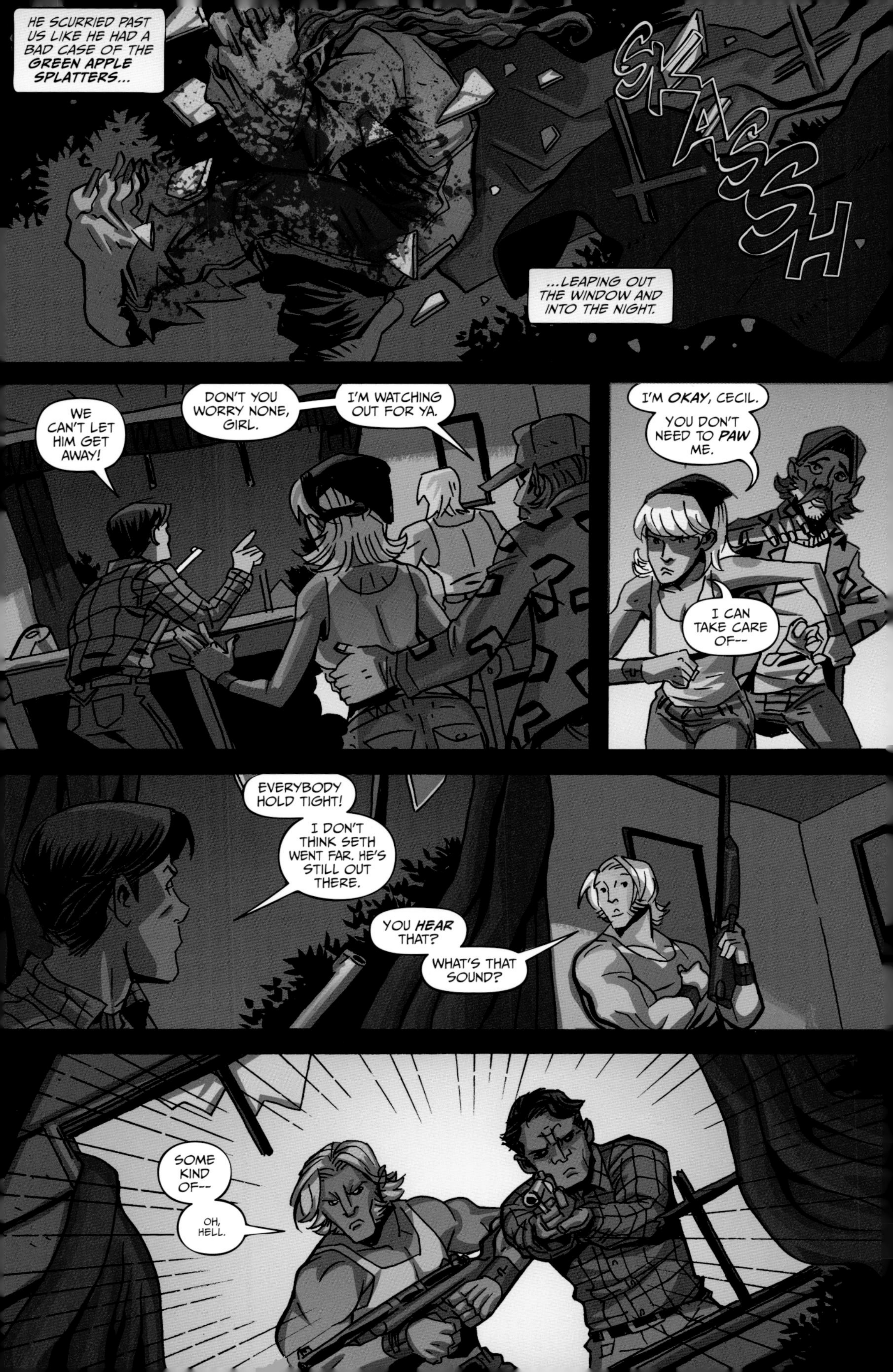
HE SCURRIED PAST US LIKE HE HAD A BAD CASE OF THE GREEN APPLE SPLATTERS...
SKASSCH
...LEAPING OUT THE WINDOW AND INTO THE NIGHT.
WE CAN'T LET HIM GET AWAY!
DON'T YOU WORRY NONE, GIRL.
I'M WATCHING OUT FOR YA.
I'M OKAY, CECIL.
YOU DON'T NEED TO PAW ME.
I CAN TAKE CARE OF--
EVERYBODY HOLD TIGHT!
I DON'T THINK SETH WENT FAR. HE'S STILL OUT THERE.
YOU HEAR THAT?
WHAT'S THAT SOUND?
SOME KIND OF--
OH, HELL.

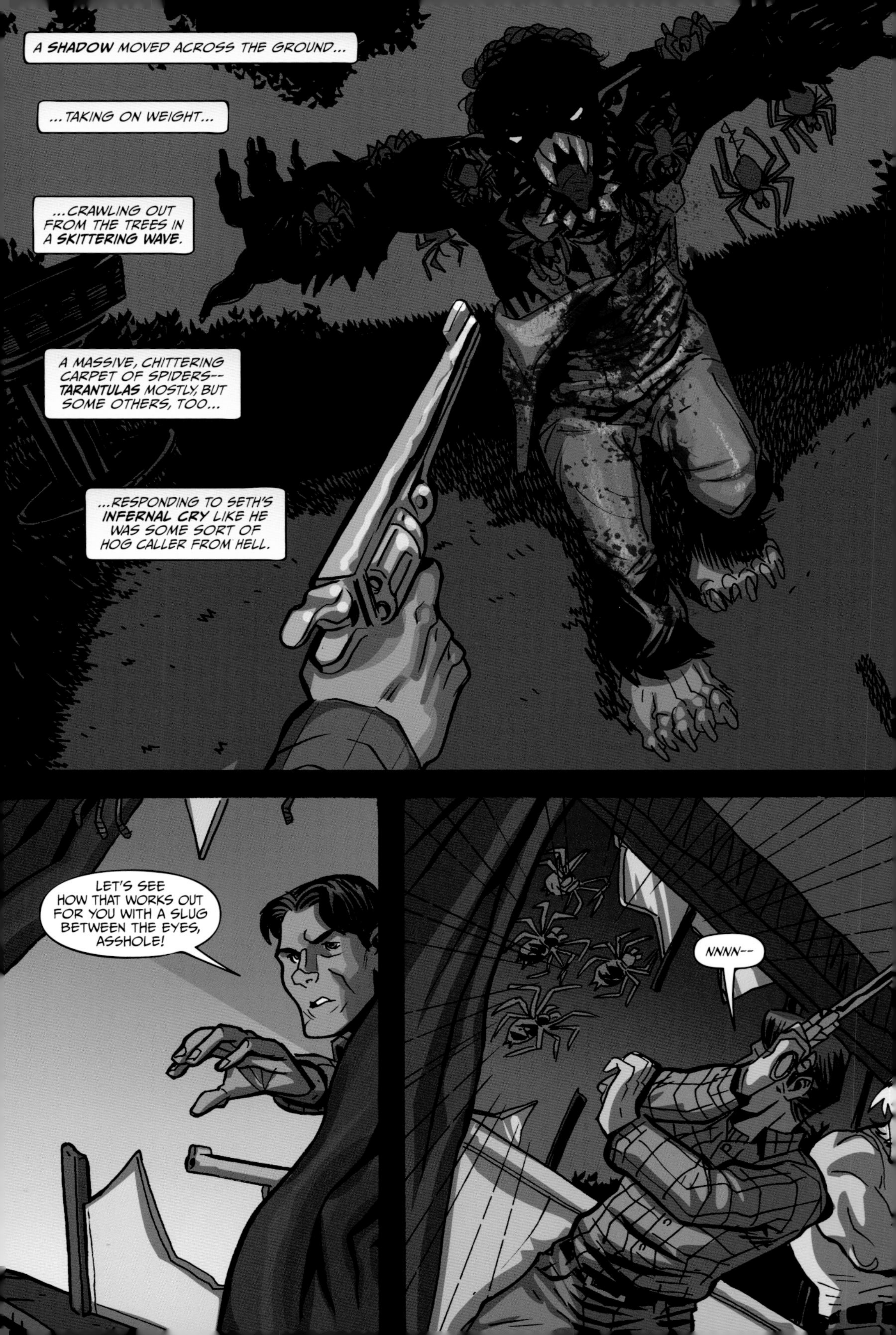
A SHADOW MOVED ACROSS THE GROUND...
...TAKING ON WEIGHT...
...CRAWLING OUT FROM THE TREES IN A SKITTERING WAVE.
A MASSIVE, CHITTERING CARPET OF SPIDERS-- TARANTULAS MOSTLY, BUT SOME OTHERS, TOO...
...RESPONDING TO SETH'S INFERNAL CRY LIKE HE WAS SOME SORT OF HOG CALLER FROM HELL.
LET'S SEE HOW THAT WORKS OUT FOR YOU WITH A SLUG BETWEEN THE EYES, ASSHOLE!
NNNN--

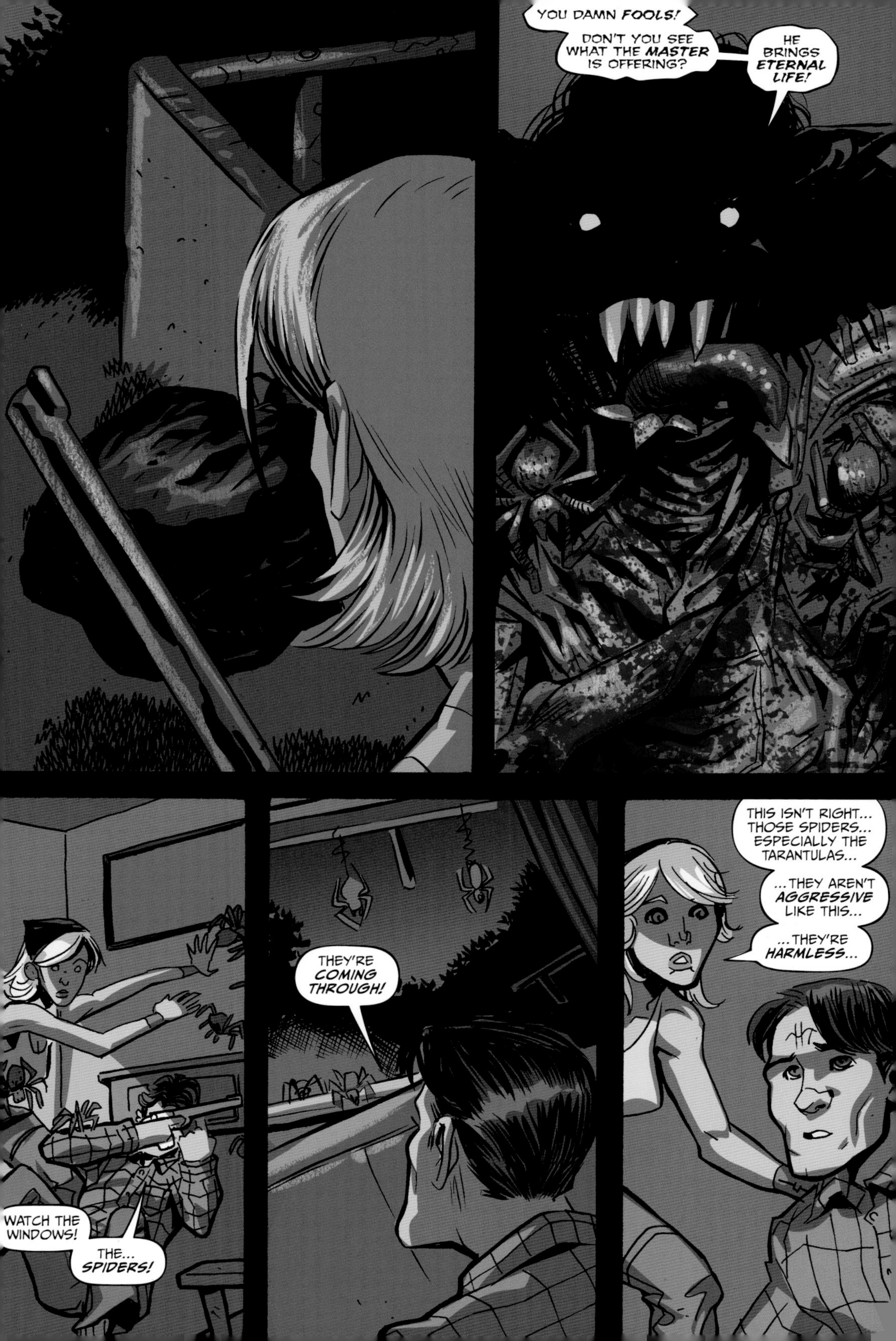
YOU DAMN FOOLS!
DON'T YOU SEE WHAT THE MASTER IS OFFERING?
HE BRINGS ETERNAL LIFE!
WATCH THE WINDOWS!
THE... SPIDERS!
THEY'RE COMING THROUGH!
THIS ISN'T RIGHT... THOSE SPIDERS... ESPECIALLY THE TARANTULAS...
...THEY AREN'T AGGRESSIVE LIKE THIS...
...THEY'RE HARMLESS...

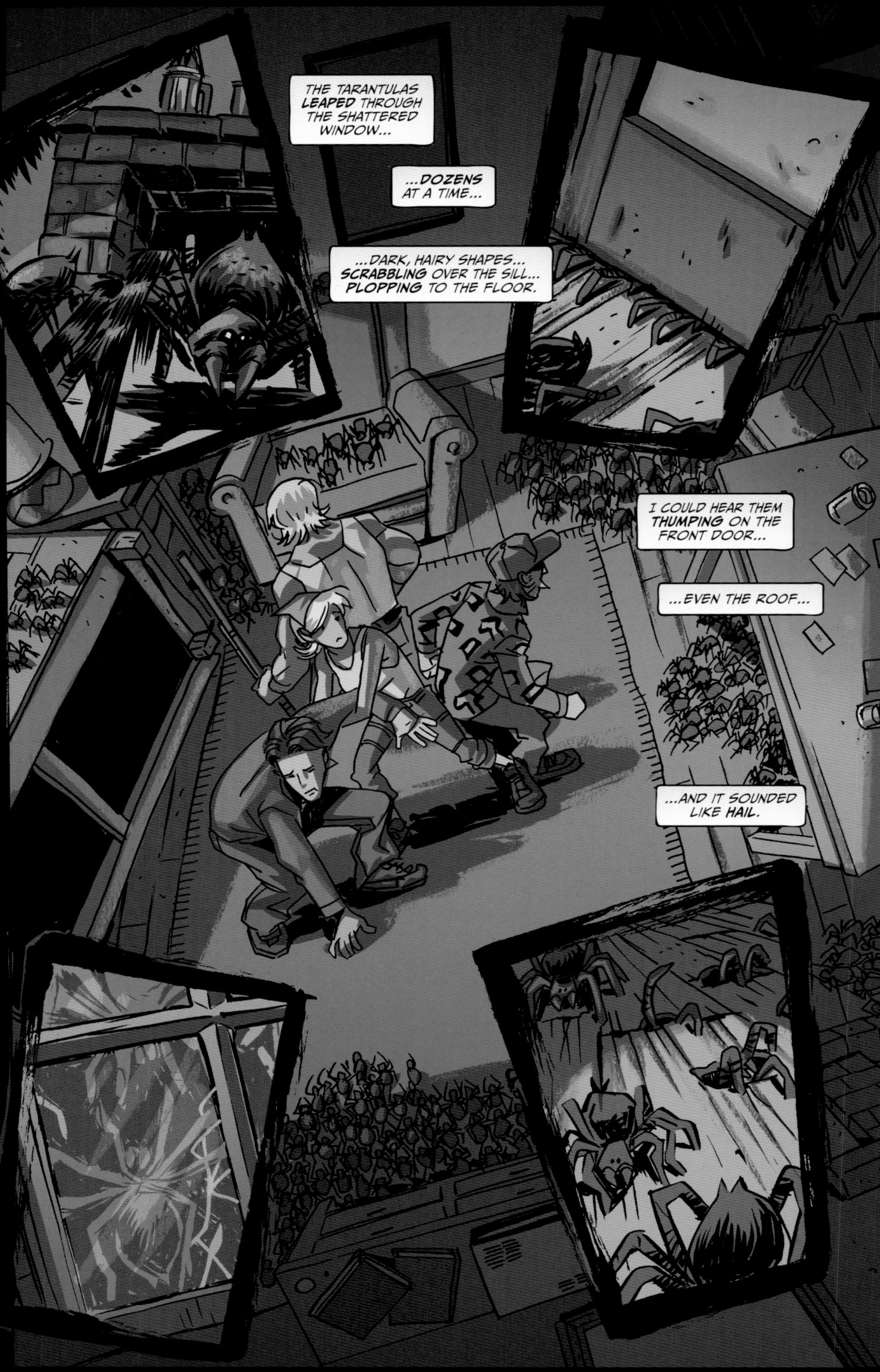
THE TARANTULAS **LEAPED** THROUGH THE SHATTERED WINDOW...
...**DOZENS** AT A TIME...
...DARK, HAIRY SHAPES... **SCRABBLING** OVER THE SILL... **PLOPPING** TO THE FLOOR.
I COULD HEAR THEM **THUMPING** ON THE FRONT DOOR...
...EVEN THE ROOF...
...AND IT SOUNDED LIKE **HAIL**.

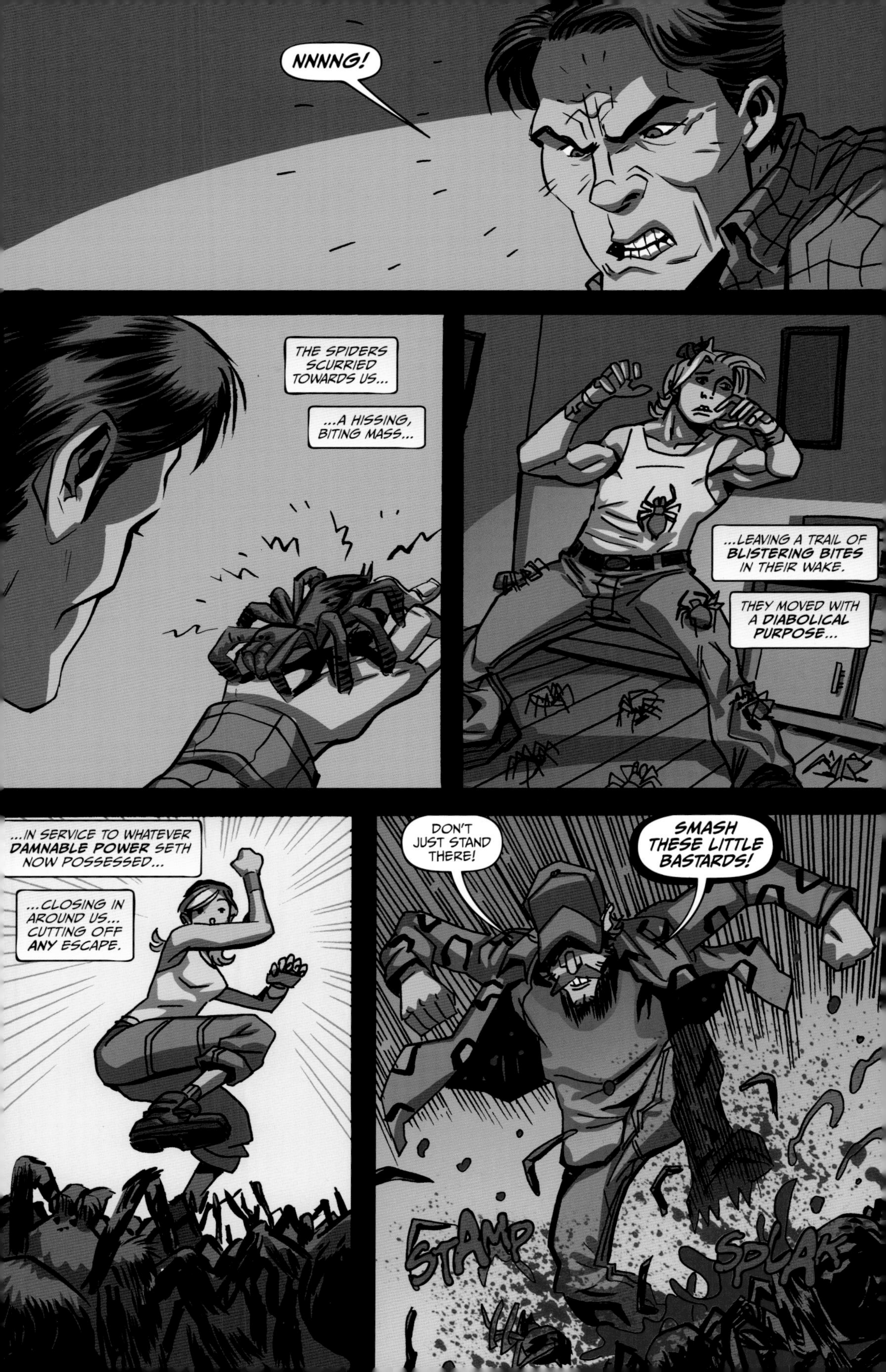
NNNNG!
THE SPIDERS SCURRIED TOWARDS US...
...A HISSING, BITING MASS...
...LEAVING A TRAIL OF BLISTERING BITES IN THEIR WAKE.
THEY MOVED WITH A DIABOLICAL PURPOSE...
...IN SERVICE TO WHATEVER DAMNABLE POWER SETH NOW POSSESSED...
...CLOSING IN AROUND US... CUTTING OFF ANY ESCAPE.
DON'T JUST STAND THERE!
SMASH THESE LITTLE BASTARDS!
STAMP
SPLAK

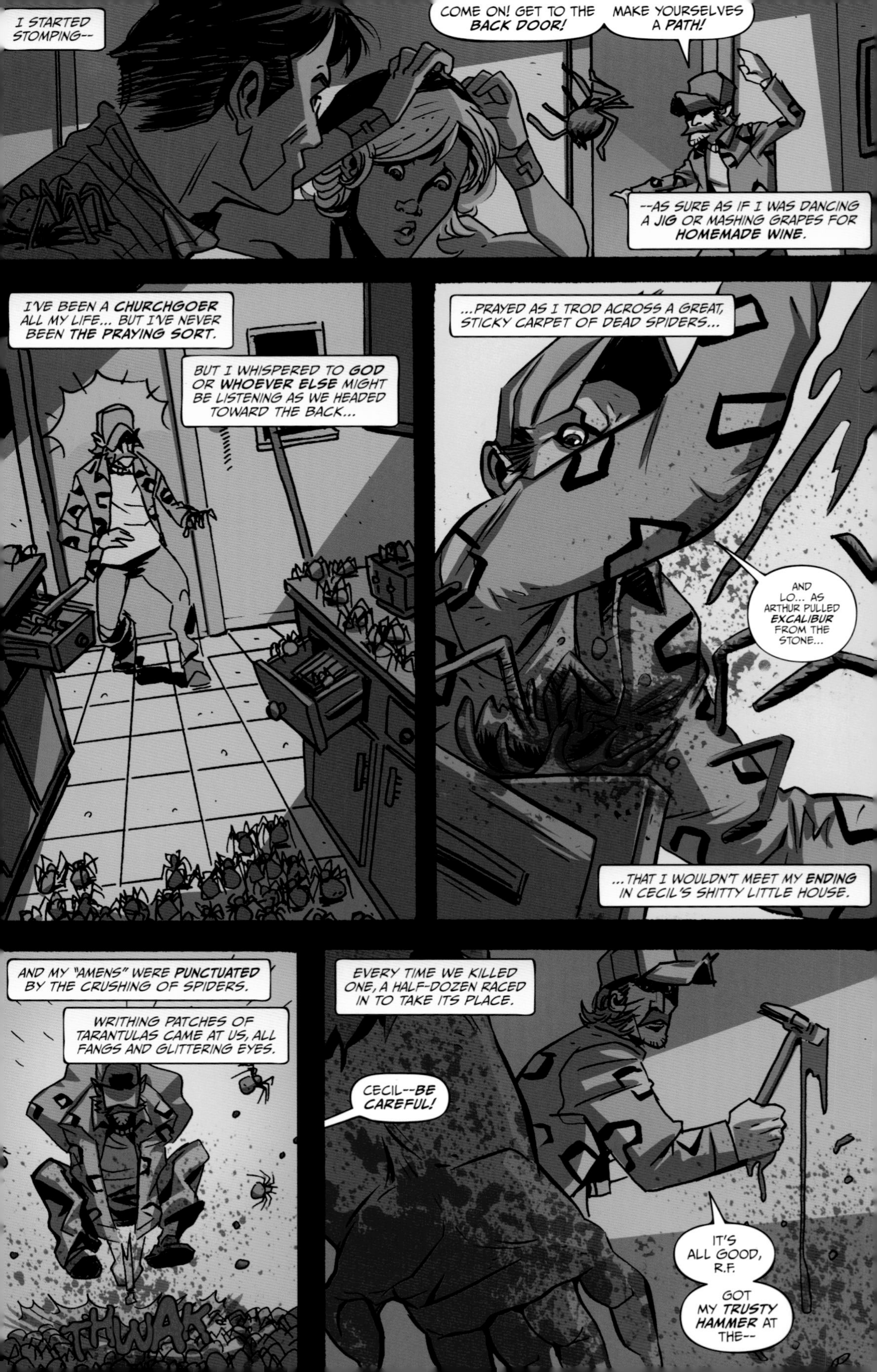
I STARTED STOMPING--
COME ON! GET TO THE BACK DOOR!
MAKE YOURSELVES A PATH!
--AS SURE AS IF I WAS DANCING A JIG OR MASHING GRAPES FOR HOMEMADE WINE.
I'VE BEEN A CHURCHGOER ALL MY LIFE... BUT I'VE NEVER BEEN THE PRAYING SORT.
BUT I WHISPERED TO GOD OR WHOEVER ELSE MIGHT BE LISTENING AS WE HEADED TOWARD THE BACK...
...PRAYED AS I TROD ACROSS A GREAT, STICKY CARPET OF DEAD SPIDERS...
AND LO... AS ARTHUR PULLED EXCALIBUR FROM THE STONE...
...THAT I WOULDN'T MEET MY ENDING IN CECIL'S SHITTY LITTLE HOUSE.
AND MY "AMENS" WERE PUNCTUATED BY THE CRUSHING OF SPIDERS.
WRITHING PATCHES OF TARANTULAS CAME AT US, ALL FANGS AND GLITTERING EYES.
THWAK
EVERY TIME WE KILLED ONE, A HALF-DOZEN RACED IN TO TAKE ITS PLACE.
CECIL--BE CAREFUL!
IT'S ALL GOOD, R.F.
GOT MY TRUSTY HAMMER AT THE--

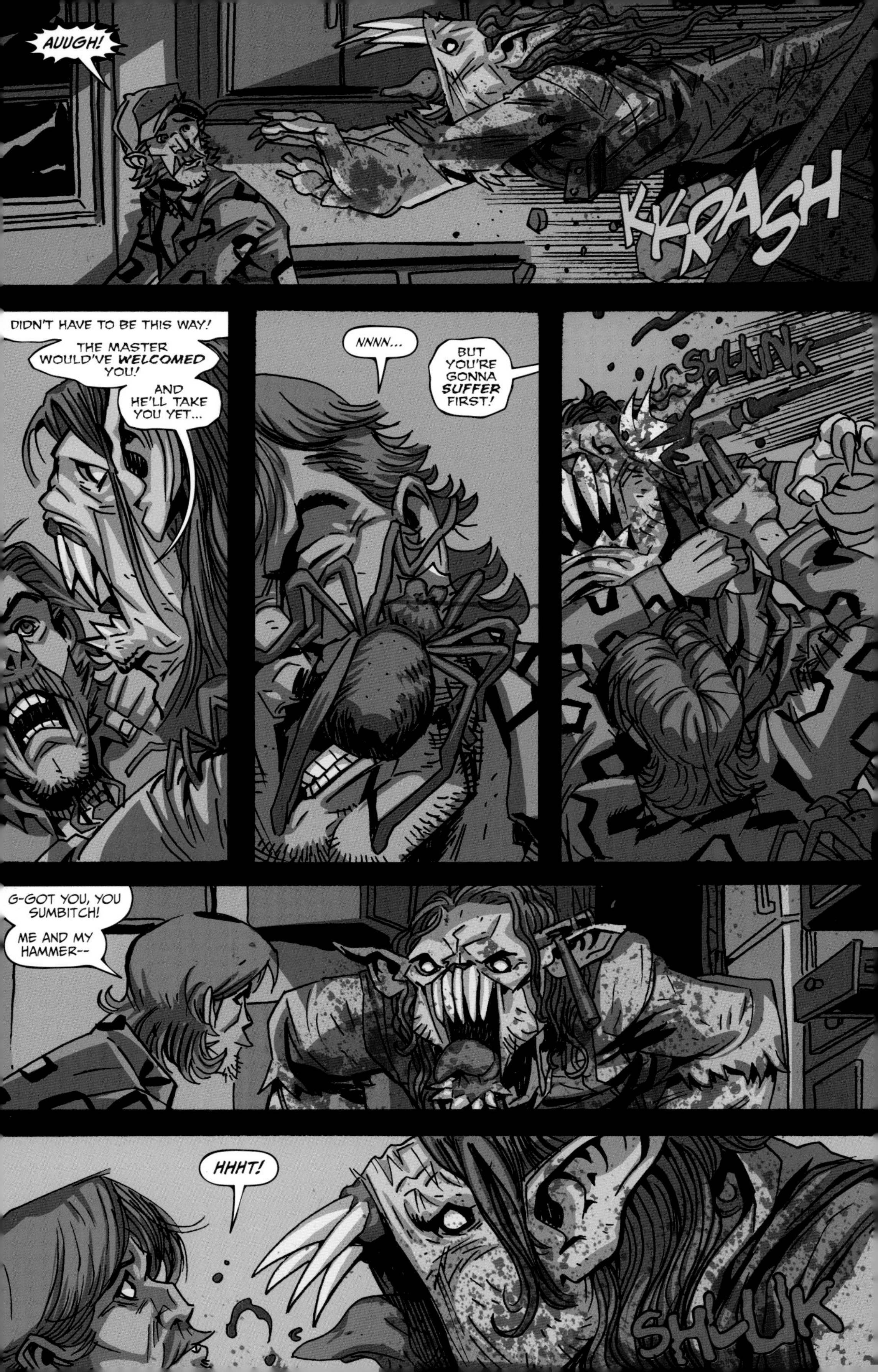

AUUGH!
KKRASH
DIDN'T HAVE TO BE THIS WAY!
THE MASTER WOULD'VE WELCOMED YOU!
AND HE'LL TAKE YOU YET...
NNNN...
BUT YOU'RE GONNA SUFFER FIRST!
SHUNK
G-GOT YOU, YOU SUMBITCH!
ME AND MY HAMMER--
HHHT!
SHLUK

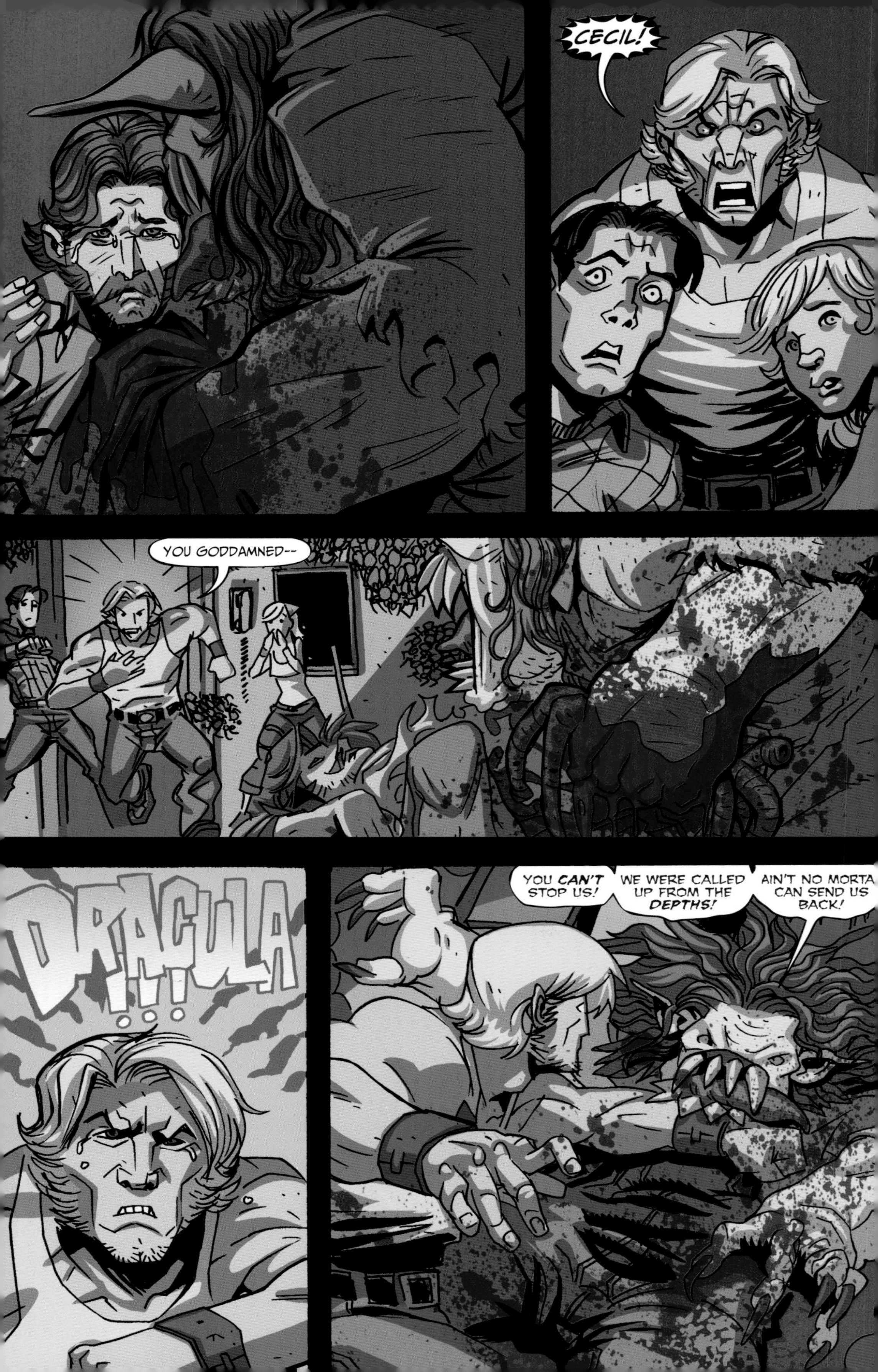
CECIL!
YOU GODDAMNED--
DRACULA!!!!
...
YOU CAN'T STOP US!
WE WERE CALLED UP FROM THE DEPTHS!
AIN'T NO MORTA CAN SEND US BACK!

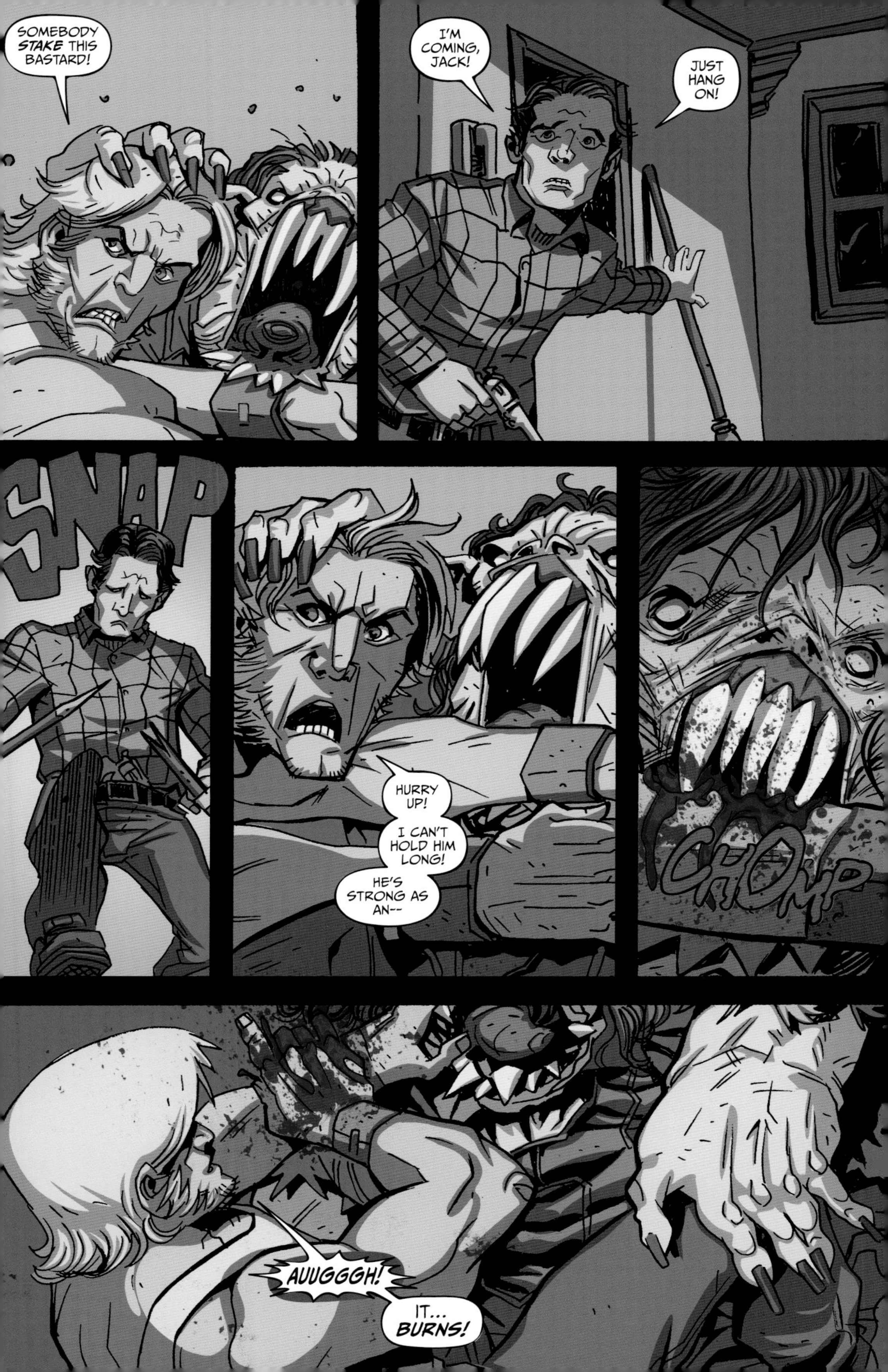
SOMEBODY STAKE THIS BASTARD!
I'M COMING, JACK!
JUST HANG ON!
SNAP
HURRY UP!
I CAN'T HOLD HIM LONG!
HE'S STRONG AS AN--
CHOMP
AUUGGGH!
IT... BURNS!

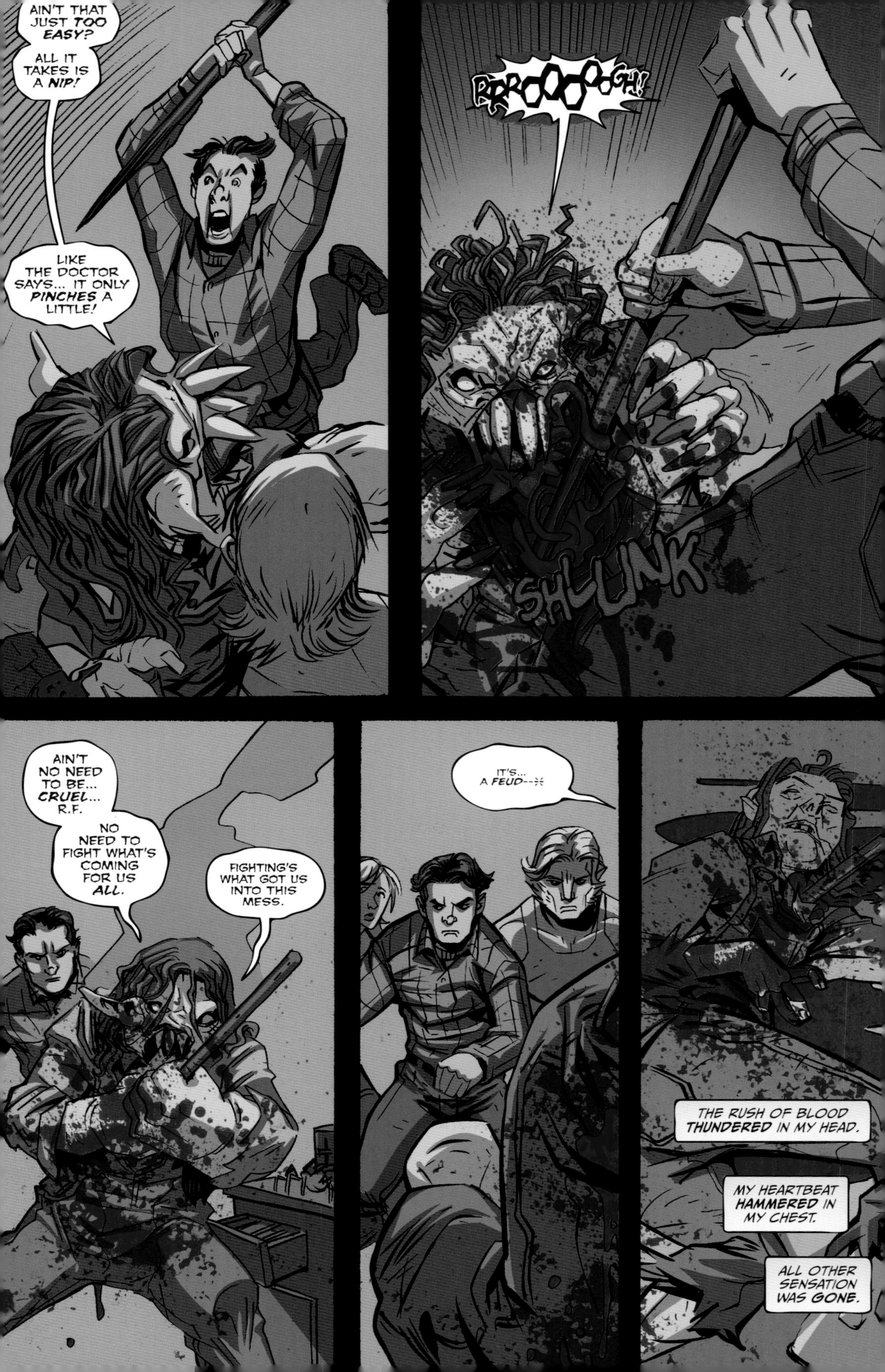
AIN'T THAT JUST TOO EASY?
ALL IT TAKES IS A NIP!
LIKE THE DOCTOR SAYS... IT ONLY PINCHES A LITTLE!
RRRROOOOOGH!!
SHLUNK
AIN'T NO NEED TO BE... CRUEL... R.F.
NO NEED TO FIGHT WHAT'S COMING FOR US ALL.
FIGHTING'S WHAT GOT US INTO THIS MESS.
IT'S... A FEUD--
THE RUSH OF BLOOD THUNDERED IN MY HEAD.
MY HEARTBEAT HAMMERED IN MY CHEST.
ALL OTHER SENSATION WAS GONE.

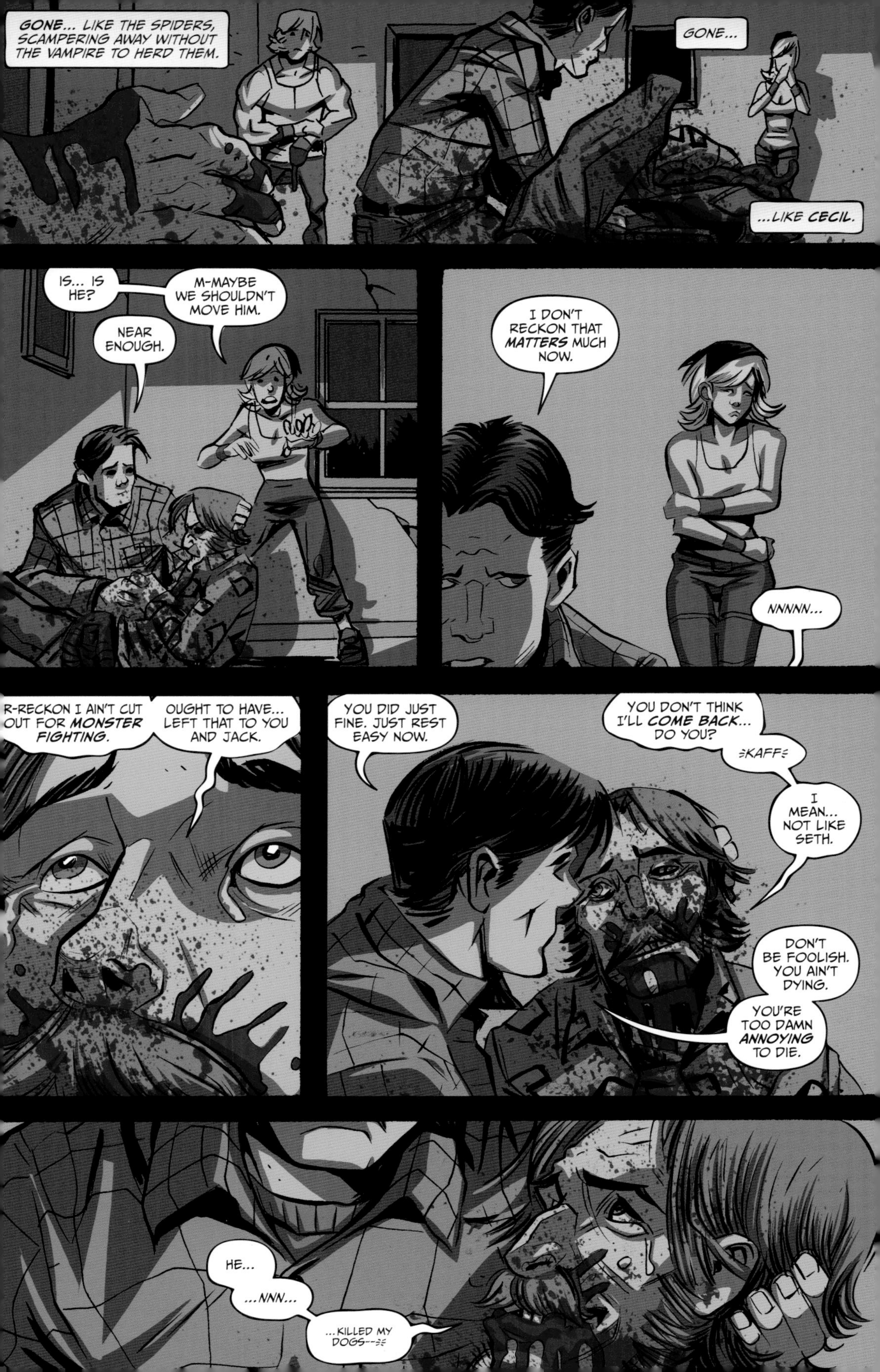
GONE... LIKE THE SPIDERS, SCAMPERING AWAY WITHOUT THE VAMPIRE TO HERD THEM.
GONE...
...LIKE CECIL.
IS... IS HE?
M-MAYBE WE SHOULDN'T MOVE HIM.
NEAR ENOUGH.
I DON'T RECKON THAT MATTERS MUCH NOW.
NNNNN...
R-RECKON I AIN'T CUT OUT FOR MONSTER FIGHTING.
OUGHT TO HAVE... LEFT THAT TO YOU AND JACK.
YOU DID JUST FINE. JUST REST EASY NOW.
YOU DON'T THINK I'LL COME BACK... DO YOU?
KAFF
I MEAN... NOT LIKE SETH.
DON'T BE FOOLISH. YOU AIN'T DYING.
YOU'RE TOO DAMN ANNOYING TO DIE.
HE...
...NNN...
...KILLED MY DOGS--

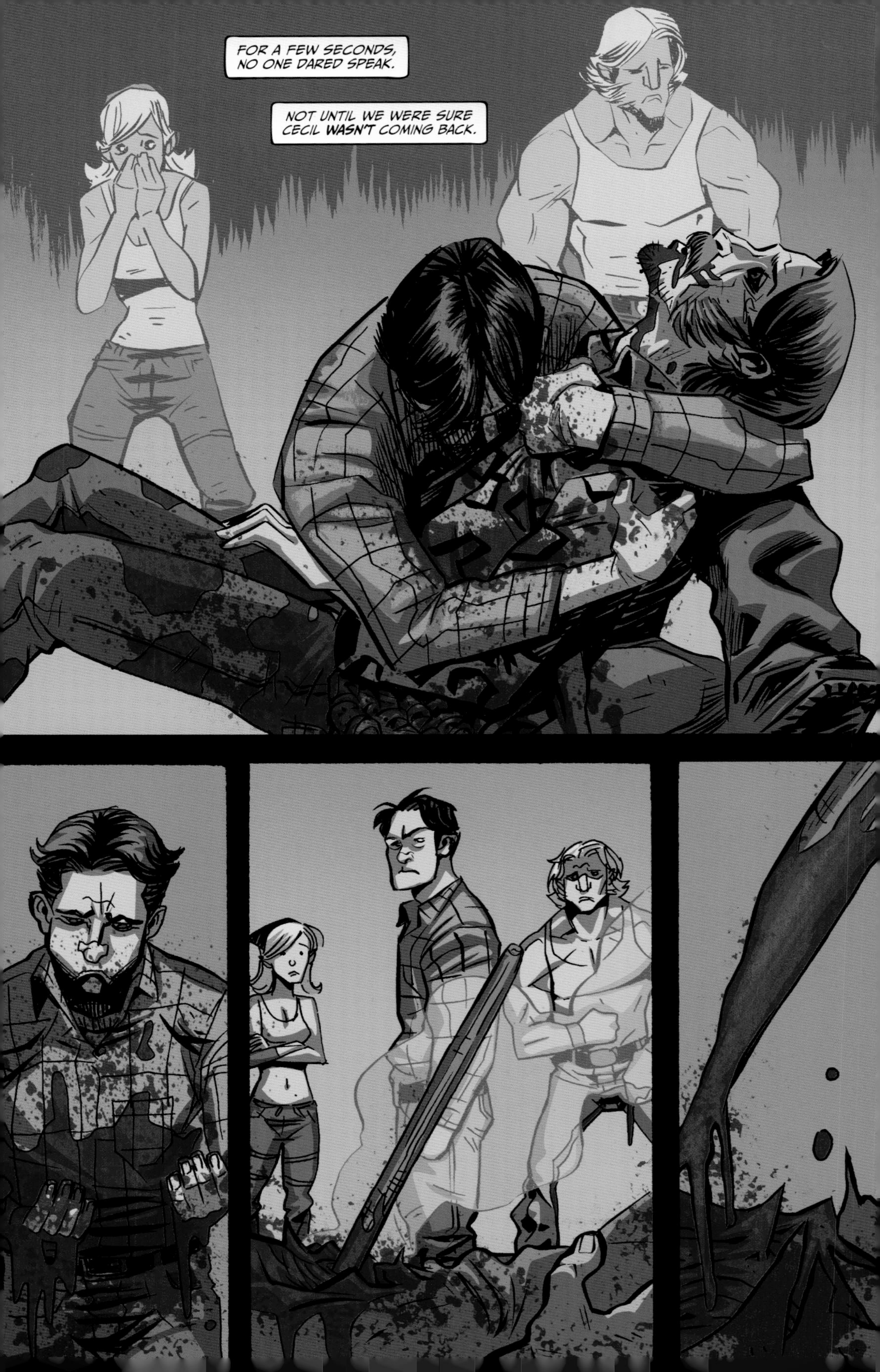
FOR A FEW SECONDS, NO ONE DARED SPEAK.
NOT UNTIL WE WERE SURE CECIL **WASN'T** COMING BACK.

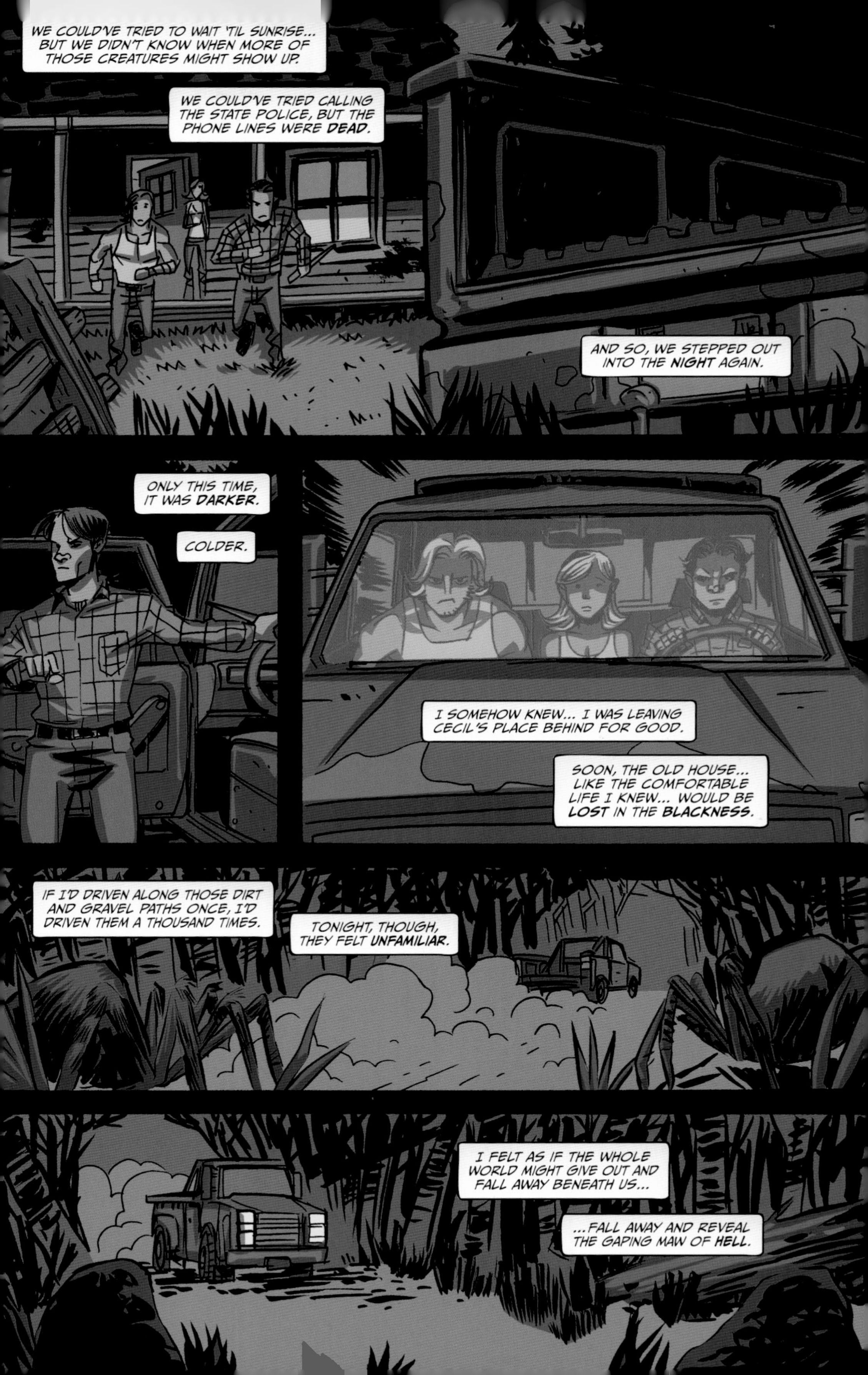

WE COULD'VE TRIED TO WAIT 'TIL SUNRISE... BUT WE DIDN'T KNOW WHEN MORE OF THOSE CREATURES MIGHT SHOW UP.
WE COULD'VE TRIED CALLING THE STATE POLICE, BUT THE PHONE LINES WERE **DEAD**.
AND SO, WE STEPPED OUT INTO THE **NIGHT** AGAIN.
ONLY THIS TIME, IT WAS **DARKER**.
COLDER.
I SOMEHOW KNEW... I WAS LEAVING CECIL'S PLACE BEHIND FOR GOOD.
SOON, THE OLD HOUSE... LIKE THE COMFORTABLE LIFE I KNEW... WOULD BE **LOST** IN THE **BLACKNESS**.
IF I'D DRIVEN ALONG THOSE DIRT AND GRAVEL PATHS ONCE, I'D DRIVEN THEM A THOUSAND TIMES.
TONIGHT, THOUGH, THEY FELT **UNFAMILIAR**.
I FELT AS IF THE WHOLE WORLD MIGHT GIVE OUT AND FALL AWAY BENEATH US...
...FALL AWAY AND REVEAL THE GAPING MAW OF **HELL**.

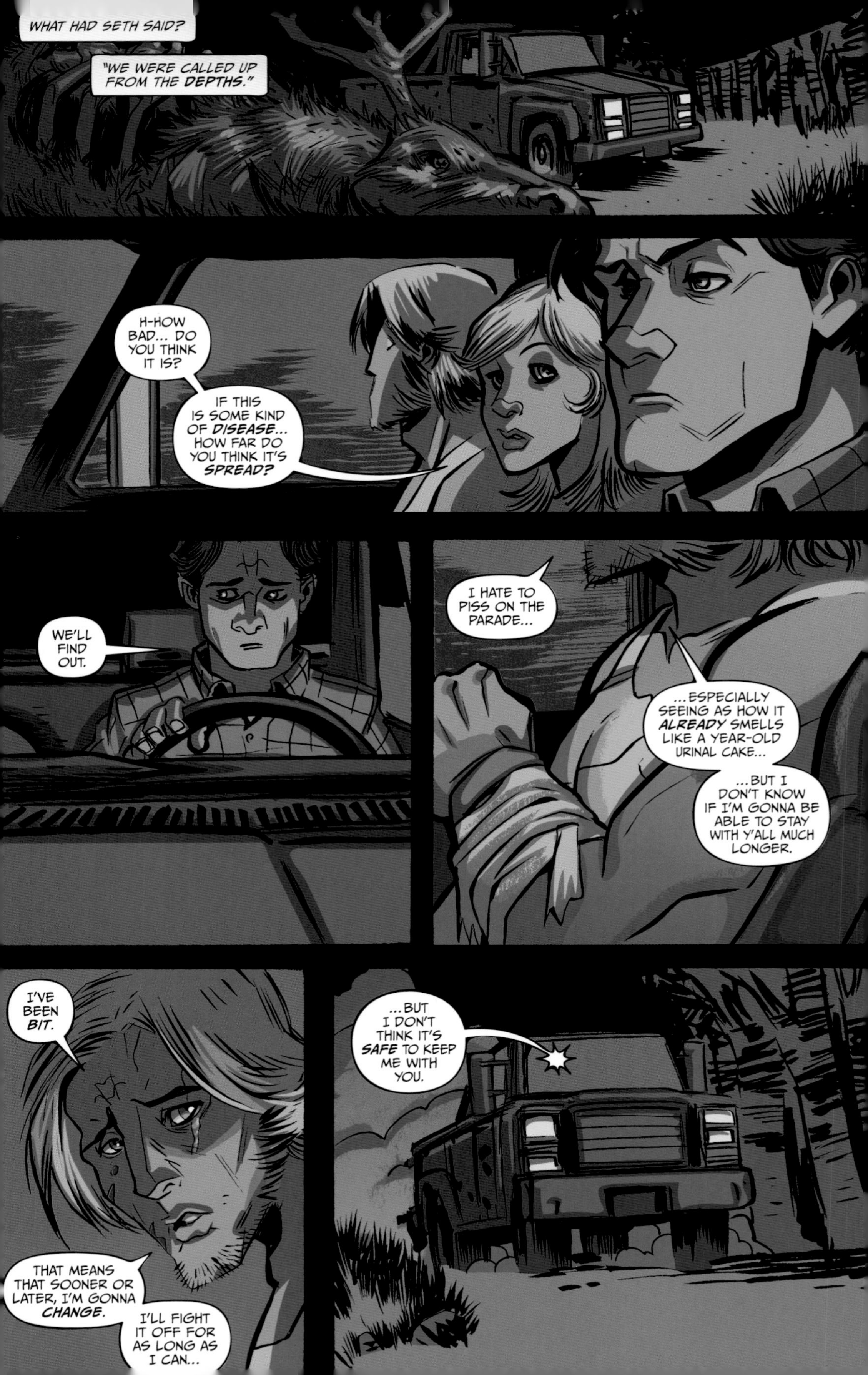

WHAT HAD SETH SAID?
"WE WERE CALLED UP FROM THE DEPTHS."
H-HOW BAD... DO YOU THINK IT IS?
IF THIS IS SOME KIND OF DISEASE... HOW FAR DO YOU THINK IT'S SPREAD?
WE'LL FIND OUT.
I HATE TO PISS ON THE PARADE...
...ESPECIALLY SEEING AS HOW IT ALREADY SMELLS LIKE A YEAR-OLD URINAL CAKE...
...BUT I DON'T KNOW IF I'M GONNA BE ABLE TO STAY WITH Y'ALL MUCH LONGER.
I'VE BEEN BIT.
THAT MEANS THAT SOONER OR LATER, I'M GONNA CHANGE.
I'LL FIGHT IT OFF FOR AS LONG AS I CAN...
...BUT I DON'T THINK IT'S SAFE TO KEEP ME WITH YOU.

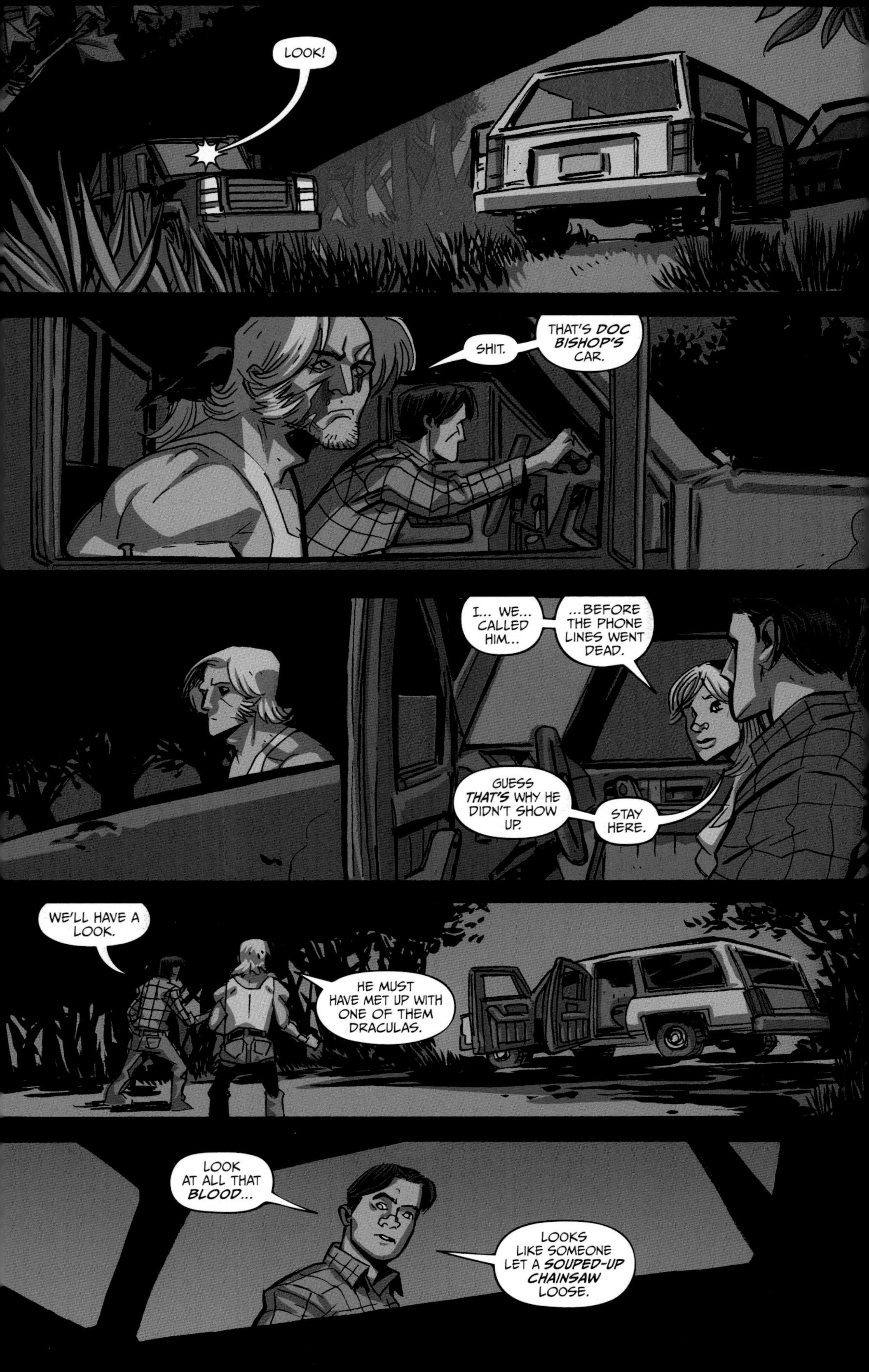
LOOK!
SHIT.
THAT'S DOC BISHOP'S CAR.
I... WE... CALLED HIM...
...BEFORE THE PHONE LINES WENT DEAD.
GUESS THAT'S WHY HE DIDN'T SHOW UP.
STAY HERE.
WE'LL HAVE A LOOK.
HE MUST HAVE MET UP WITH ONE OF THEM DRACULAS.
LOOK AT ALL THAT BLOOD...
LOOKS LIKE SOMEONE LET A SOUPED-UP CHAINSAW LOOSE.

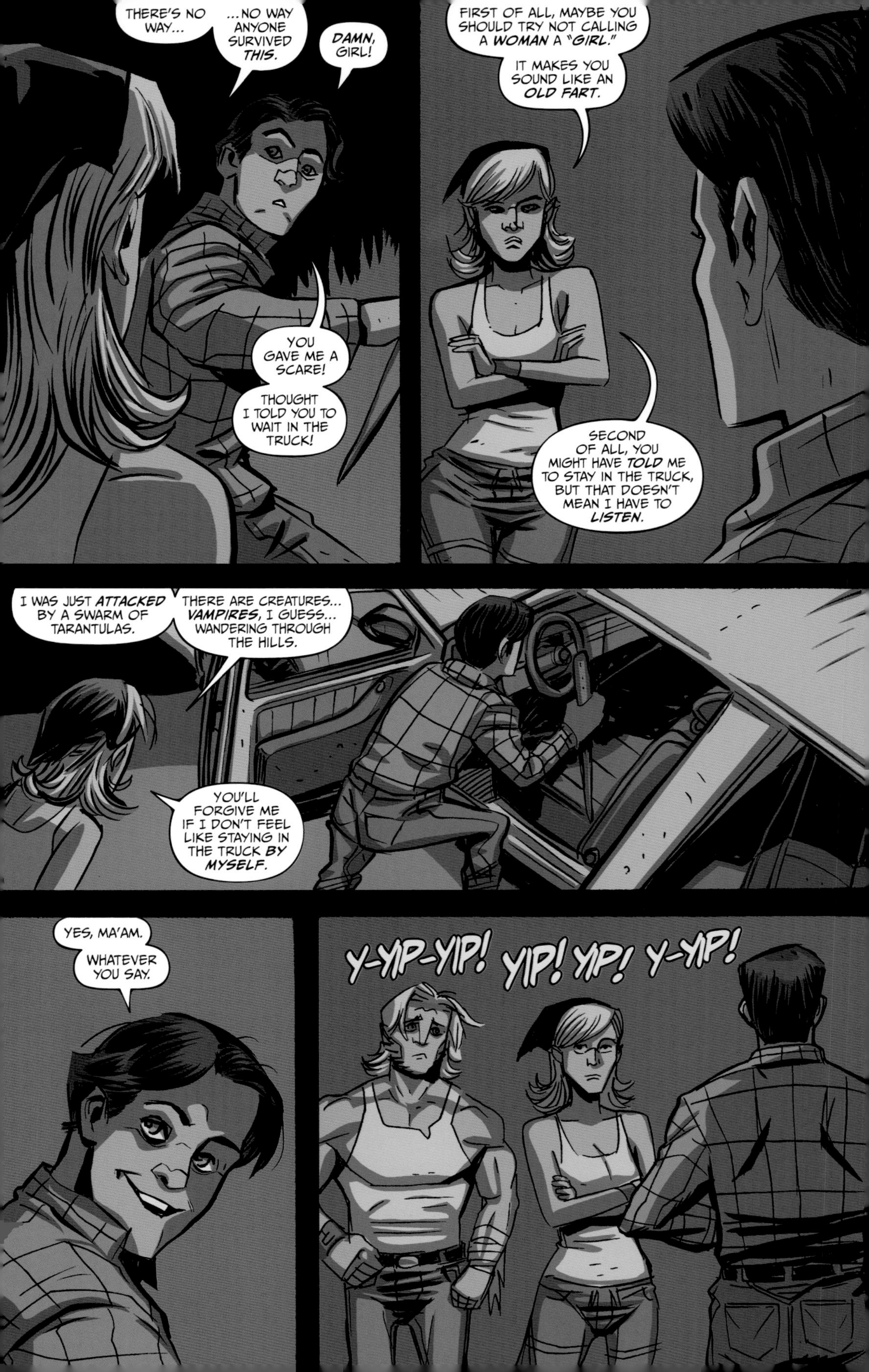
THERE'S NO WAY...
...NO WAY ANYONE SURVIVED THIS.
DAMN, GIRL!
YOU GAVE ME A SCARE!
THOUGHT I TOLD YOU TO WAIT IN THE TRUCK!
FIRST OF ALL, MAYBE YOU SHOULD TRY NOT CALLING A WOMAN A "GIRL."
IT MAKES YOU SOUND LIKE AN OLD FART.
SECOND OF ALL, YOU MIGHT HAVE TOLD ME TO STAY IN THE TRUCK, BUT THAT DOESN'T MEAN I HAVE TO LISTEN.
I WAS JUST ATTACKED BY A SWARM OF TARANTULAS.
THERE ARE CREATURES... VAMPIRES, I GUESS... WANDERING THROUGH THE HILLS.
YOU'LL FORGIVE ME IF I DON'T FEEL LIKE STAYING IN THE TRUCK BY MYSELF.
YES, MA'AM.
WHATEVER YOU SAY.
Y-YIP-YIP! YIP! YIP! Y-YIP!

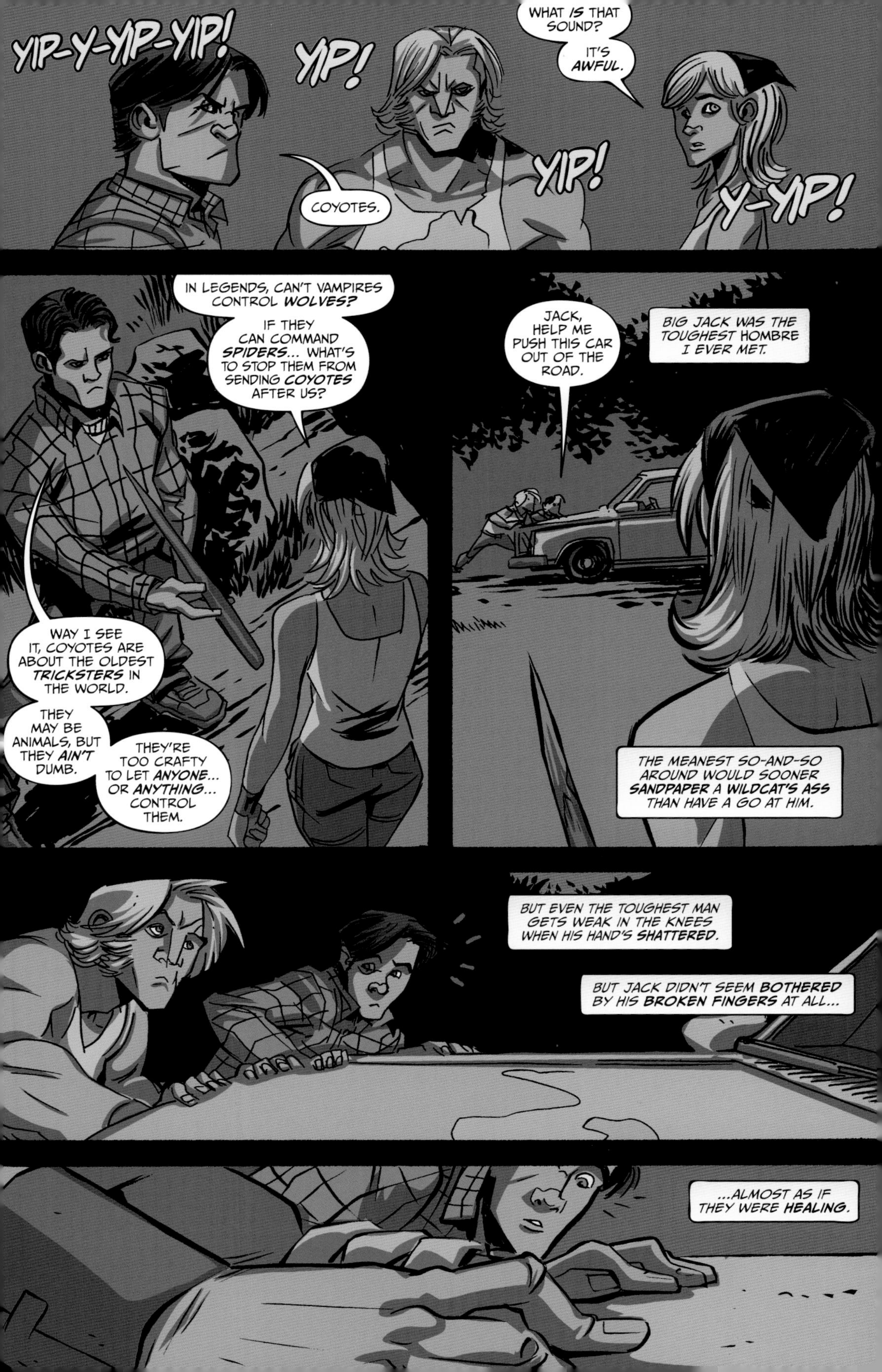
YIP-Y-YIP-YIP!
YIP!
WHAT IS THAT SOUND?
IT'S AWFUL.
COYOTES.
YIP!
Y-YIP!
IN LEGENDS, CAN'T VAMPIRES CONTROL WOLVES?
IF THEY CAN COMMAND SPIDERS... WHAT'S TO STOP THEM FROM SENDING COYOTES AFTER US?
WAY I SEE IT, COYOTES ARE ABOUT THE OLDEST TRICKSTERS IN THE WORLD.
THEY MAY BE ANIMALS, BUT THEY AIN'T DUMB.
THEY'RE TOO CRAFTY TO LET ANYONE... OR ANYTHING... CONTROL THEM.
BIG JACK WAS THE TOUGHEST HOMBRE I EVER MET.
JACK, HELP ME PUSH THIS CAR OUT OF THE ROAD.
THE MEANEST SO-AND-SO AROUND WOULD SOONER SANDPAPER A WILDCAT'S ASS THAN HAVE A GO AT HIM.
BUT EVEN THE TOUGHEST MAN GETS WEAK IN THE KNEES WHEN HIS HAND'S SHATTERED.
BUT JACK DIDN'T SEEM BOTHERED BY HIS BROKEN FINGERS AT ALL...
...ALMOST AS IF THEY WERE HEALING.

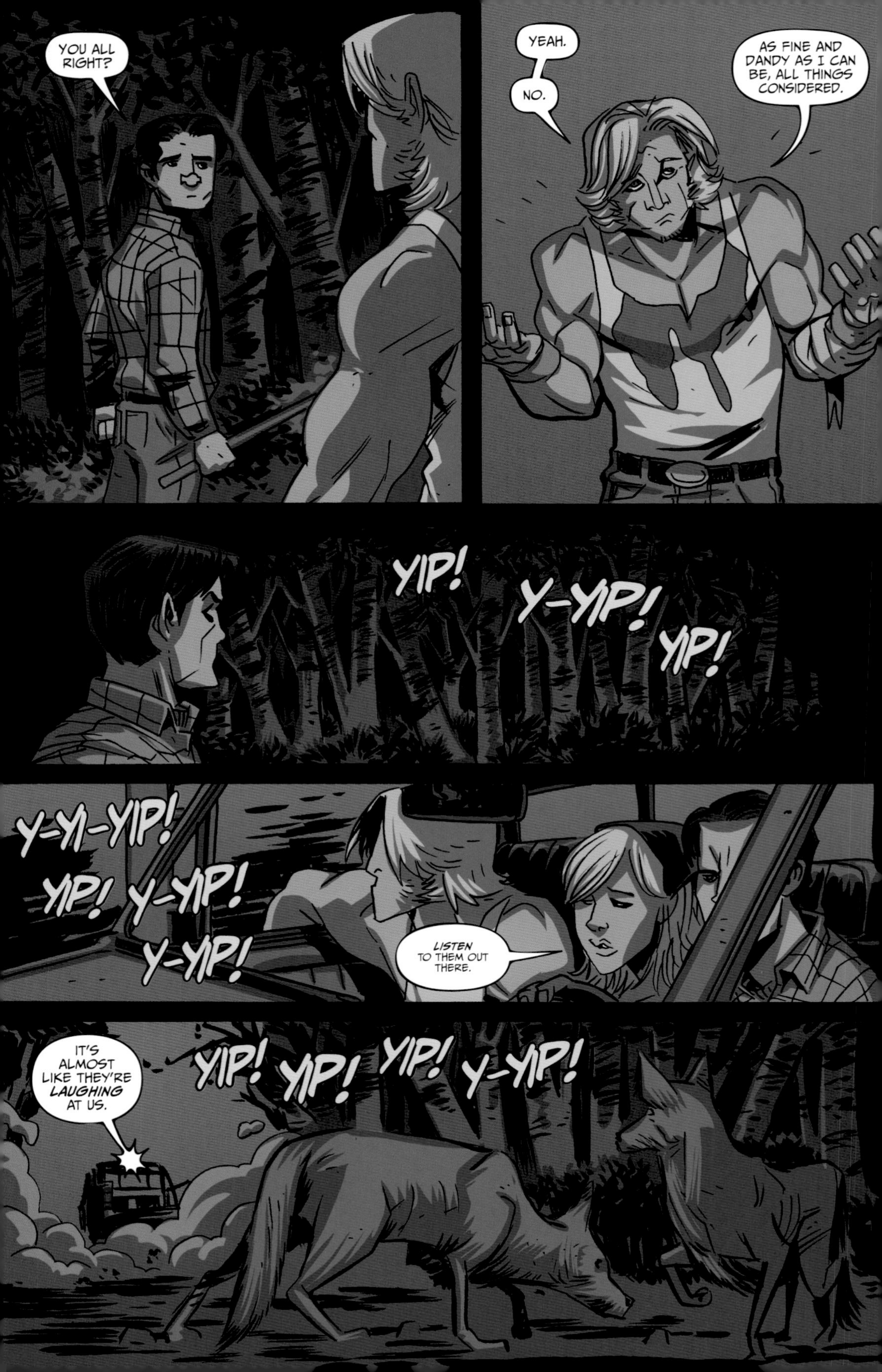
YOU ALL RIGHT?
YEAH.
NO.
AS FINE AND DANDY AS I CAN BE, ALL THINGS CONSIDERED.
YIP!
Y-YIP!
YIP!
Y-YI-YIP!
YIP! Y-YIP!
Y-YIP!
LISTEN TO THEM OUT THERE.
IT'S ALMOST LIKE THEY'RE LAUGHING AT US.
YIP! YIP! YIP! Y-YIP!

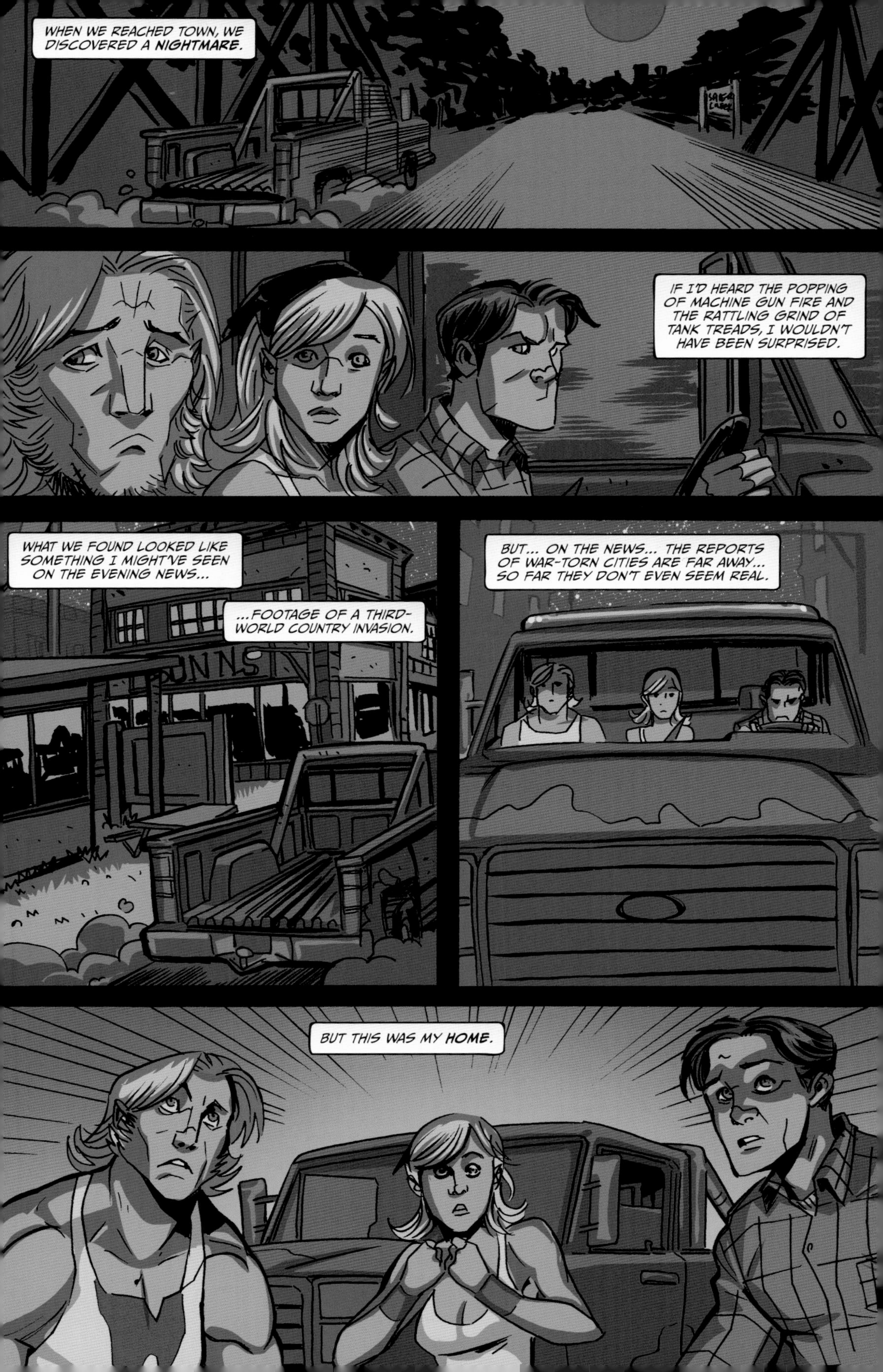
WHEN WE REACHED TOWN, WE DISCOVERED A **NIGHTMARE**.
IF I'D HEARD THE POPPING OF MACHINE GUN FIRE AND THE RATTLING GRIND OF TANK TREADS, I WOULDN'T HAVE BEEN SURPRISED.
WHAT WE FOUND LOOKED LIKE SOMETHING I MIGHT'VE SEEN ON THE EVENING NEWS...
...FOOTAGE OF A THIRD-WORLD COUNTRY INVASION.
BUT... ON THE NEWS... THE REPORTS OF WAR-TORN CITIES ARE FAR AWAY... SO FAR THEY DON'T EVEN SEEM REAL.
BUT THIS WAS MY **HOME**.

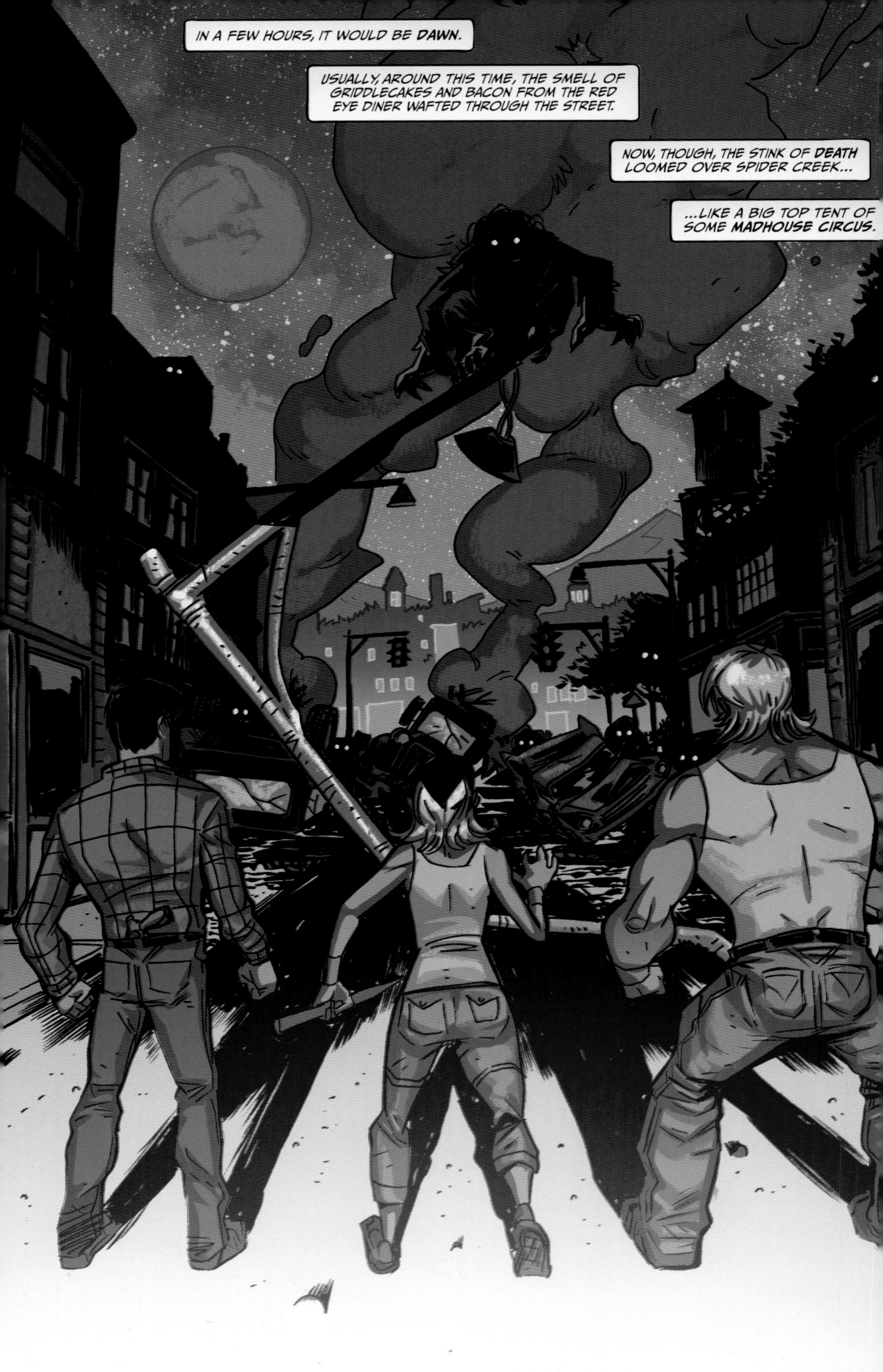
IN A FEW HOURS, IT WOULD BE DAWN.
USUALLY, AROUND THIS TIME, THE SMELL OF GRIDDLECAKES AND BACON FROM THE RED EYE DINER WAFTED THROUGH THE STREET.
NOW, THOUGH, THE STINK OF DEATH LOOMED OVER SPIDER CREEK...
...LIKE A BIG TOP TENT OF SOME MADHOUSE CIRCUS.

CHAPTER 4

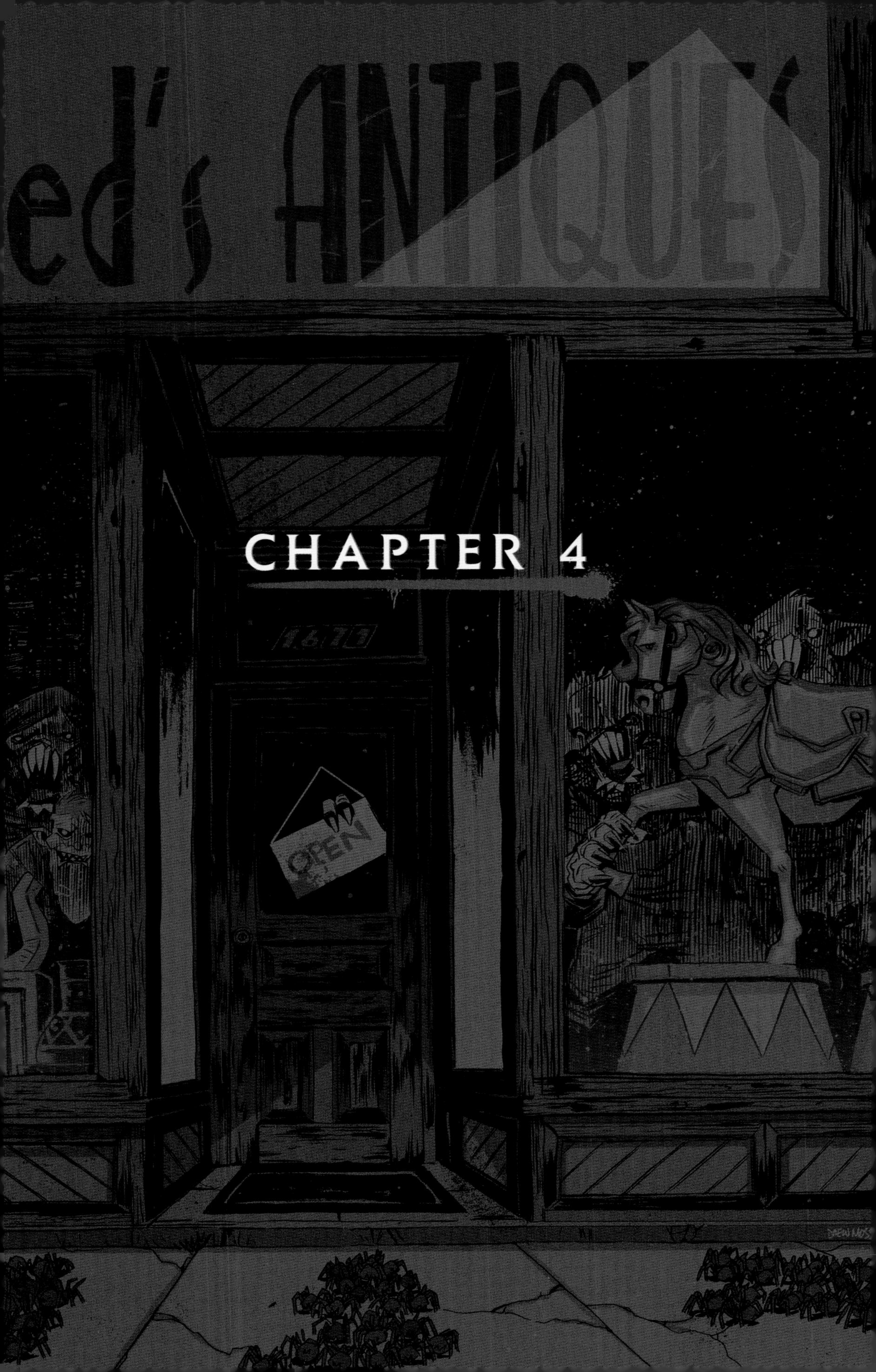

ed's ANTIQUES
OPEN

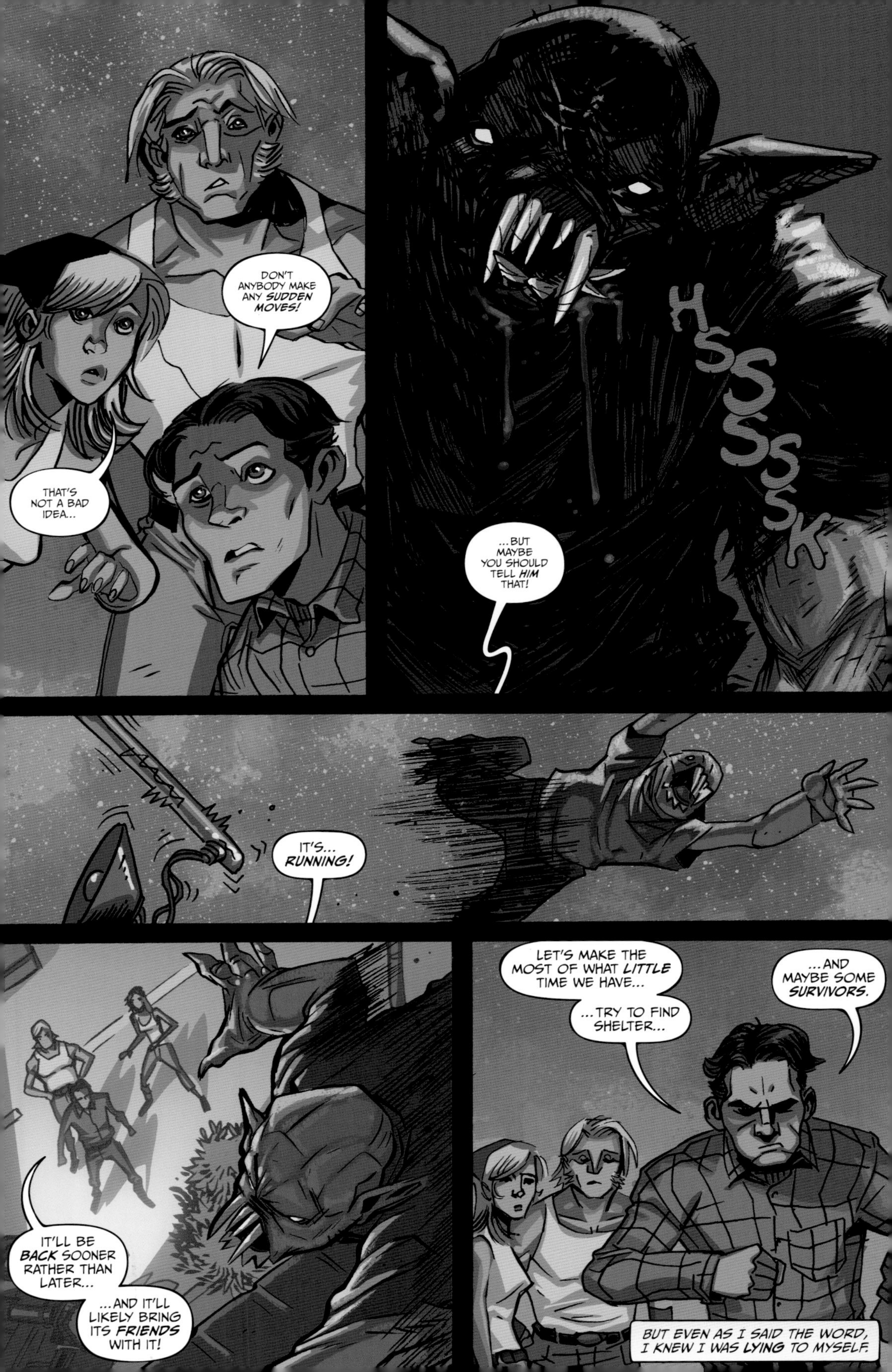
DON'T ANYBODY MAKE ANY SUDDEN MOVES!
THAT'S NOT A BAD IDEA...
...BUT MAYBE YOU SHOULD TELL HIM THAT!
HSSSSSK
IT'S... RUNNING!
IT'LL BE BACK SOONER RATHER THAN LATER...
...AND IT'LL LIKELY BRING ITS FRIENDS WITH IT!
LET'S MAKE THE MOST OF WHAT LITTLE TIME WE HAVE...
...TRY TO FIND SHELTER...
...AND MAYBE SOME SURVIVORS.
BUT EVEN AS I SAID THE WORD, I KNEW I WAS LYING TO MYSELF.

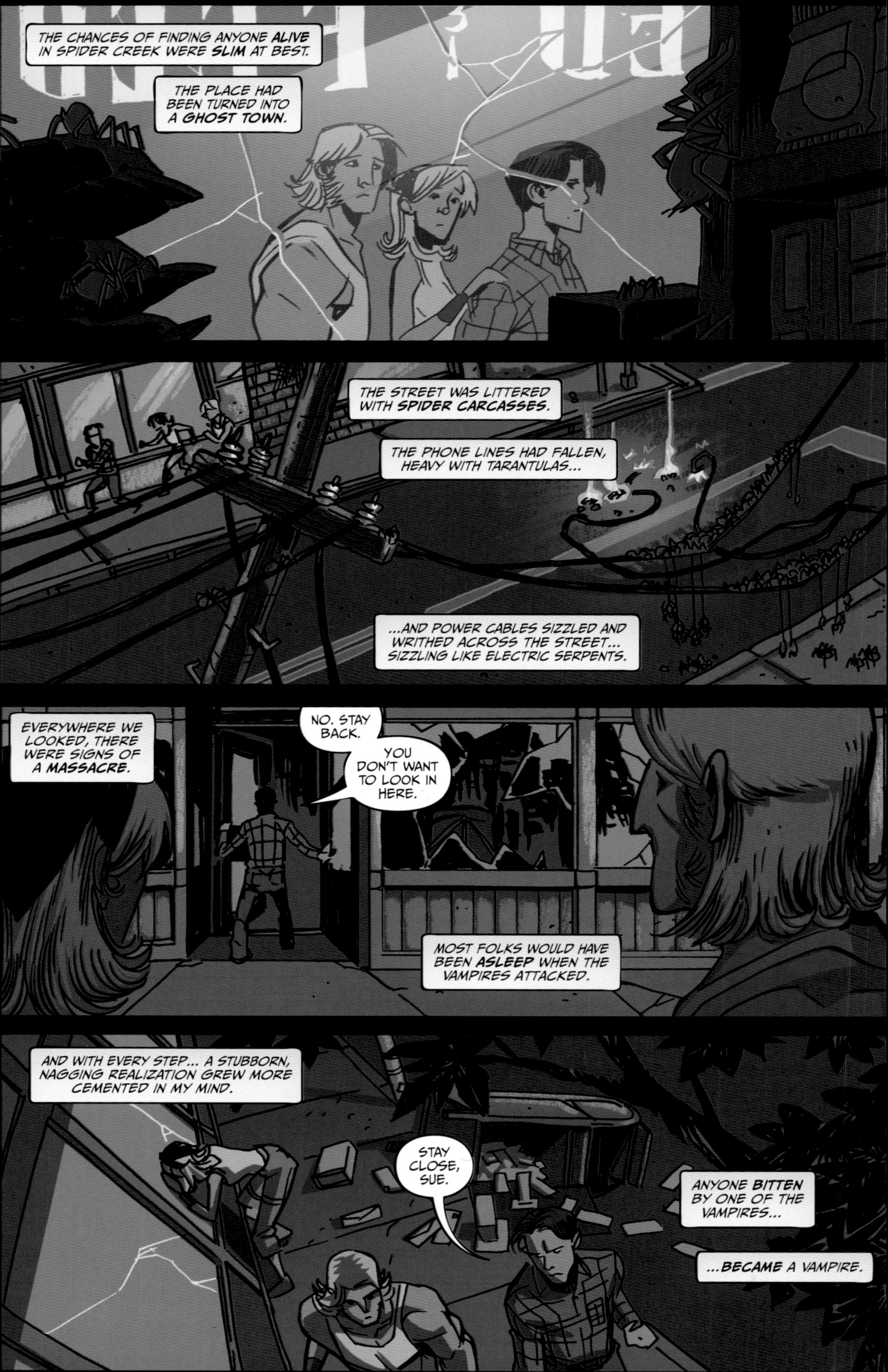

THE CHANCES OF FINDING ANYONE ALIVE IN SPIDER CREEK WERE SLIM AT BEST.
THE PLACE HAD BEEN TURNED INTO A GHOST TOWN.
THE STREET WAS LITTERED WITH SPIDER CARCASSES.
THE PHONE LINES HAD FALLEN, HEAVY WITH TARANTULAS...
...AND POWER CABLES SIZZLED AND WRITHED ACROSS THE STREET... SIZZLING LIKE ELECTRIC SERPENTS.
EVERYWHERE WE LOOKED, THERE WERE SIGNS OF A MASSACRE.
NO. STAY BACK.
YOU DON'T WANT TO LOOK IN HERE.
MOST FOLKS WOULD HAVE BEEN ASLEEP WHEN THE VAMPIRES ATTACKED.
AND WITH EVERY STEP... A STUBBORN, NAGGING REALIZATION GREW MORE CEMENTED IN MY MIND.
STAY CLOSE, SUE.
ANYONE BITTEN BY ONE OF THE VAMPIRES...
...BECAME A VAMPIRE.

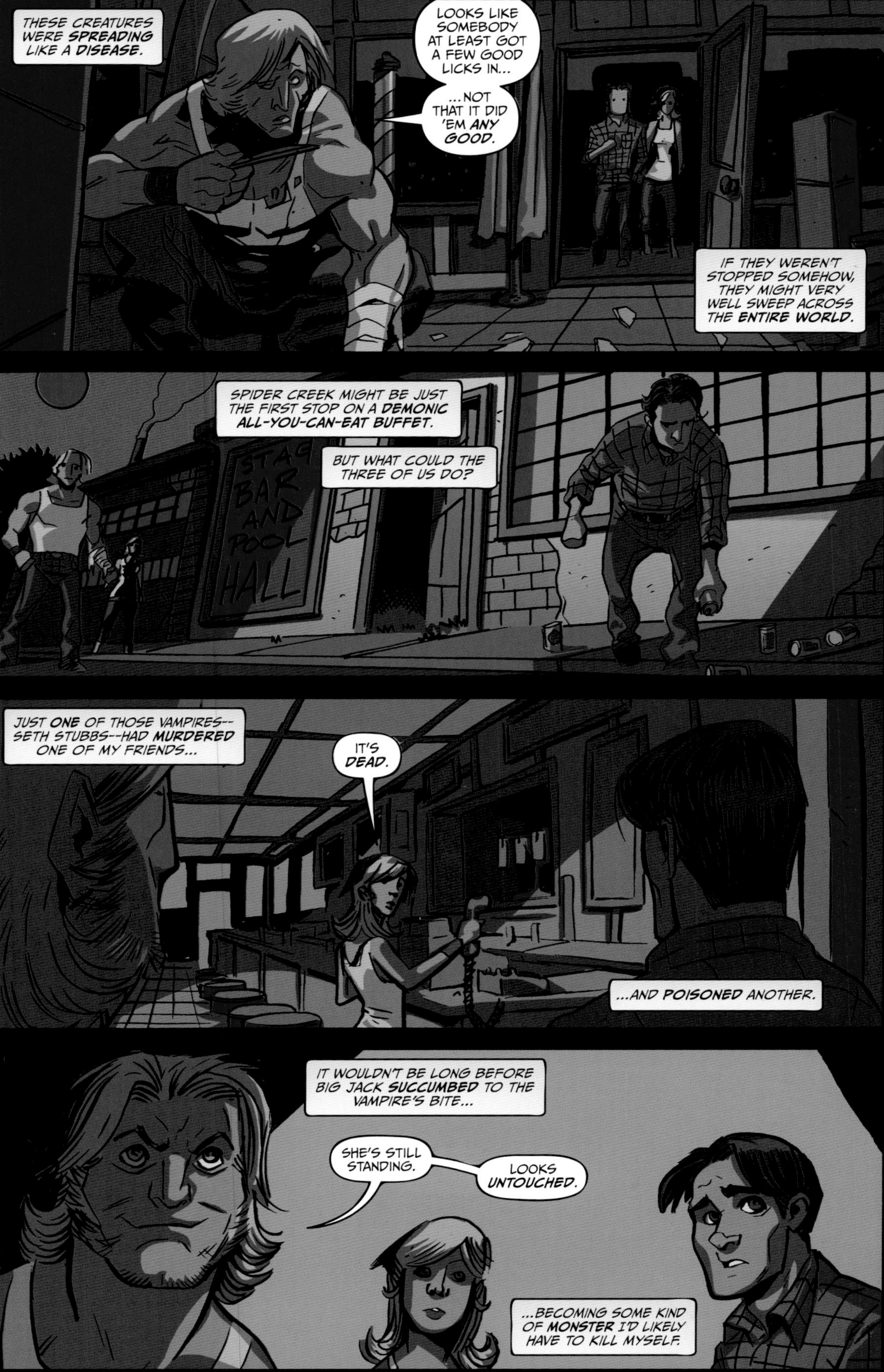
THESE CREATURES WERE SPREADING LIKE A DISEASE.
LOOKS LIKE SOMEBODY AT LEAST GOT A FEW GOOD LICKS IN...
...NOT THAT IT DID 'EM ANY GOOD.
IF THEY WEREN'T STOPPED SOMEHOW, THEY MIGHT VERY WELL SWEEP ACROSS THE ENTIRE WORLD.
SPIDER CREEK MIGHT BE JUST THE FIRST STOP ON A DEMONIC ALL-YOU-CAN-EAT BUFFET.
BUT WHAT COULD THE THREE OF US DO?
STAG BAR AND POOL HALL
JUST ONE OF THOSE VAMPIRES--SETH STUBBS--HAD MURDERED ONE OF MY FRIENDS...
IT'S DEAD.
...AND POISONED ANOTHER.
IT WOULDN'T BE LONG BEFORE BIG JACK SUCCUMBED TO THE VAMPIRE'S BITE...
SHE'S STILL STANDING.
LOOKS UNTOUCHED.
...BECOMING SOME KIND OF MONSTER I'D LIKELY HAVE TO KILL MYSELF.

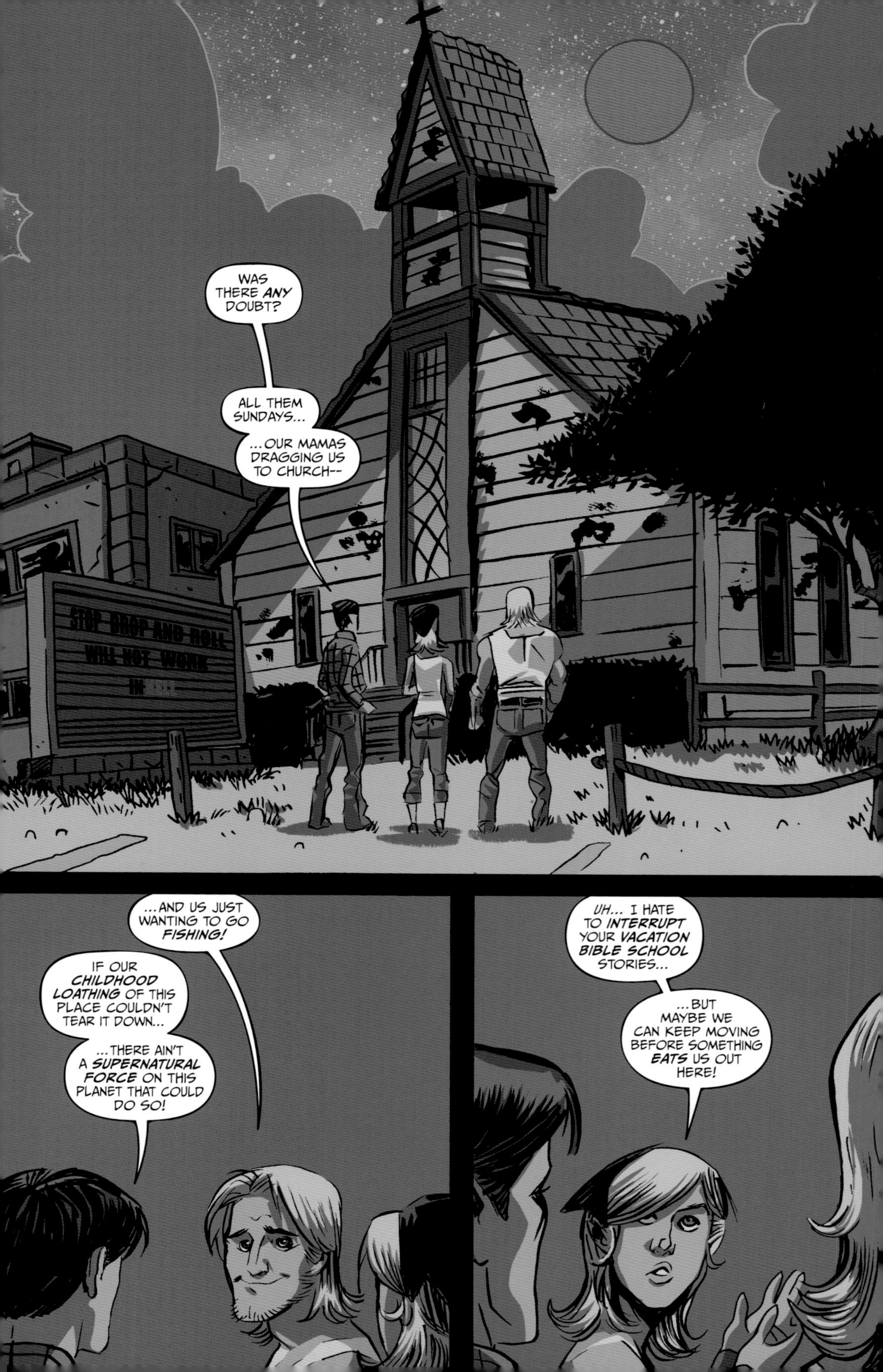

WAS THERE *ANY* DOUBT?
ALL THEM SUNDAYS...
...OUR MAMAS DRAGGING US TO CHURCH--
STOP DROP AND ROLL
WILL NOT WORK
IN
...AND US JUST WANTING TO GO *FISHING!*
IF OUR *CHILDHOOD LOATHING* OF THIS PLACE COULDN'T TEAR IT DOWN...
...THERE AIN'T A *SUPERNATURAL FORCE* ON THIS PLANET THAT COULD DO SO!
UH... I HATE TO *INTERRUPT* YOUR *VACATION BIBLE SCHOOL* STORIES...
...BUT MAYBE WE CAN KEEP MOVING BEFORE SOMETHING *EATS* US OUT HERE!

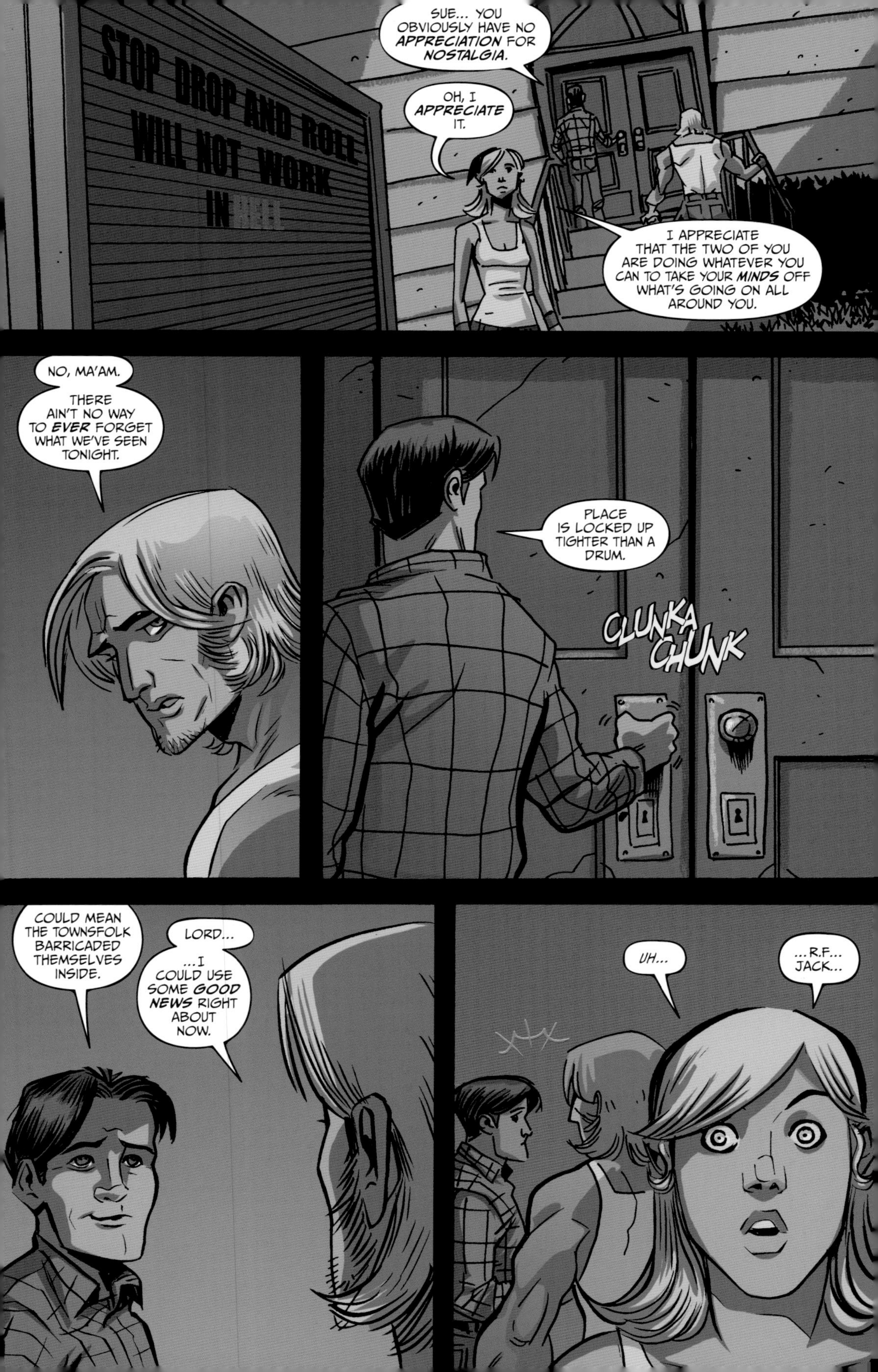
STOP DROP AND ROLL WILL NOT WORK IN HELL
SUE... YOU OBVIOUSLY HAVE NO APPRECIATION FOR NOSTALGIA.
OH, I APPRECIATE IT.
I APPRECIATE THAT THE TWO OF YOU ARE DOING WHATEVER YOU CAN TO TAKE YOUR MINDS OFF WHAT'S GOING ON ALL AROUND YOU.
NO, MA'AM.
THERE AIN'T NO WAY TO EVER FORGET WHAT WE'VE SEEN TONIGHT.
PLACE IS LOCKED UP TIGHTER THAN A DRUM.
CLUNKA CHUNK
COULD MEAN THE TOWNSFOLK BARRICADED THEMSELVES INSIDE.
LORD...
...I COULD USE SOME GOOD NEWS RIGHT ABOUT NOW.
UH...
...R.F... JACK...

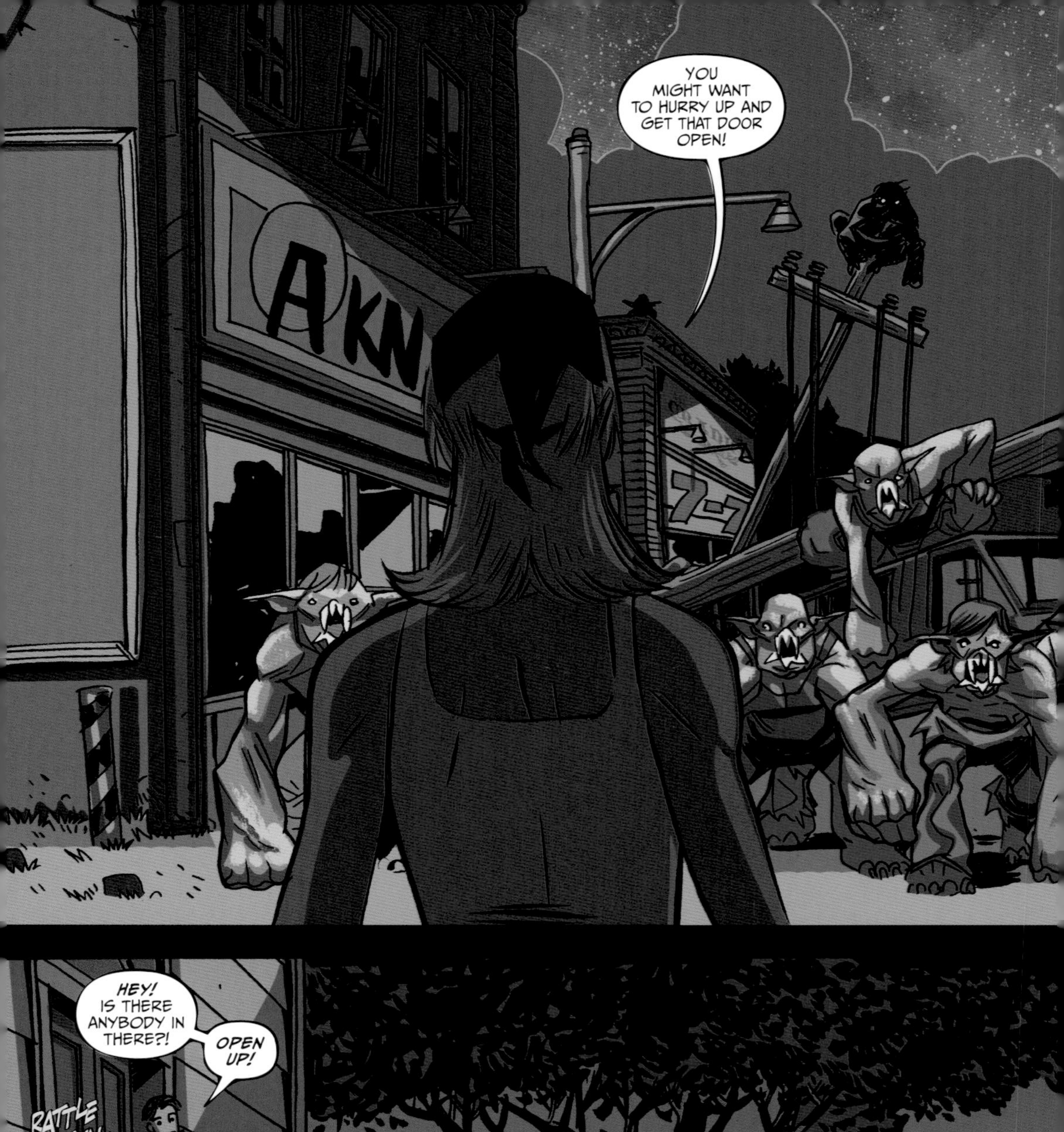
YOU MIGHT WANT TO HURRY UP AND GET THAT DOOR OPEN!

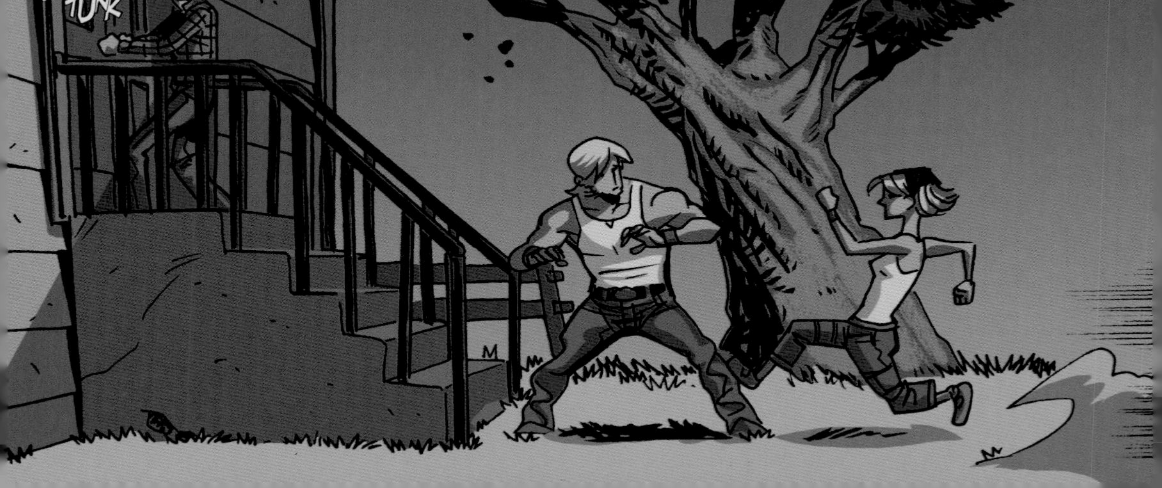
HEY! IS THERE ANYBODY IN THERE?!
OPEN UP!
RATTLE
TUNK

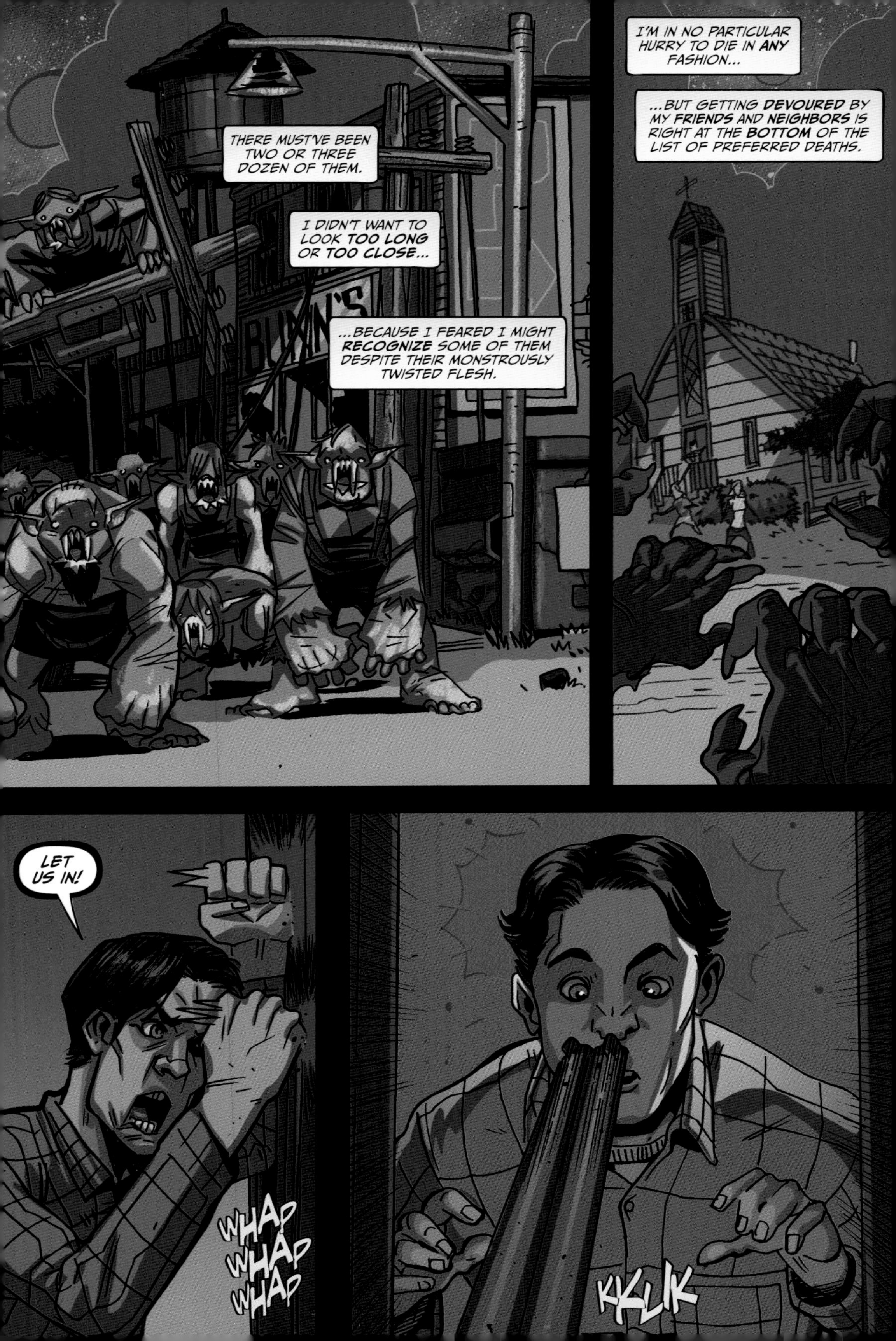

THERE MUST'VE BEEN TWO OR THREE DOZEN OF THEM.
I DIDN'T WANT TO LOOK TOO LONG OR TOO CLOSE...
...BECAUSE I FEARED I MIGHT RECOGNIZE SOME OF THEM DESPITE THEIR MONSTROUSLY TWISTED FLESH.
I'M IN NO PARTICULAR HURRY TO DIE IN ANY FASHION...
...BUT GETTING DEVOURED BY MY FRIENDS AND NEIGHBORS IS RIGHT AT THE BOTTOM OF THE LIST OF PREFERRED DEATHS.
LET US IN!
WHAP WHAP WHAP
KKLIK

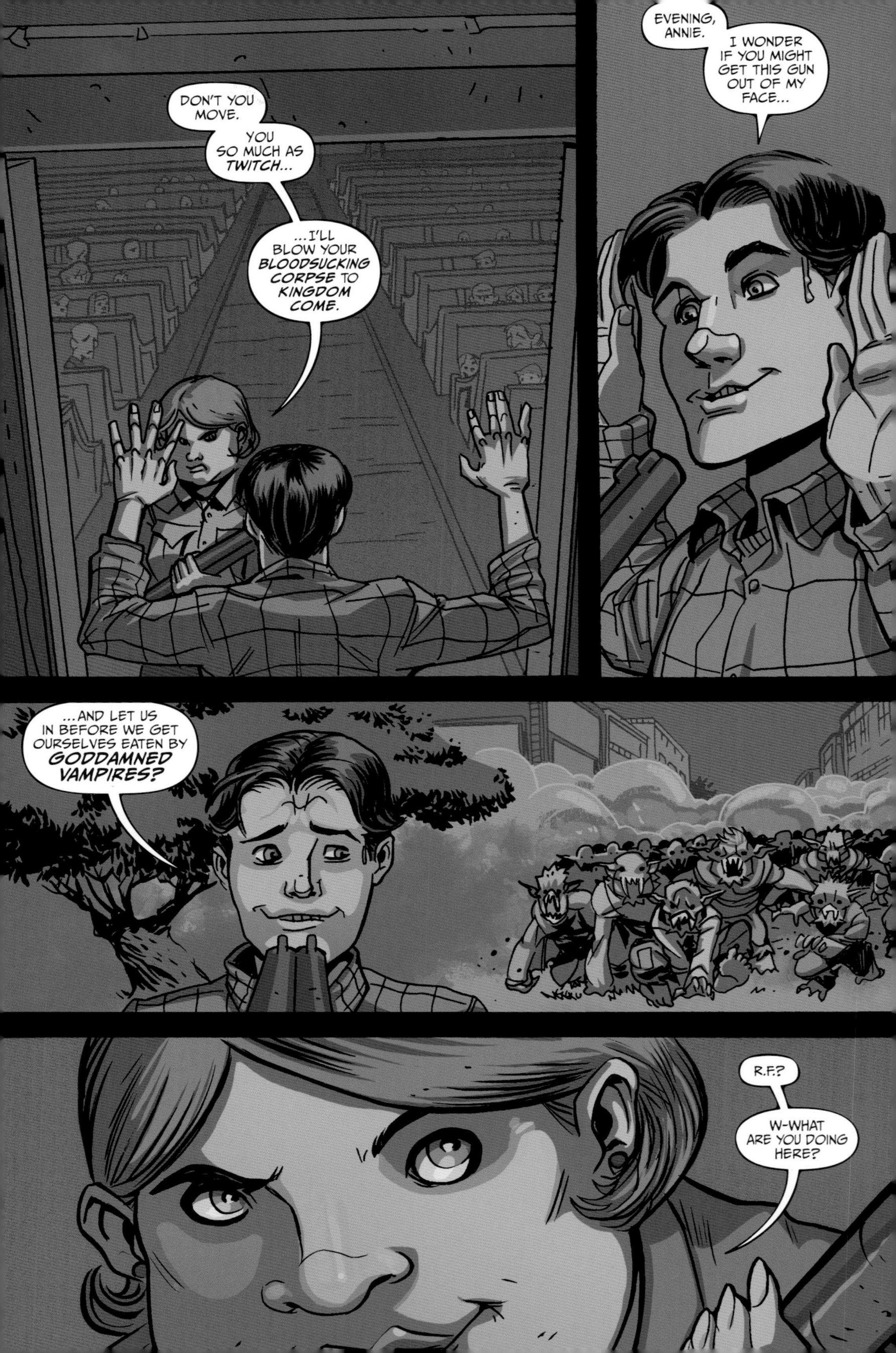
DON'T YOU MOVE.
YOU SO MUCH AS *TWITCH*...
...I'LL BLOW YOUR ***BLOODSUCKING CORPSE*** TO ***KINGDOM COME***.
EVENING, ANNIE.
I WONDER IF YOU MIGHT GET THIS GUN OUT OF MY FACE...
...AND LET US IN BEFORE WE GET OURSELVES EATEN BY ***GODDAMNED VAMPIRES?***
R.F.?
W-WHAT ARE YOU DOING HERE?

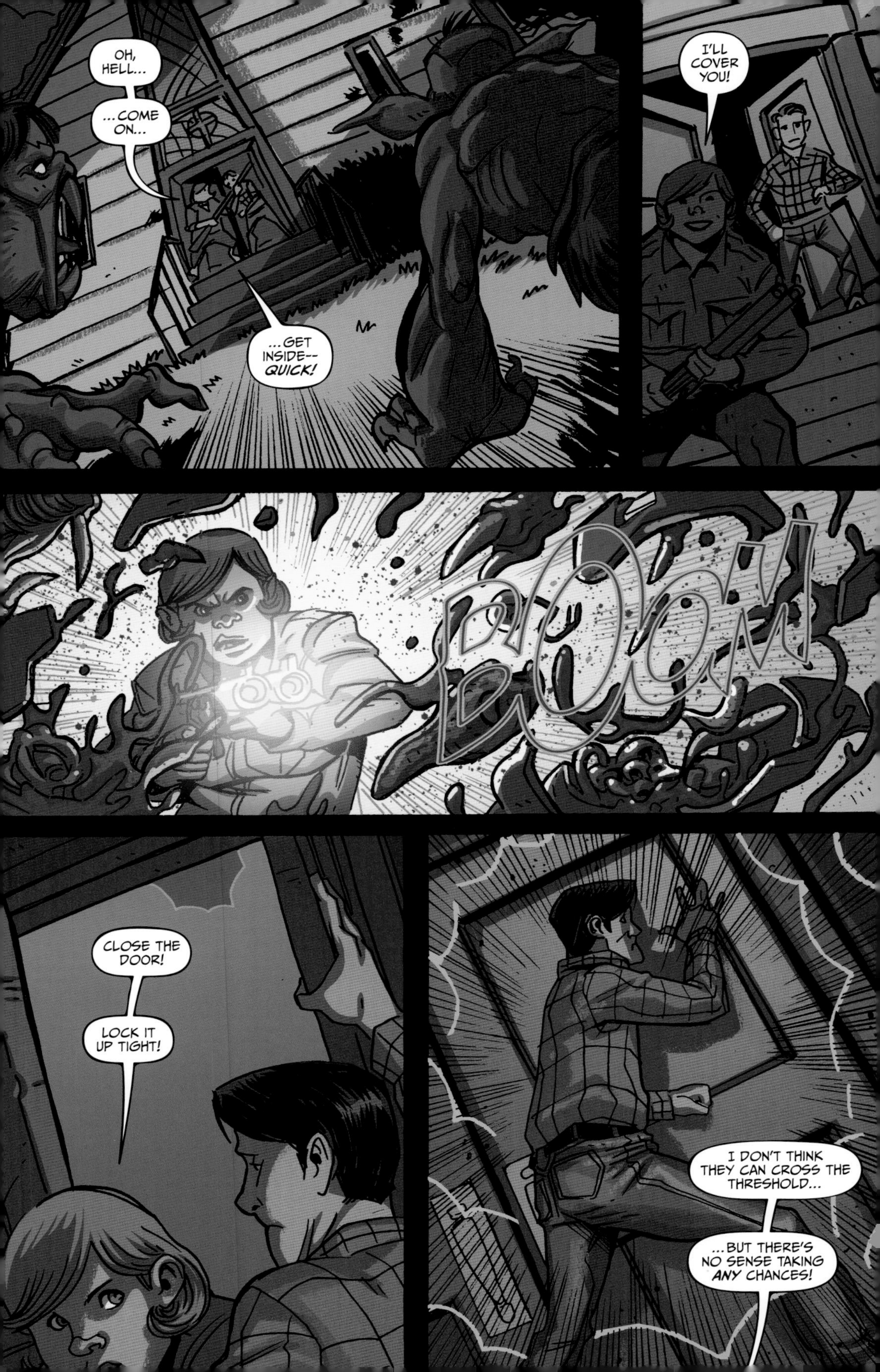
OH, HELL...
...COME ON...
...GET INSIDE-- QUICK!
I'LL COVER YOU!
BOOM
BOOM
CLOSE THE DOOR!
LOCK IT UP TIGHT!
I DON'T THINK THEY CAN CROSS THE THRESHOLD...
...BUT THERE'S NO SENSE TAKING ANY CHANCES!

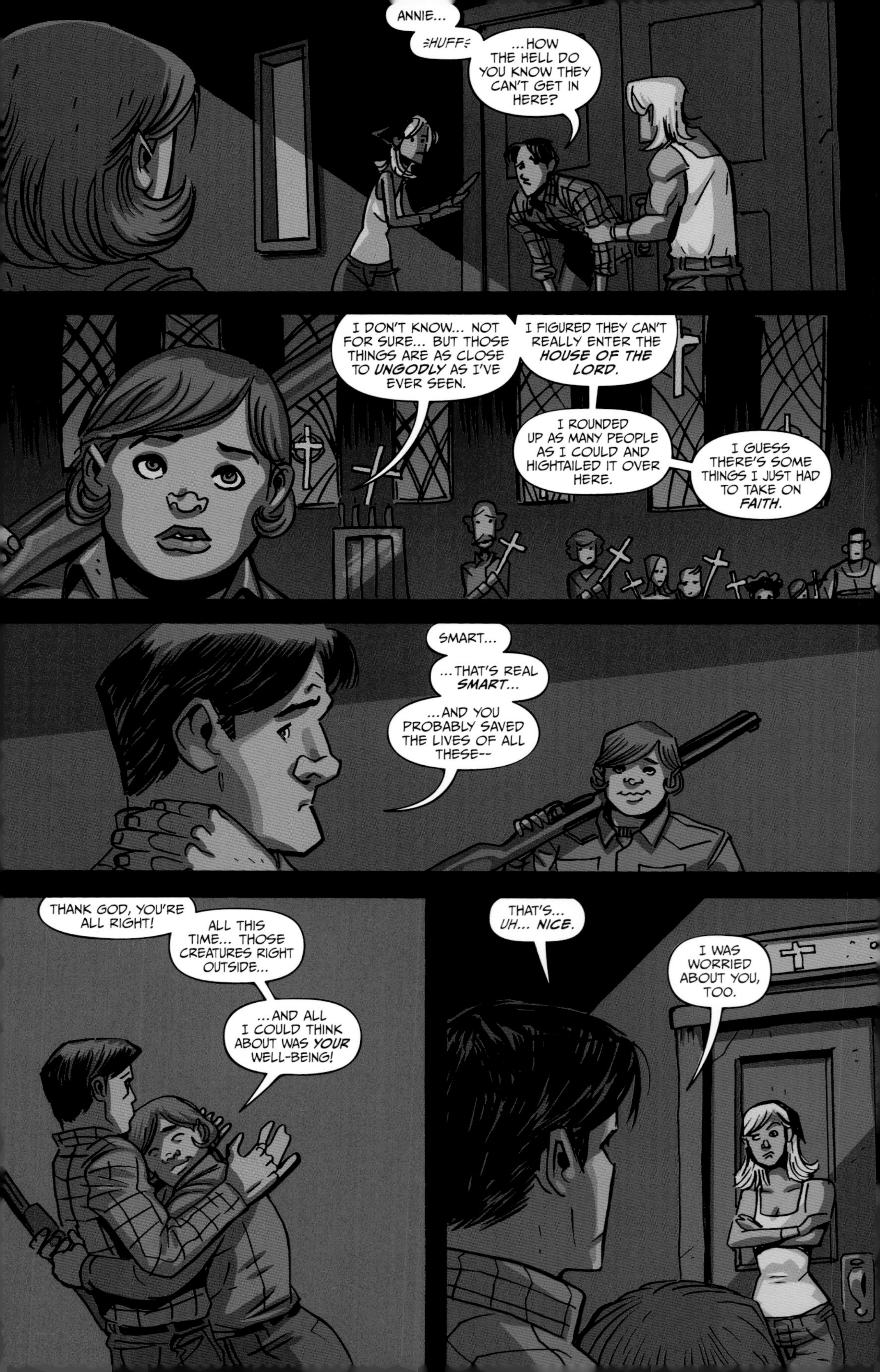
ANNIE...
HUFF
...HOW THE HELL DO YOU KNOW THEY CAN'T GET IN HERE?
I DON'T KNOW... NOT FOR SURE... BUT THOSE THINGS ARE AS CLOSE TO UNGODLY AS I'VE EVER SEEN.
I FIGURED THEY CAN'T REALLY ENTER THE HOUSE OF THE LORD.
I ROUNDED UP AS MANY PEOPLE AS I COULD AND HIGHTAILED IT OVER HERE.
I GUESS THERE'S SOME THINGS I JUST HAD TO TAKE ON FAITH.
SMART...
...THAT'S REAL SMART...
...AND YOU PROBABLY SAVED THE LIVES OF ALL THESE--
THANK GOD, YOU'RE ALL RIGHT!
ALL THIS TIME... THOSE CREATURES RIGHT OUTSIDE...
...AND ALL I COULD THINK ABOUT WAS YOUR WELL-BEING!
THAT'S... UH... NICE.
I WAS WORRIED ABOUT YOU, TOO.

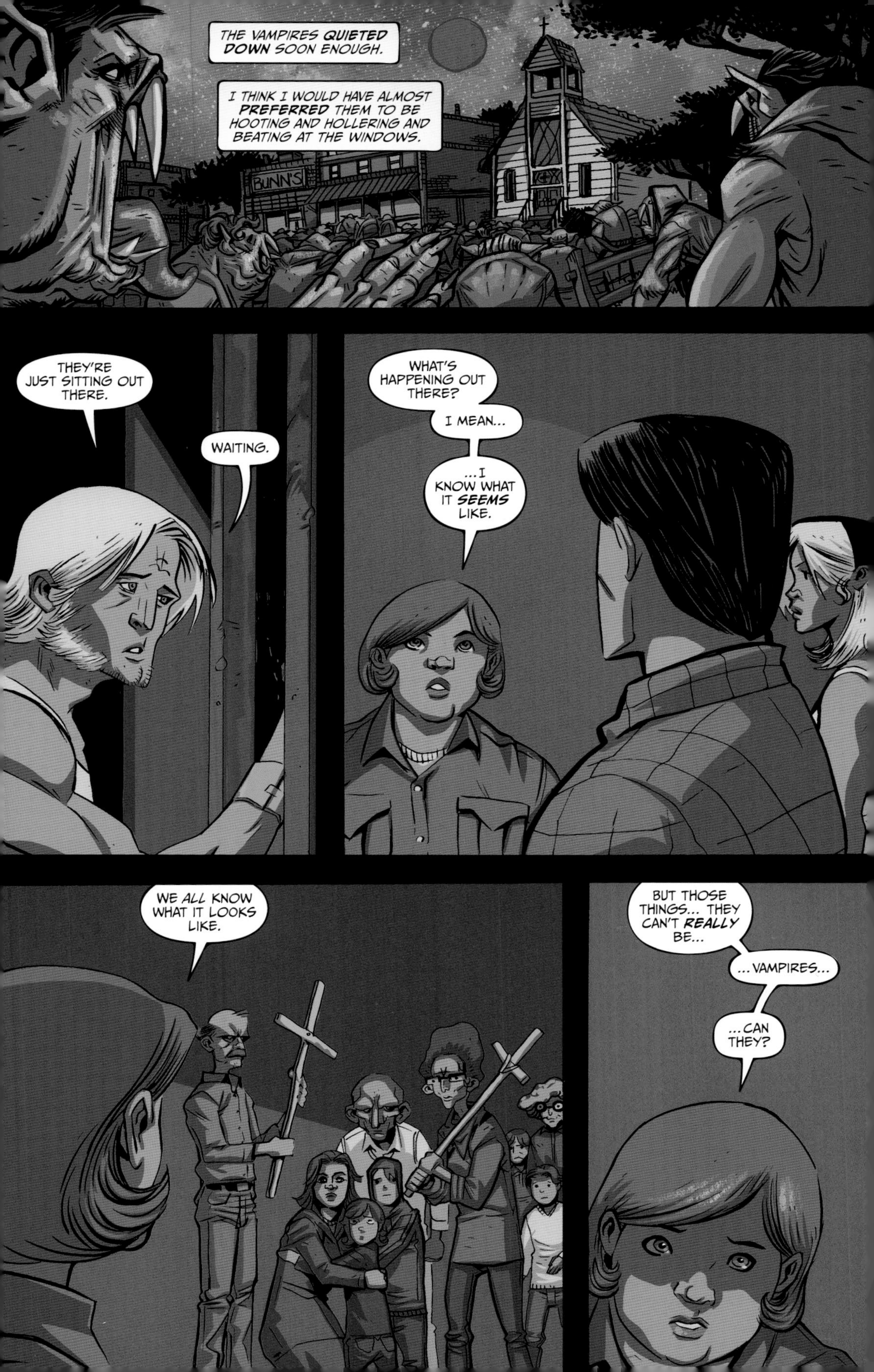
THE VAMPIRES QUIETED DOWN SOON ENOUGH.
I THINK I WOULD HAVE ALMOST PREFERRED THEM TO BE HOOTING AND HOLLERING AND BEATING AT THE WINDOWS.
BUNN'S
THEY'RE JUST SITTING OUT THERE.
WAITING.
WHAT'S HAPPENING OUT THERE?
I MEAN...
...I KNOW WHAT IT SEEMS LIKE.
WE ALL KNOW WHAT IT LOOKS LIKE.
BUT THOSE THINGS... THEY CAN'T REALLY BE...
...VAMPIRES...
...CAN THEY?

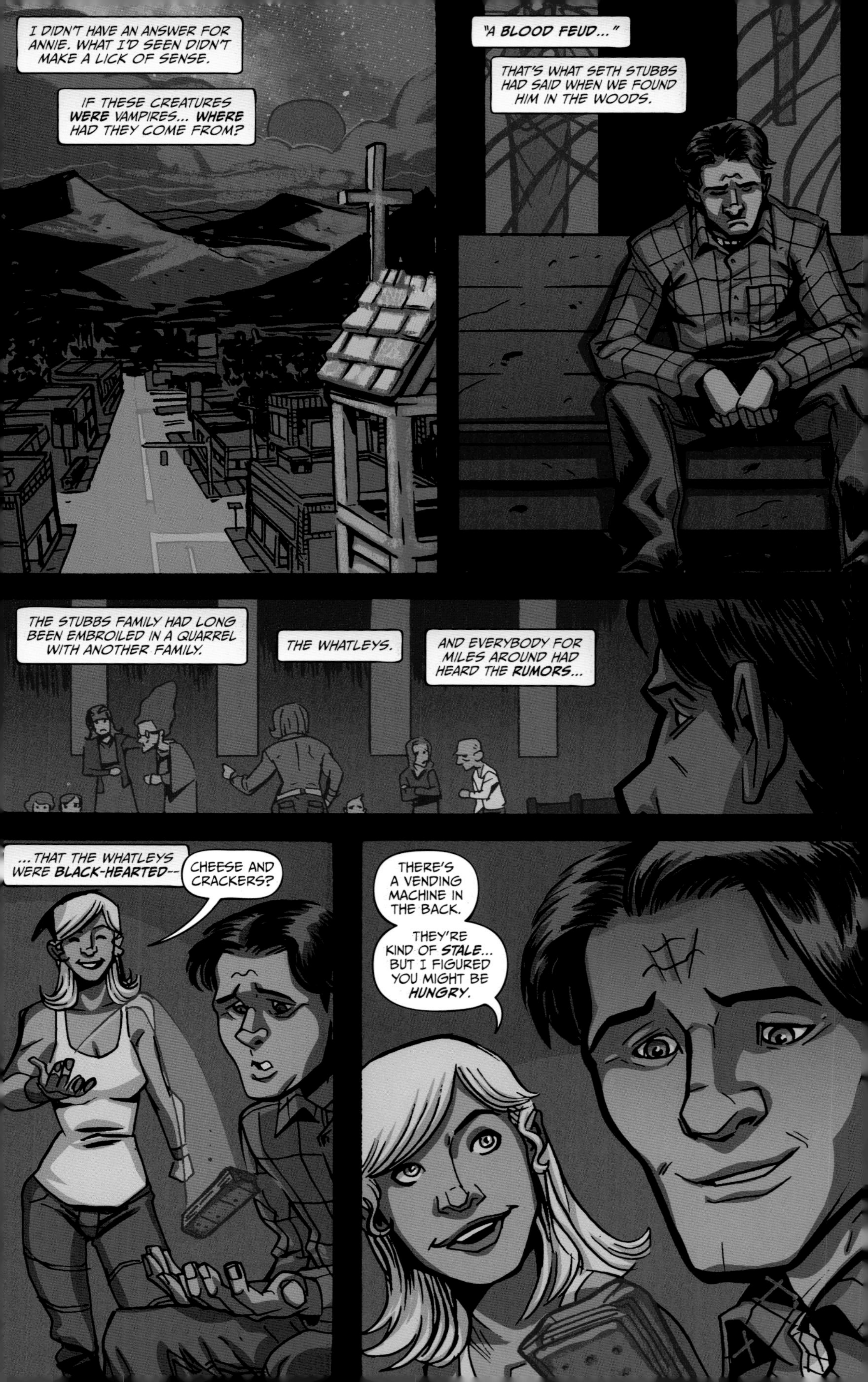

I DIDN'T HAVE AN ANSWER FOR ANNIE. WHAT I'D SEEN DIDN'T MAKE A LICK OF SENSE.
IF THESE CREATURES WERE VAMPIRES... WHERE HAD THEY COME FROM?
"A BLOOD FEUD..."
THAT'S WHAT SETH STUBBS HAD SAID WHEN WE FOUND HIM IN THE WOODS.
THE STUBBS FAMILY HAD LONG BEEN EMBROILED IN A QUARREL WITH ANOTHER FAMILY.
THE WHATLEYS.
AND EVERYBODY FOR MILES AROUND HAD HEARD THE RUMORS...
...THAT THE WHATLEYS WERE BLACK-HEARTED--
CHEESE AND CRACKERS?
THERE'S A VENDING MACHINE IN THE BACK.
THEY'RE KIND OF STALE... BUT I FIGURED YOU MIGHT BE HUNGRY.

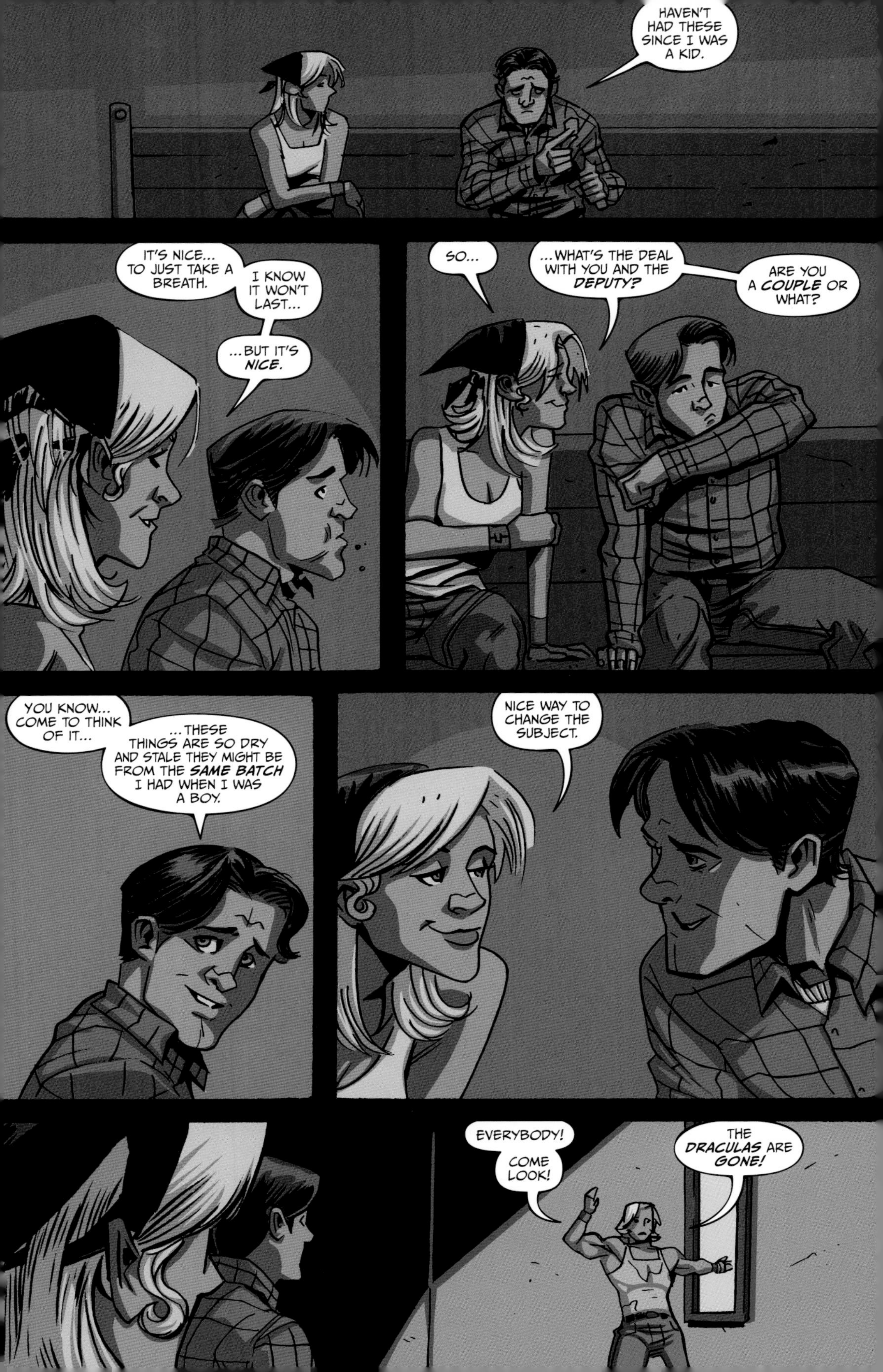
HAVEN'T HAD THESE SINCE I WAS A KID.
IT'S NICE... TO JUST TAKE A BREATH.
I KNOW IT WON'T LAST...
...BUT IT'S NICE.
SO...
...WHAT'S THE DEAL WITH YOU AND THE DEPUTY?
ARE YOU A COUPLE OR WHAT?
YOU KNOW... COME TO THINK OF IT...
...THESE THINGS ARE SO DRY AND STALE THEY MIGHT BE FROM THE SAME BATCH I HAD WHEN I WAS A BOY.
NICE WAY TO CHANGE THE SUBJECT.
EVERYBODY!
COME LOOK!
THE DRACULAS ARE GONE!

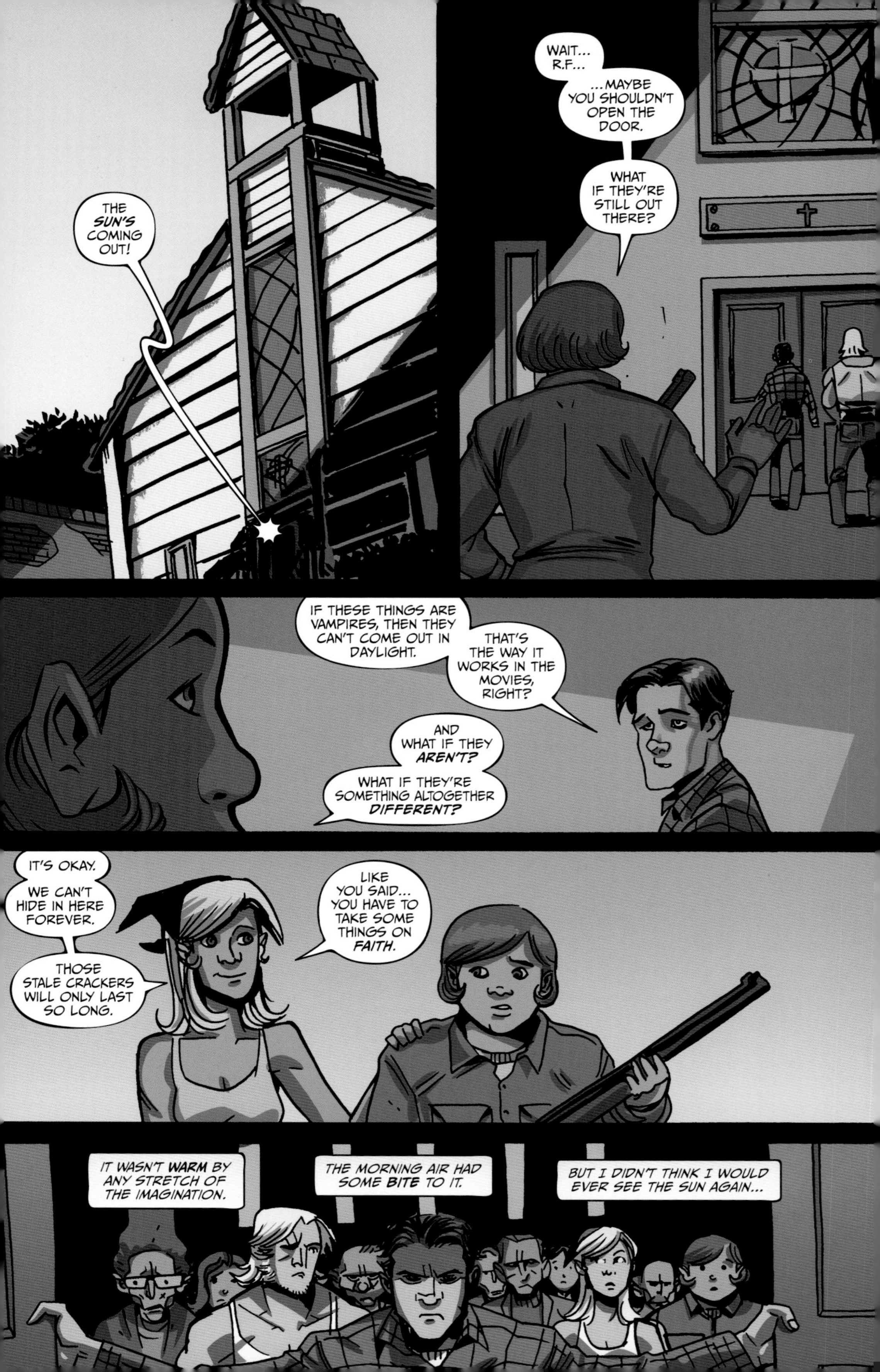
THE SUN'S COMING OUT!
WAIT... R.F...
...MAYBE YOU SHOULDN'T OPEN THE DOOR.
WHAT IF THEY'RE STILL OUT THERE?
IF THESE THINGS ARE VAMPIRES, THEN THEY CAN'T COME OUT IN DAYLIGHT.
THAT'S THE WAY IT WORKS IN THE MOVIES, RIGHT?
AND WHAT IF THEY AREN'T?
WHAT IF THEY'RE SOMETHING ALTOGETHER DIFFERENT?
IT'S OKAY.
WE CAN'T HIDE IN HERE FOREVER.
THOSE STALE CRACKERS WILL ONLY LAST SO LONG.
LIKE YOU SAID... YOU HAVE TO TAKE SOME THINGS ON FAITH.
IT WASN'T WARM BY ANY STRETCH OF THE IMAGINATION.
THE MORNING AIR HAD SOME BITE TO IT.
BUT I DIDN'T THINK I WOULD EVER SEE THE SUN AGAIN...

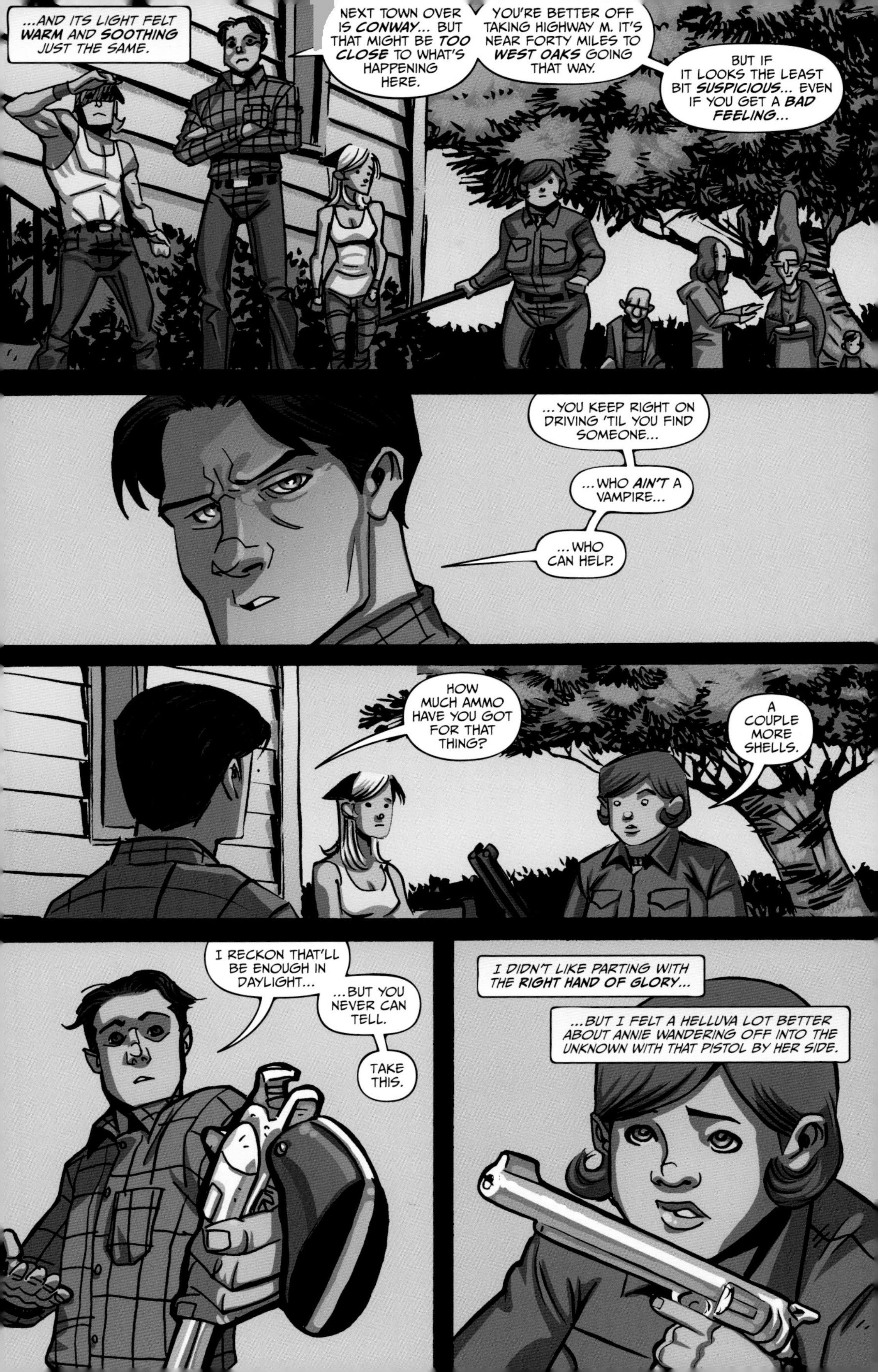
...AND ITS LIGHT FELT WARM AND SOOTHING JUST THE SAME.
NEXT TOWN OVER IS CONWAY... BUT THAT MIGHT BE TOO CLOSE TO WHAT'S HAPPENING HERE.
YOU'RE BETTER OFF TAKING HIGHWAY M. IT'S NEAR FORTY MILES TO WEST OAKS GOING THAT WAY.
BUT IF IT LOOKS THE LEAST BIT SUSPICIOUS... EVEN IF YOU GET A BAD FEELING...
...YOU KEEP RIGHT ON DRIVING 'TIL YOU FIND SOMEONE...
...WHO AIN'T A VAMPIRE...
...WHO CAN HELP.
HOW MUCH AMMO HAVE YOU GOT FOR THAT THING?
A COUPLE MORE SHELLS.
I RECKON THAT'LL BE ENOUGH IN DAYLIGHT...
...BUT YOU NEVER CAN TELL.
TAKE THIS.
I DIDN'T LIKE PARTING WITH THE RIGHT HAND OF GLORY...
...BUT I FELT A HELLUVA LOT BETTER ABOUT ANNIE WANDERING OFF INTO THE UNKNOWN WITH THAT PISTOL BY HER SIDE.

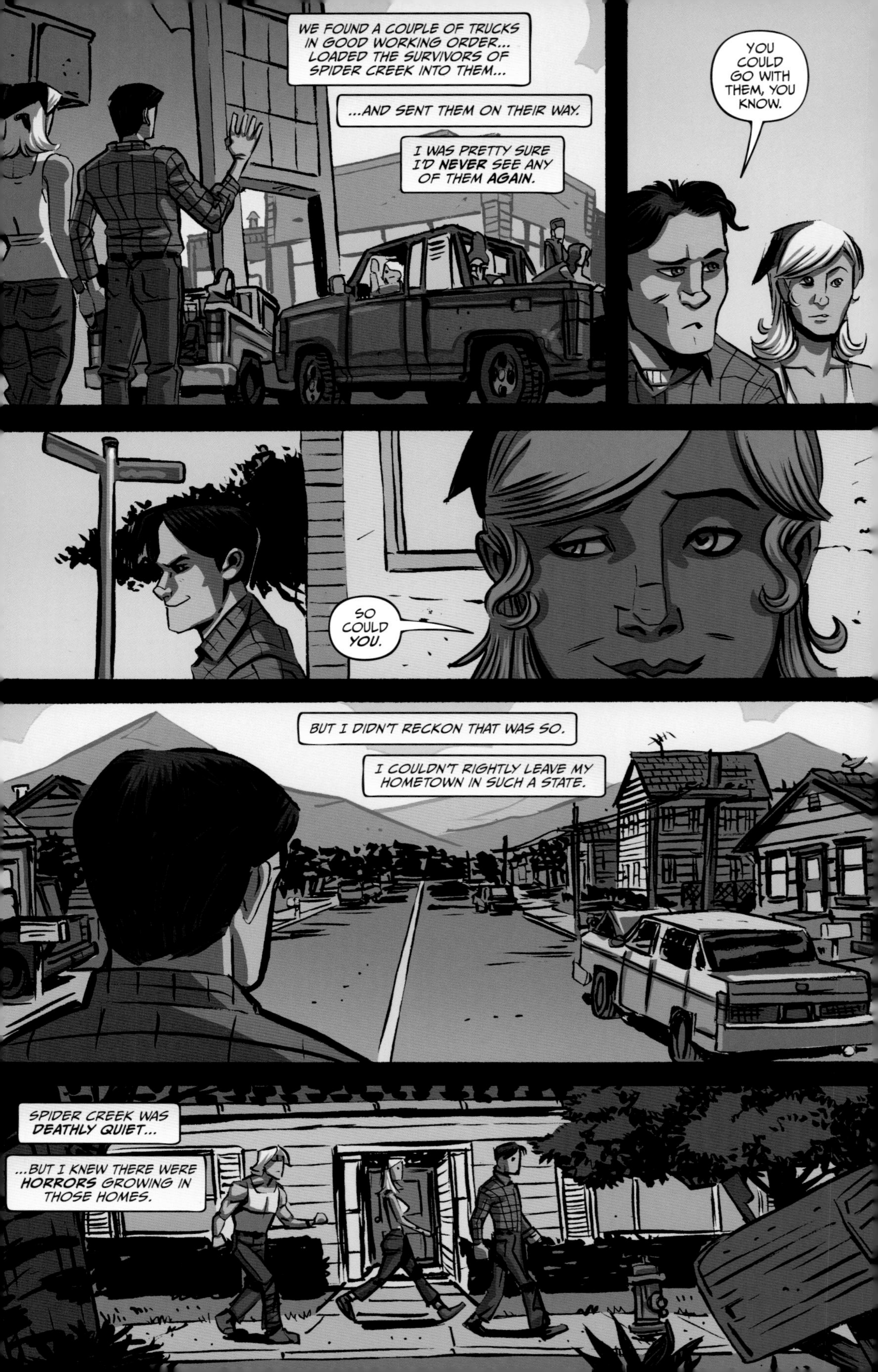

WE FOUND A COUPLE OF TRUCKS IN GOOD WORKING ORDER... LOADED THE SURVIVORS OF SPIDER CREEK INTO THEM...
...AND SENT THEM ON THEIR WAY.
I WAS PRETTY SURE I'D NEVER SEE ANY OF THEM AGAIN.
YOU COULD GO WITH THEM, YOU KNOW.
SO COULD YOU.
BUT I DIDN'T RECKON THAT WAS SO.
I COULDN'T RIGHTLY LEAVE MY HOMETOWN IN SUCH A STATE.
SPIDER CREEK WAS DEATHLY QUIET...
...BUT I KNEW THERE WERE HORRORS GROWING IN THOSE HOMES.

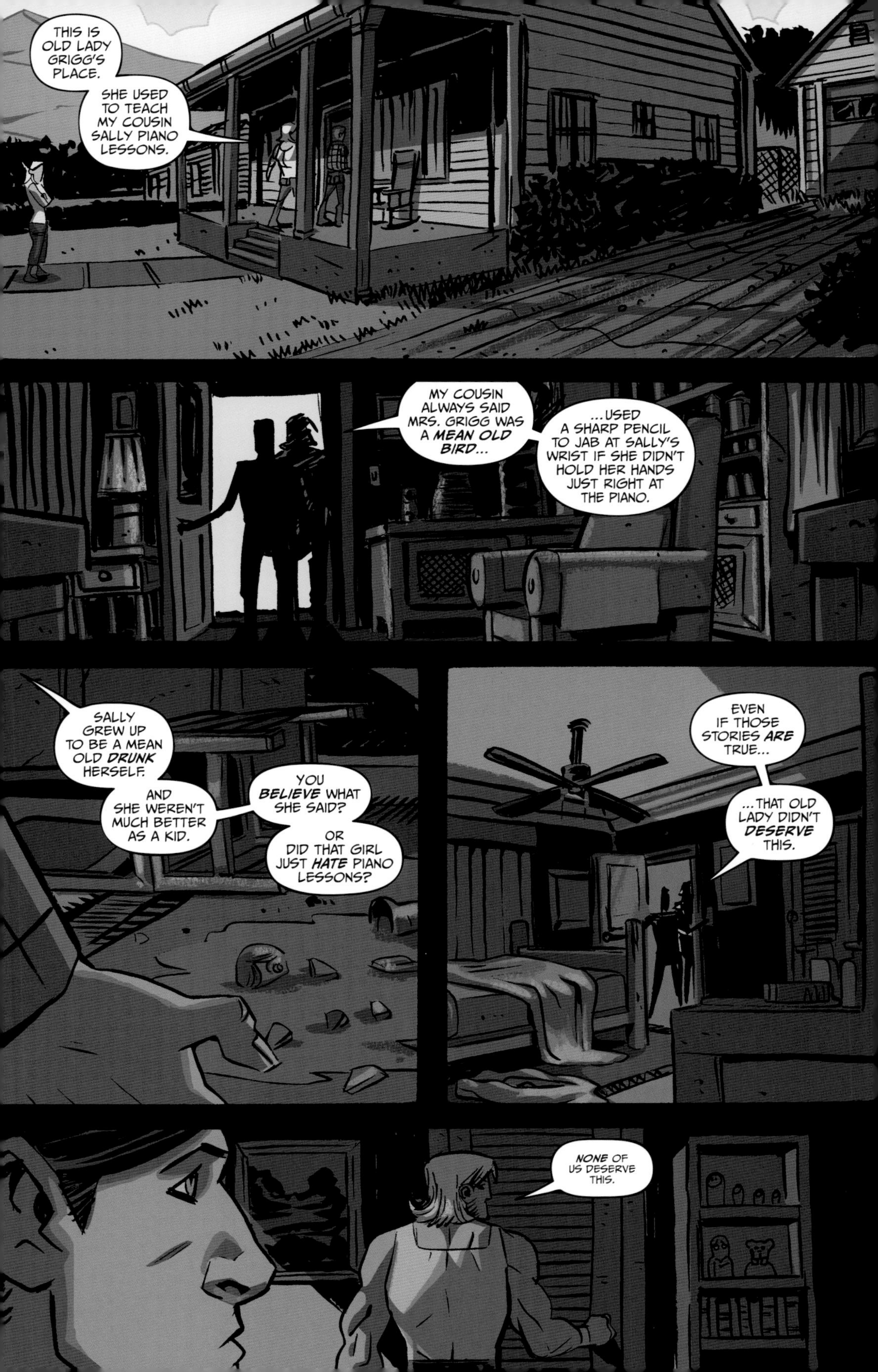
THIS IS OLD LADY GRIGG'S PLACE.
SHE USED TO TEACH MY COUSIN SALLY PIANO LESSONS.
MY COUSIN ALWAYS SAID MRS. GRIGG WAS A *MEAN OLD BIRD*...
...USED A SHARP PENCIL TO JAB AT SALLY'S WRIST IF SHE DIDN'T HOLD HER HANDS JUST RIGHT AT THE PIANO.
SALLY GREW UP TO BE A MEAN OLD *DRUNK* HERSELF.
AND SHE WEREN'T MUCH BETTER AS A KID.
YOU *BELIEVE* WHAT SHE SAID?
OR DID THAT GIRL JUST *HATE* PIANO LESSONS?
EVEN IF THOSE STORIES *ARE* TRUE...
...THAT OLD LADY DIDN'T *DESERVE* THIS.
NONE OF US DESERVE THIS.

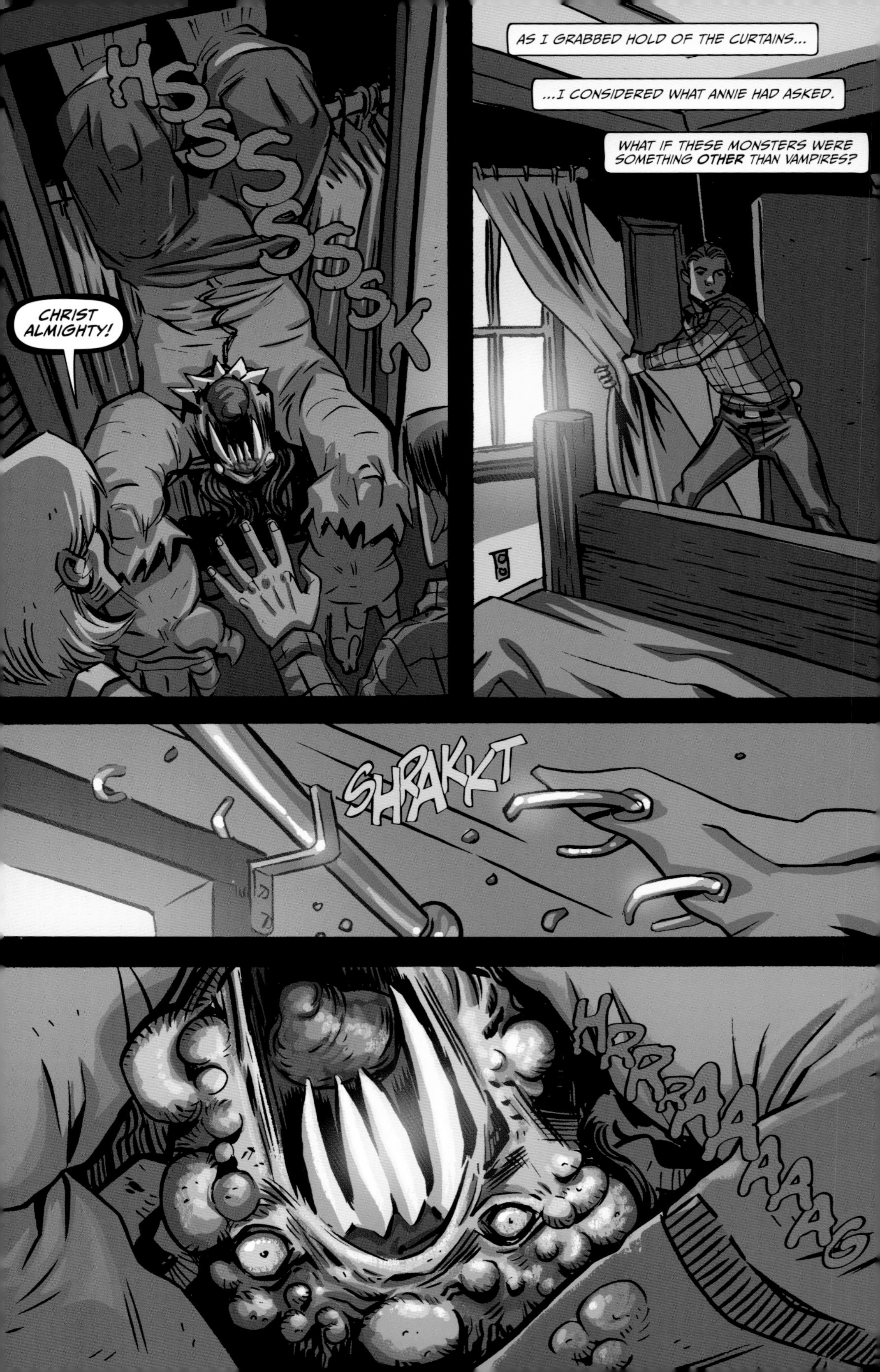
HSSSSSSK
CHRIST ALMIGHTY!
AS I GRABBED HOLD OF THE CURTAINS...
...I CONSIDERED WHAT ANNIE HAD ASKED.
WHAT IF THESE MONSTERS WERE SOMETHING OTHER THAN VAMPIRES?
SHRAKKT
HRRRAAAAAAG

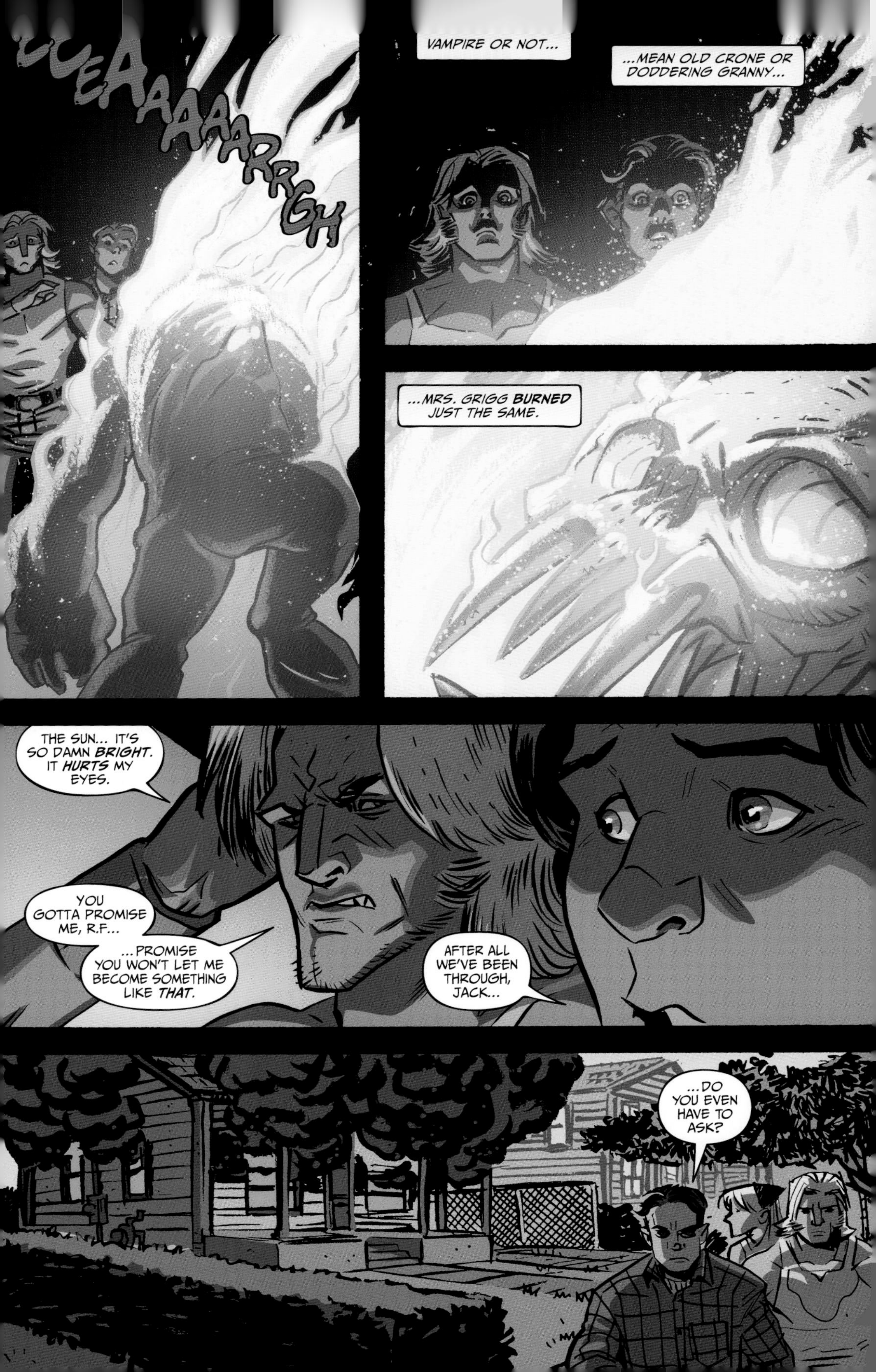
CCEAAAAAARRRGH
VAMPIRE OR NOT...
...MEAN OLD CRONE OR DODDERING GRANNY...
...MRS. GRIGG BURNED JUST THE SAME.
THE SUN... IT'S SO DAMN BRIGHT. IT HURTS MY EYES.
YOU GOTTA PROMISE ME, R.F...
...PROMISE YOU WON'T LET ME BECOME SOMETHING LIKE THAT.
AFTER ALL WE'VE BEEN THROUGH, JACK...
...DO YOU EVEN HAVE TO ASK?

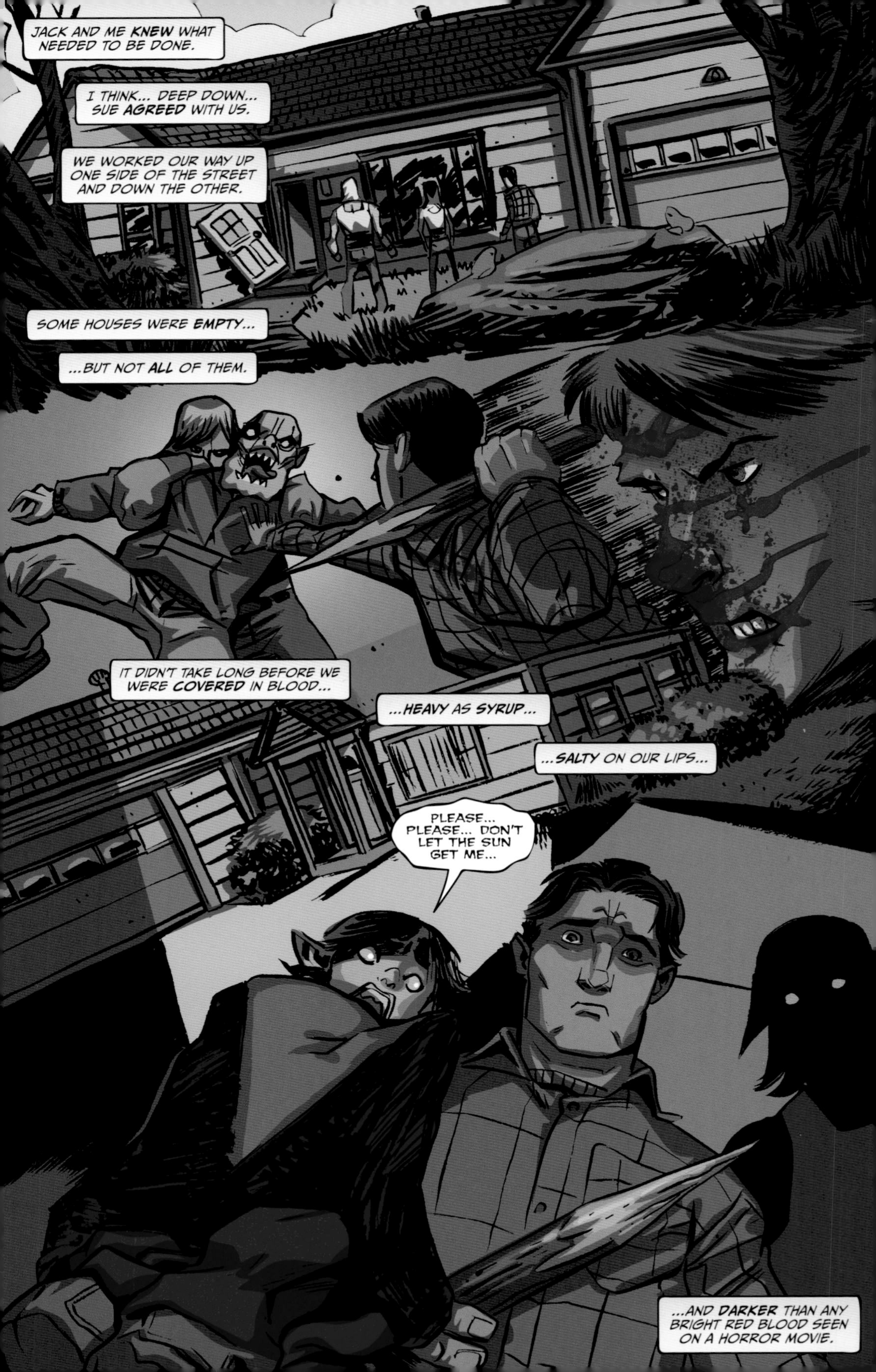
JACK AND ME KNEW WHAT NEEDED TO BE DONE.
I THINK... DEEP DOWN... SUE AGREED WITH US.
WE WORKED OUR WAY UP ONE SIDE OF THE STREET AND DOWN THE OTHER.
SOME HOUSES WERE EMPTY...
...BUT NOT ALL OF THEM.
IT DIDN'T TAKE LONG BEFORE WE WERE COVERED IN BLOOD...
...HEAVY AS SYRUP...
...SALTY ON OUR LIPS...
PLEASE... PLEASE... DON'T LET THE SUN GET ME...
...AND DARKER THAN ANY BRIGHT RED BLOOD SEEN ON A HORROR MOVIE.

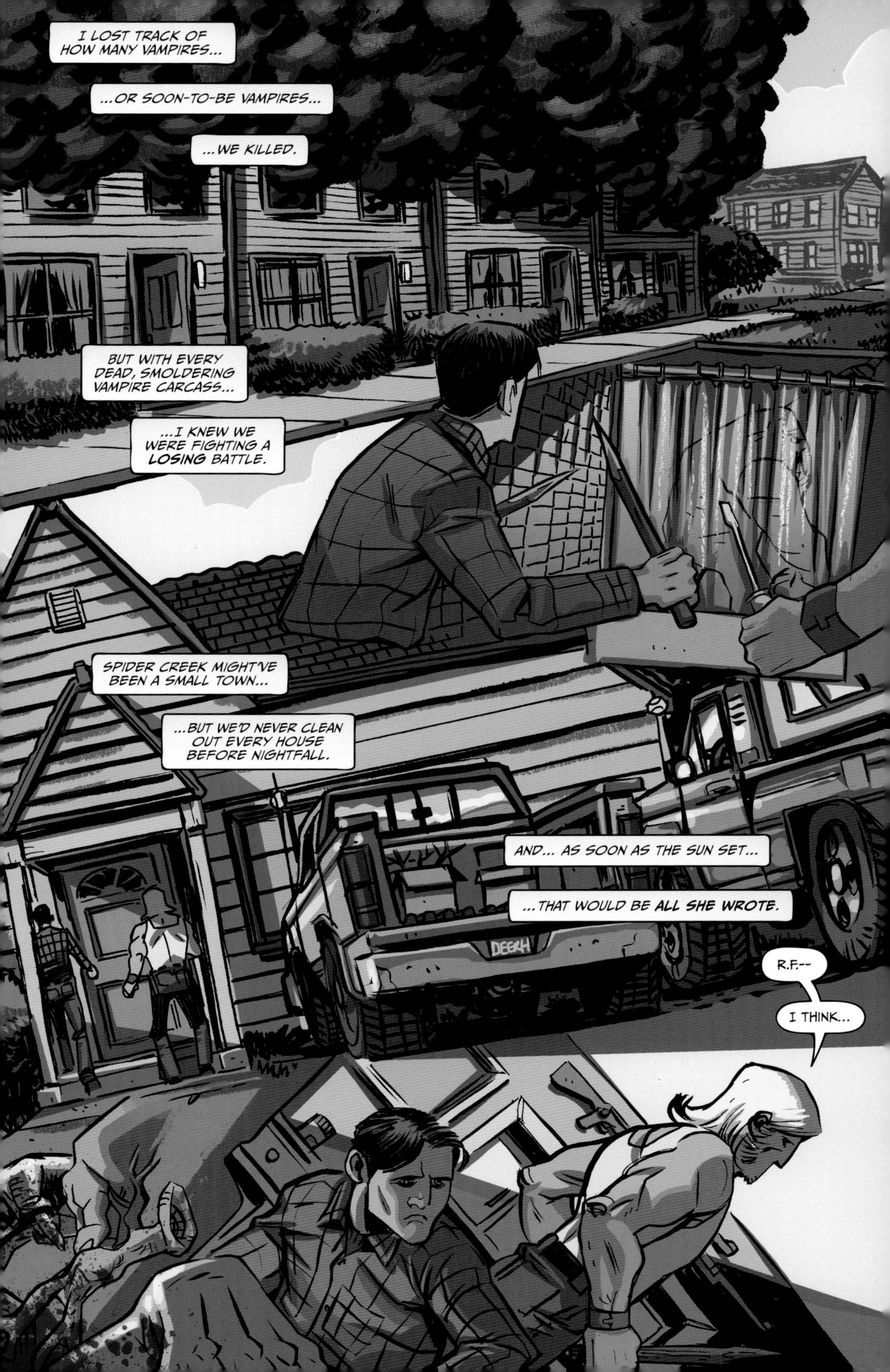
I LOST TRACK OF HOW MANY VAMPIRES...
...OR SOON-TO-BE VAMPIRES...
...WE KILLED.
BUT WITH EVERY DEAD, SMOLDERING VAMPIRE CARCASS...
...I KNEW WE WERE FIGHTING A LOSING BATTLE.
SPIDER CREEK MIGHT'VE BEEN A SMALL TOWN...
...BUT WE'D NEVER CLEAN OUT EVERY HOUSE BEFORE NIGHTFALL.
AND... AS SOON AS THE SUN SET...
...THAT WOULD BE ALL SHE WROTE.
DEERH
R.F.--
I THINK...

"...WE NEED TO *TALK*."

WHERE'D YOU GET ALL THOSE GUNS?

THIS IS SPIDER CREEK, MISSOURI. *EVERYBODY'S* ARMED.

AND IT'S A GOOD THING, TOO.

WE'LL *NEED* THESE GUNS FOR WHAT COMES NEXT.

TELL HER WHAT YOU TOLD ME.

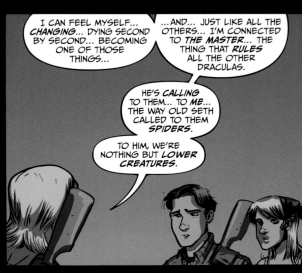

I CAN FEEL MYSELF... *CHANGING*... DYING SECOND BY SECOND... BECOMING ONE OF THOSE THINGS...

...AND... JUST LIKE ALL THE OTHERS... I'M CONNECTED TO *THE MASTER*... THE THING THAT *RULES* ALL THE OTHER DRACULAS.

HE'S *CALLING* TO THEM... TO *ME*... THE WAY OLD SETH CALLED TO THEM *SPIDERS*.

TO HIM, WE'RE NOTHING BUT *LOWER CREATURES*.

HE'S *POWERFUL*... BUT HE'S *AFRAID*, TOO.

HE'S NEVER HAD ANYONE DESTROY ONE OF HIS BROOD BEFORE.

HE'S AFRAID OF WHAT MIGHT HAPPEN IF YOU FIND HIM.

AND YOU KNOW WHERE HE IS?

I CAN SEE IT IN MY MIND'S EYE. HE'S HOLED UP NEAR THE *WHATLEY* PLACE.

THAT'S WHERE HE'S *HIDING*.

AND THAT'S WHERE WE'LL *KILL* HIS *UNDEAD ASS*.

CHAPTER 5

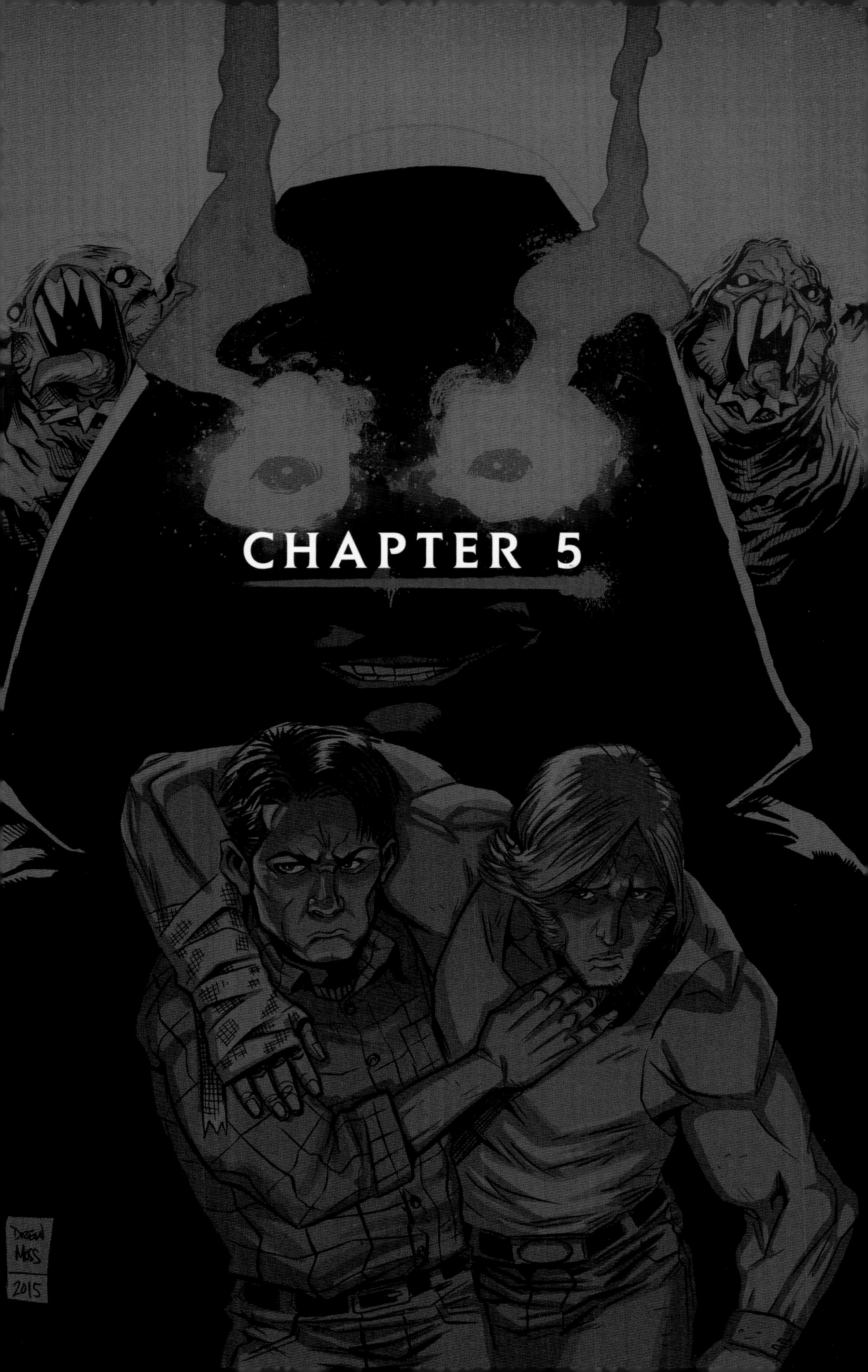
DREW MOSS
2015

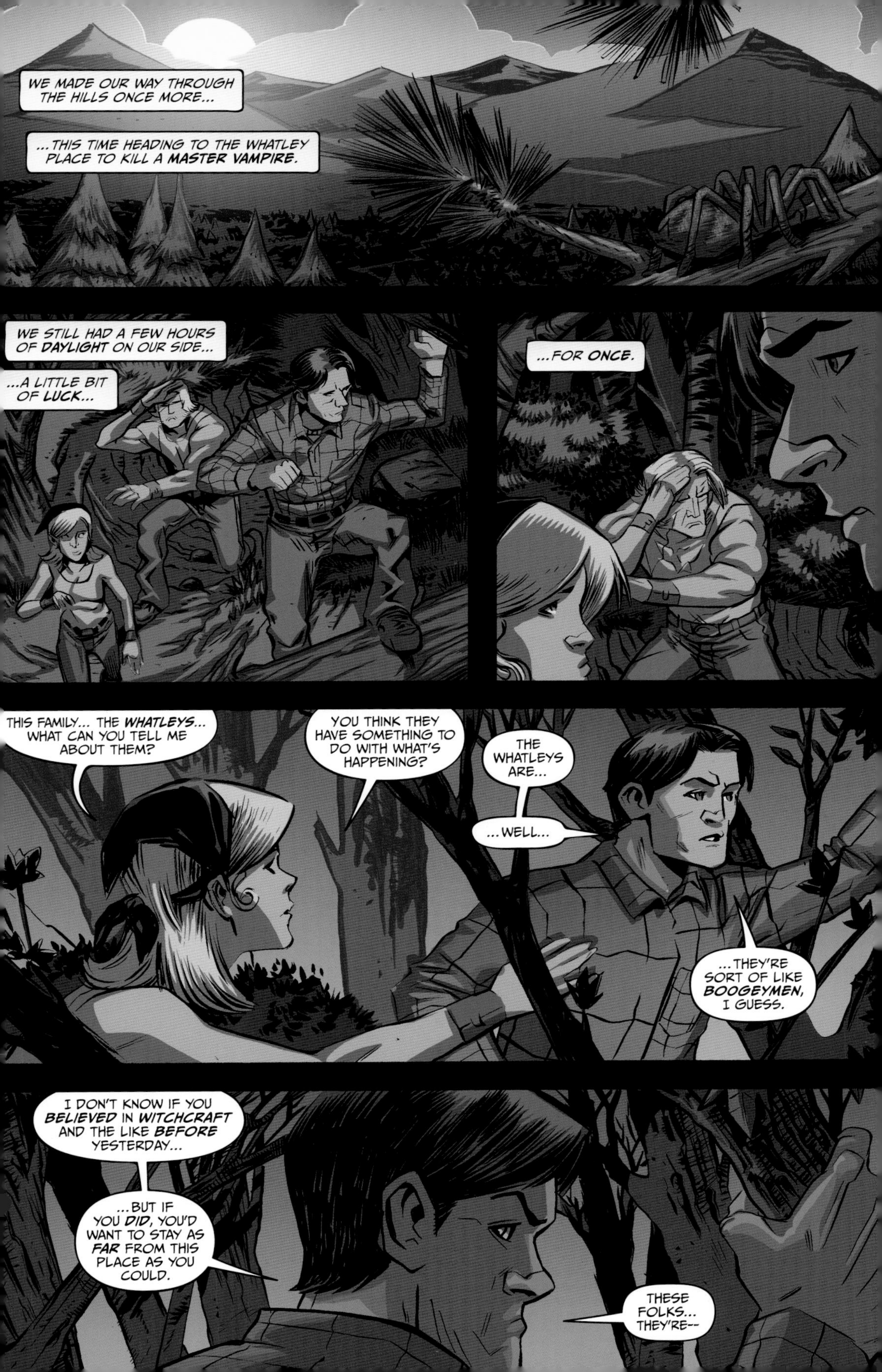
WE MADE OUR WAY THROUGH THE HILLS ONCE MORE...
...THIS TIME HEADING TO THE WHATLEY PLACE TO KILL A MASTER VAMPIRE.
WE STILL HAD A FEW HOURS OF DAYLIGHT ON OUR SIDE...
...A LITTLE BIT OF LUCK...
...FOR ONCE.
THIS FAMILY... THE WHATLEYS... WHAT CAN YOU TELL ME ABOUT THEM?
YOU THINK THEY HAVE SOMETHING TO DO WITH WHAT'S HAPPENING?
THE WHATLEYS ARE...
...WELL...
...THEY'RE SORT OF LIKE BOOGEYMEN, I GUESS.
I DON'T KNOW IF YOU BELIEVED IN WITCHCRAFT AND THE LIKE BEFORE YESTERDAY...
...BUT IF YOU DID, YOU'D WANT TO STAY AS FAR FROM THIS PLACE AS YOU COULD.
THESE FOLKS... THEY'RE--

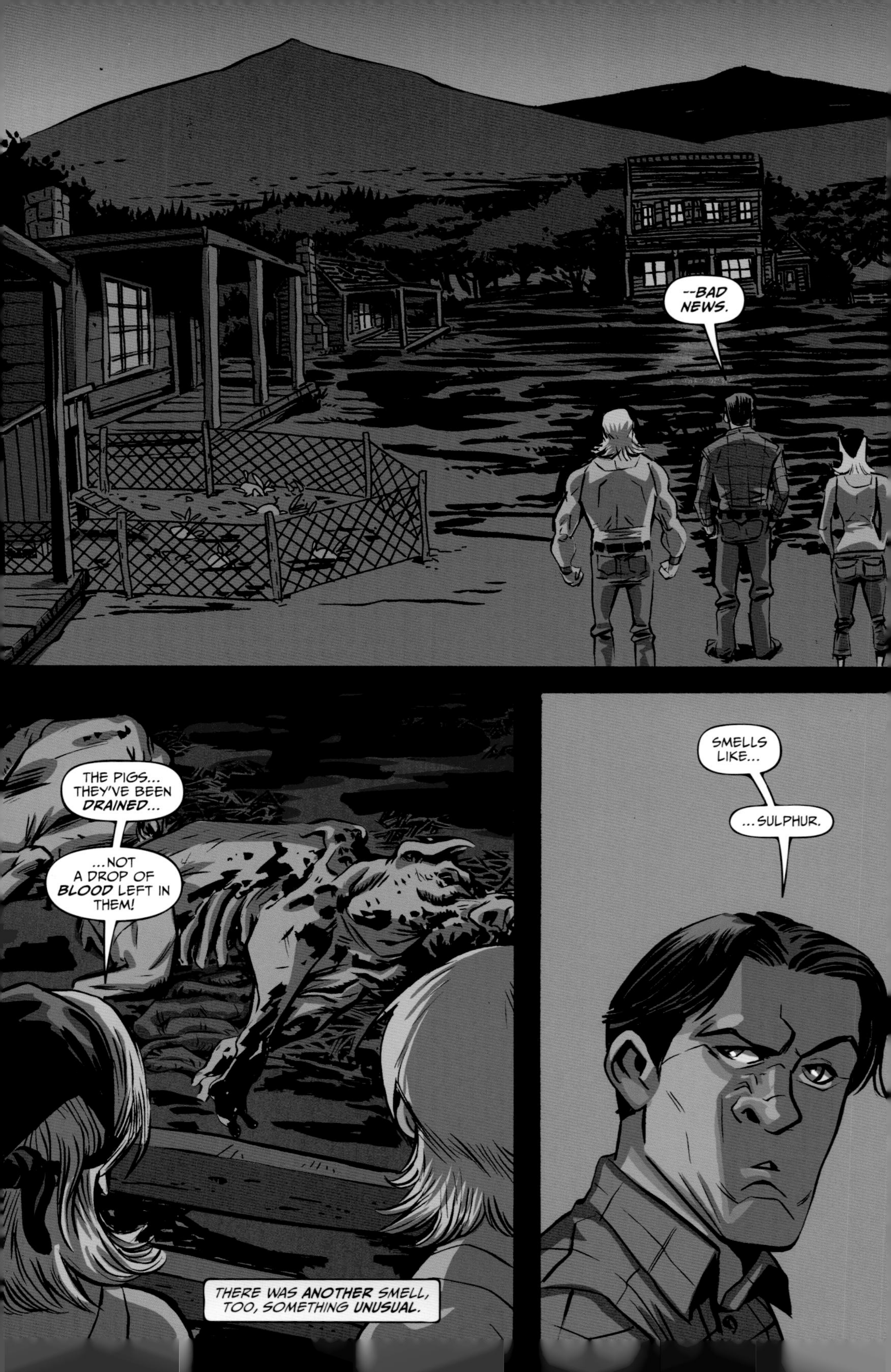
--BAD NEWS.
THE PIGS... THEY'VE BEEN DRAINED...
...NOT A DROP OF BLOOD LEFT IN THEM!
THERE WAS ANOTHER SMELL, TOO, SOMETHING UNUSUAL.
SMELLS LIKE...
...SULPHUR.

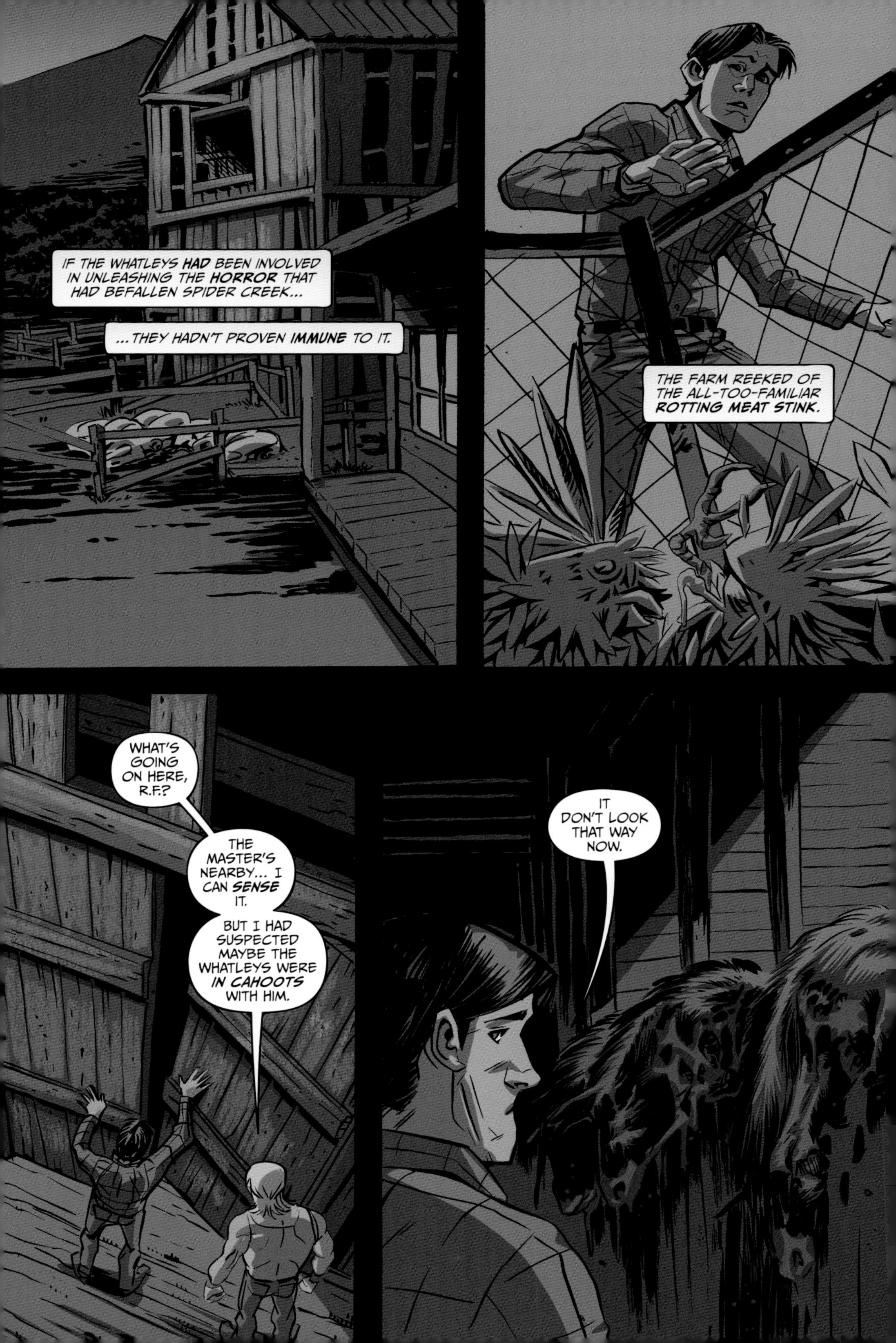
IF THE WHATLEYS HAD BEEN INVOLVED IN UNLEASHING THE HORROR THAT HAD BEFALLEN SPIDER CREEK...
...THEY HADN'T PROVEN IMMUNE TO IT.
THE FARM REEKED OF THE ALL-TOO-FAMILIAR ROTTING MEAT STINK.
WHAT'S GOING ON HERE, R.F.?
THE MASTER'S NEARBY... I CAN SENSE IT.
BUT I HAD SUSPECTED MAYBE THE WHATLEYS WERE IN CAHOOTS WITH HIM.
IT DON'T LOOK THAT WAY NOW.

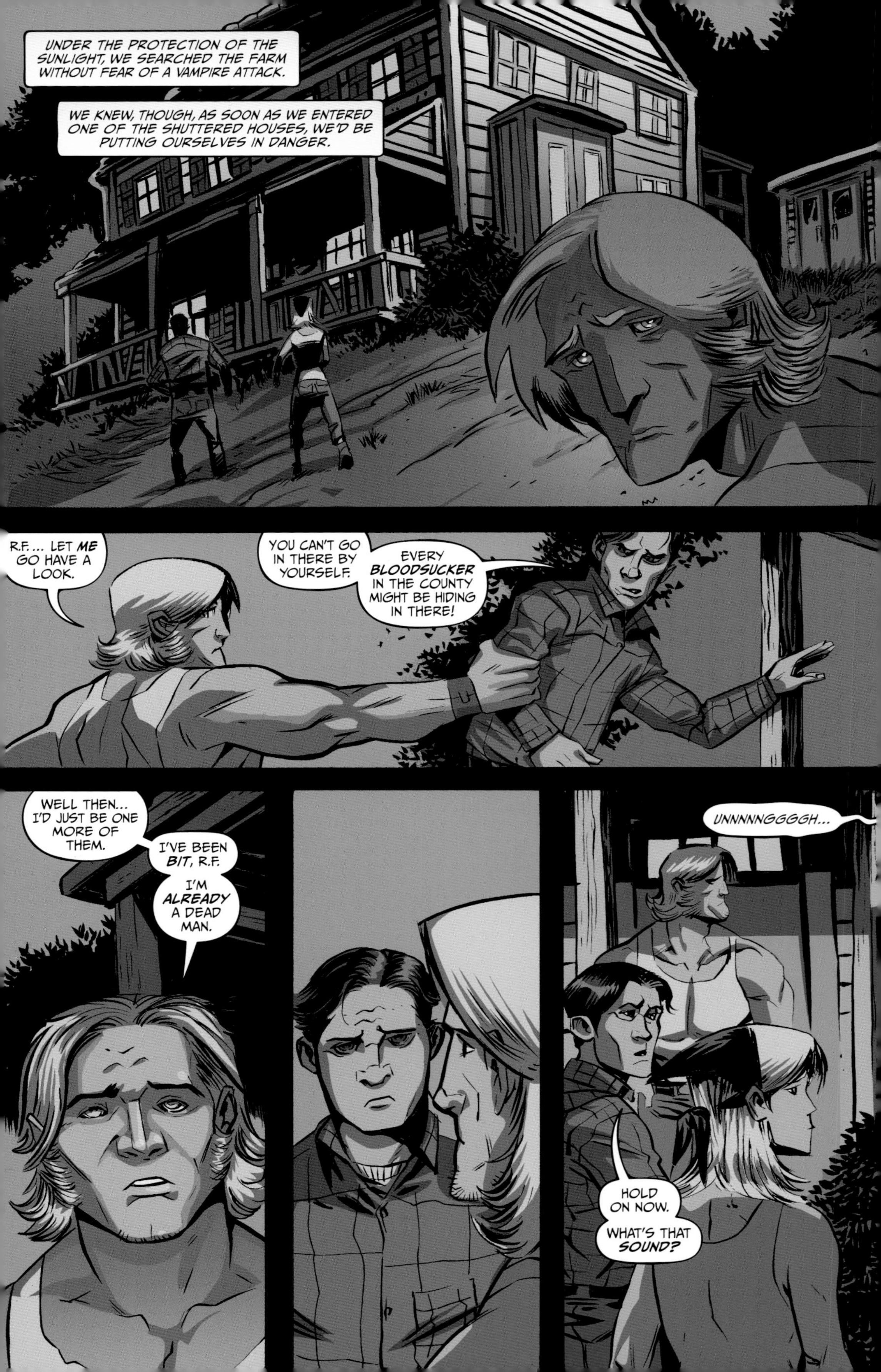
UNDER THE PROTECTION OF THE SUNLIGHT, WE SEARCHED THE FARM WITHOUT FEAR OF A VAMPIRE ATTACK.
WE KNEW, THOUGH, AS SOON AS WE ENTERED ONE OF THE SHUTTERED HOUSES, WE'D BE PUTTING OURSELVES IN DANGER.
R.F. ... LET ME GO HAVE A LOOK.
YOU CAN'T GO IN THERE BY YOURSELF.
EVERY BLOODSUCKER IN THE COUNTY MIGHT BE HIDING IN THERE!
WELL THEN... I'D JUST BE ONE MORE OF THEM.
I'VE BEEN BIT, R.F.
I'M ALREADY A DEAD MAN.
UNNNNNGGGGH...
HOLD ON NOW.
WHAT'S THAT SOUND?

WHO...

...WHO'S THERE?

SHOULDN'T BE HERE.

BAD THINGS ABOUT.

I RECOGNIZED HIM STRAIGHT AWAY...

B-BAD THINGS.

...OLD MAN EZEKIEL... THE *PATRIARCH* OF THE WHATLEY CLAN.

MR. WHATLEY... IT'S R.F. COVEN.

ARE YOU ALL RIGHT? ARE YOU--

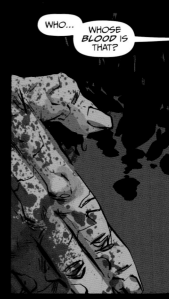

WHO...

WHOSE *BLOOD* IS THAT?

WE... WE SHOULDN'T HAVE DONE IT.

WE SHOULDN'T HAVE CALLED UP WHAT COULD NOT BE PUT DOWN.

BUT WE DID... WE CALLED *HIM* UP...

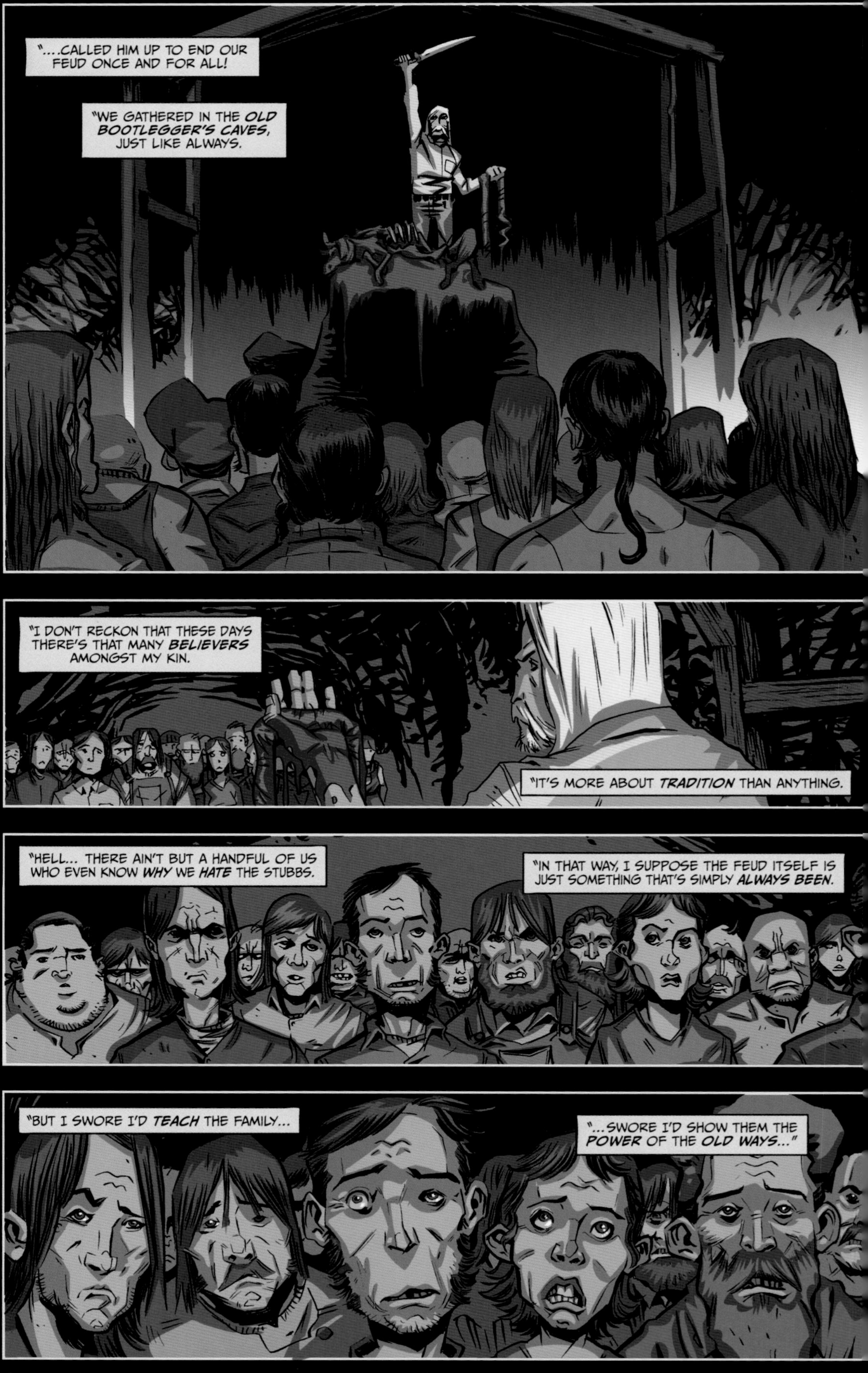
"....CALLED HIM UP TO END OUR FEUD ONCE AND FOR ALL!
"WE GATHERED IN THE *OLD BOOTLEGGER'S CAVES*, JUST LIKE ALWAYS.
"I DON'T RECKON THAT THESE DAYS THERE'S THAT MANY *BELIEVERS* AMONGST MY KIN.
"IT'S MORE ABOUT *TRADITION* THAN ANYTHING.
"HELL... THERE AIN'T BUT A HANDFUL OF US WHO EVEN KNOW *WHY* WE *HATE* THE STUBBS.
"IN THAT WAY, I SUPPOSE THE FEUD ITSELF IS JUST SOMETHING THAT'S SIMPLY *ALWAYS BEEN*.
"BUT I SWORE I'D *TEACH* THE FAMILY...
"...SWORE I'D SHOW THEM THE *POWER* OF THE *OLD WAYS*..."

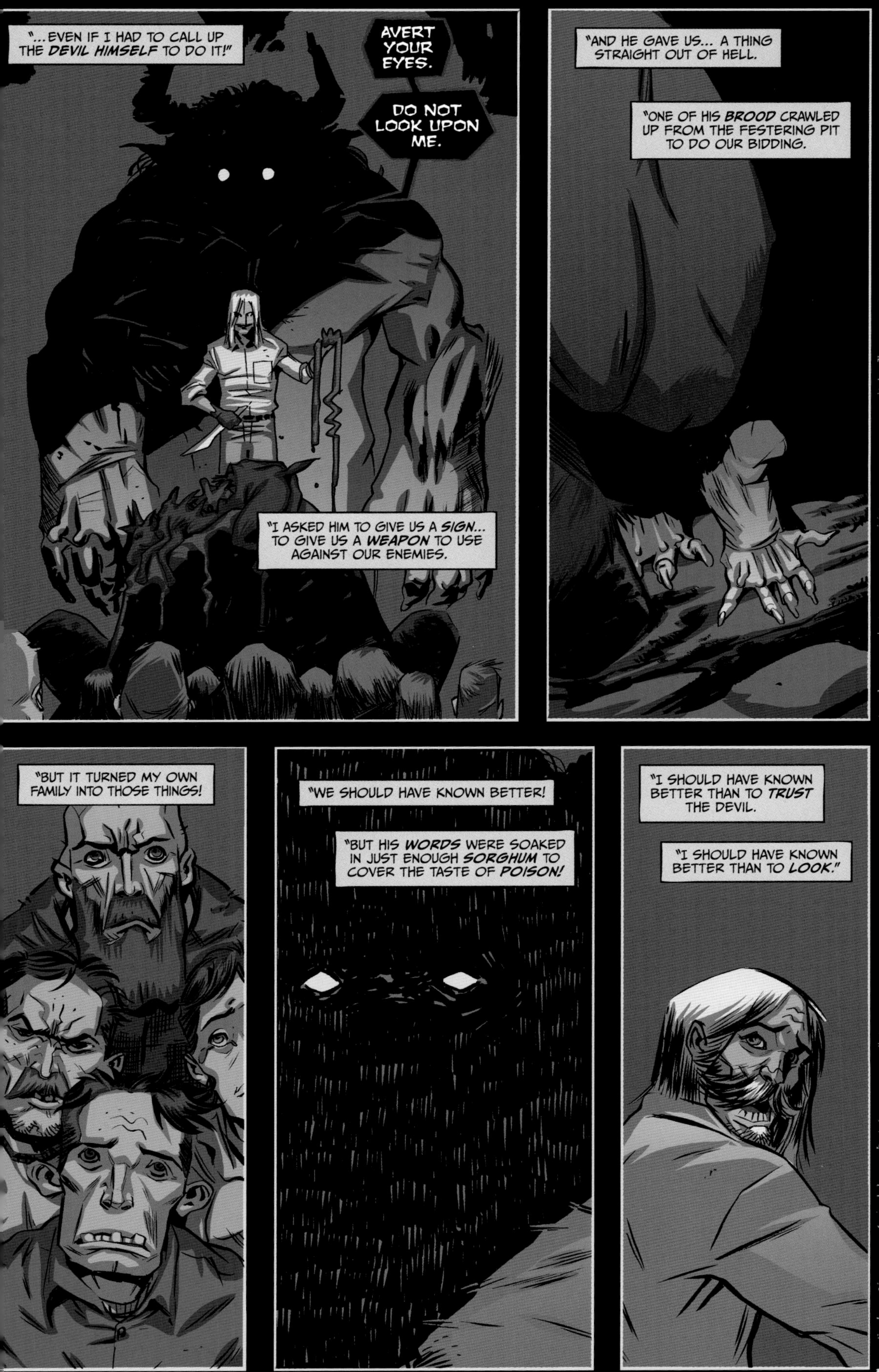
"...EVEN IF I HAD TO CALL UP THE DEVIL HIMSELF TO DO IT!"
AVERT YOUR EYES.
DO NOT LOOK UPON ME.
"I ASKED HIM TO GIVE US A SIGN... TO GIVE US A WEAPON TO USE AGAINST OUR ENEMIES.
"AND HE GAVE US... A THING STRAIGHT OUT OF HELL.
"ONE OF HIS BROOD CRAWLED UP FROM THE FESTERING PIT TO DO OUR BIDDING.
"BUT IT TURNED MY OWN FAMILY INTO THOSE THINGS!
"WE SHOULD HAVE KNOWN BETTER!
"BUT HIS WORDS WERE SOAKED IN JUST ENOUGH SORGHUM TO COVER THE TASTE OF POISON!
"I SHOULD HAVE KNOWN BETTER THAN TO TRUST THE DEVIL.
"I SHOULD HAVE KNOWN BETTER THAN TO LOOK."

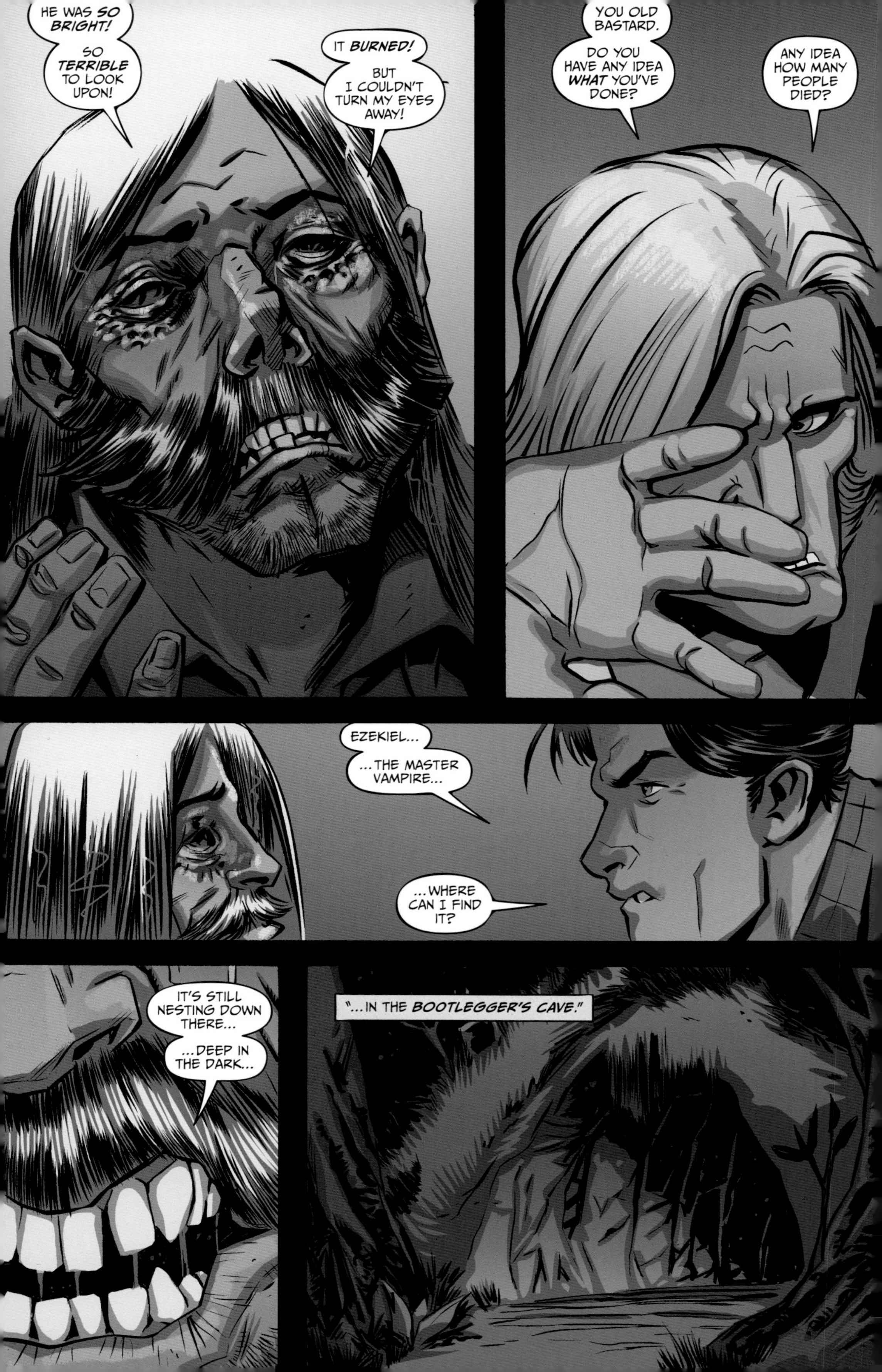
HE WAS SO BRIGHT!
SO TERRIBLE TO LOOK UPON!
IT BURNED!
BUT I COULDN'T TURN MY EYES AWAY!
YOU OLD BASTARD.
DO YOU HAVE ANY IDEA WHAT YOU'VE DONE?
ANY IDEA HOW MANY PEOPLE DIED?
EZEKIEL...
...THE MASTER VAMPIRE...
...WHERE CAN I FIND IT?
IT'S STILL NESTING DOWN THERE...
...DEEP IN THE DARK...
"...IN THE BOOTLEGGER'S CAVE."

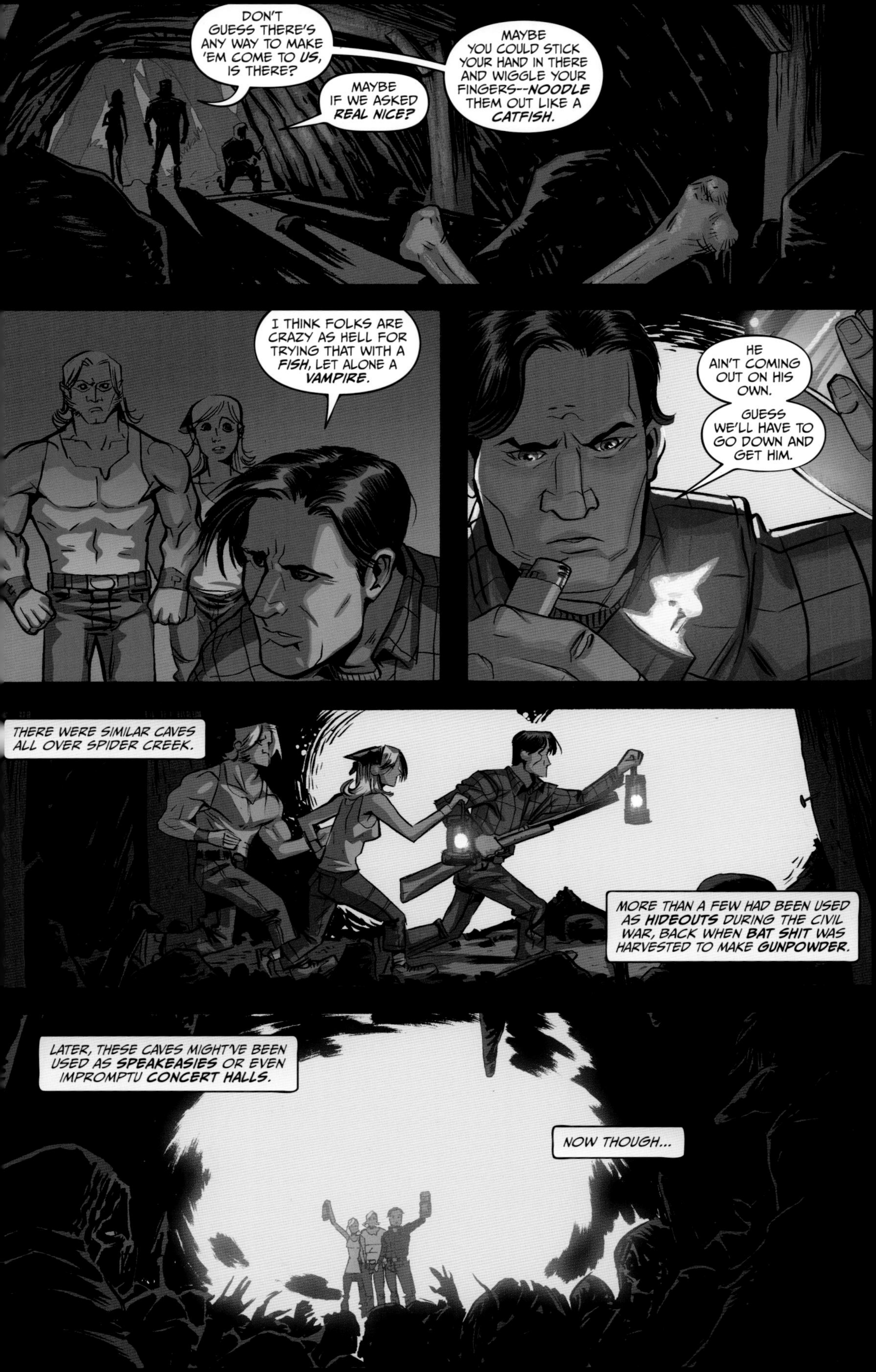
DON'T GUESS THERE'S ANY WAY TO MAKE 'EM COME TO US, IS THERE?
MAYBE IF WE ASKED REAL NICE?
MAYBE YOU COULD STICK YOUR HAND IN THERE AND WIGGLE YOUR FINGERS--NOODLE THEM OUT LIKE A CATFISH.
I THINK FOLKS ARE CRAZY AS HELL FOR TRYING THAT WITH A FISH, LET ALONE A VAMPIRE.
HE AIN'T COMING OUT ON HIS OWN.
GUESS WE'LL HAVE TO GO DOWN AND GET HIM.
THERE WERE SIMILAR CAVES ALL OVER SPIDER CREEK.
MORE THAN A FEW HAD BEEN USED AS HIDEOUTS DURING THE CIVIL WAR, BACK WHEN BAT SHIT WAS HARVESTED TO MAKE GUNPOWDER.
LATER, THESE CAVES MIGHT'VE BEEN USED AS SPEAKEASIES OR EVEN IMPROMPTU CONCERT HALLS.
NOW THOUGH...

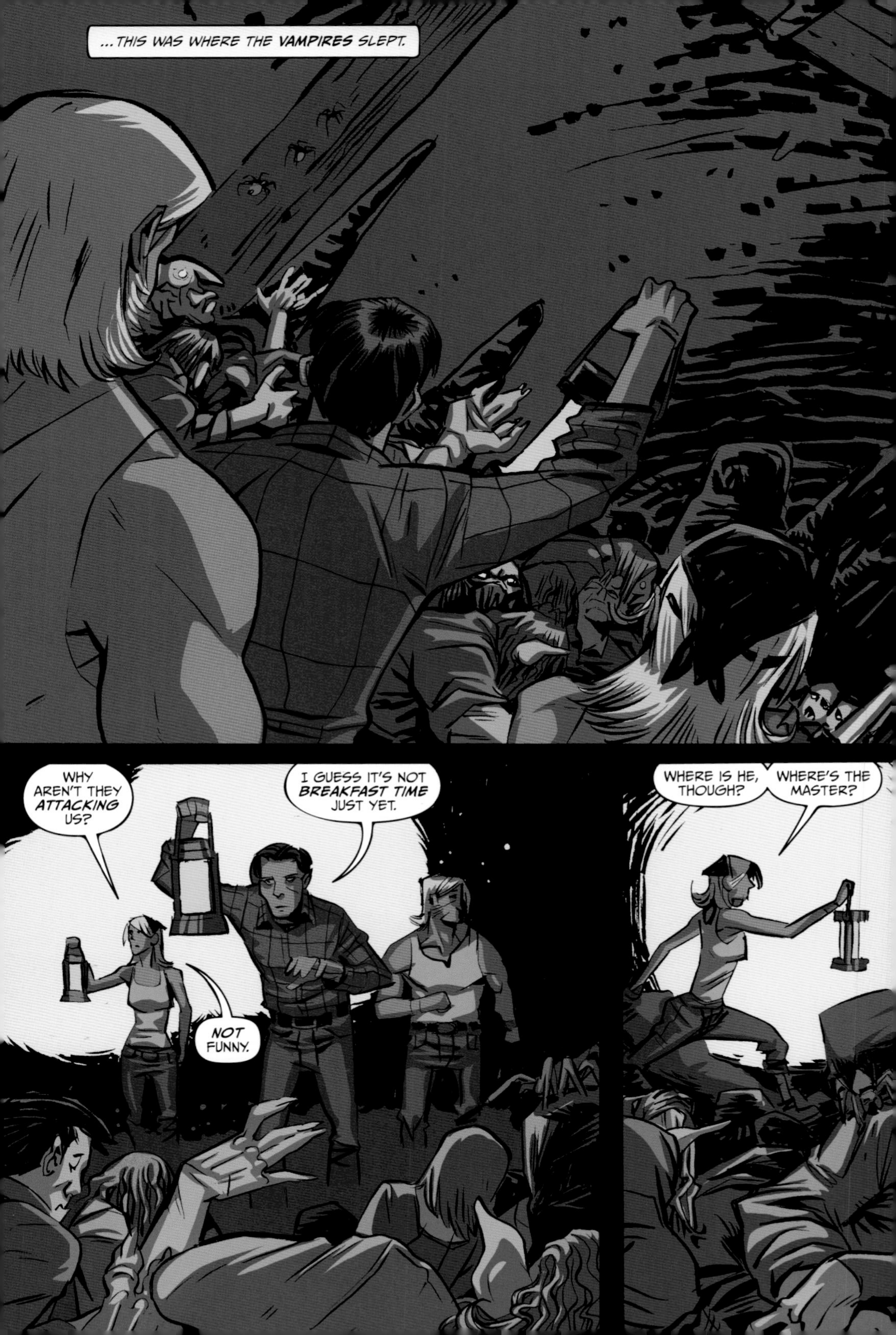

...THIS WAS WHERE THE **VAMPIRES** SLEPT.
WHY AREN'T THEY ***ATTACKING*** US?
I GUESS IT'S NOT ***BREAKFAST TIME*** JUST YET.
NOT FUNNY.
WHERE IS HE, THOUGH?
WHERE'S THE MASTER?

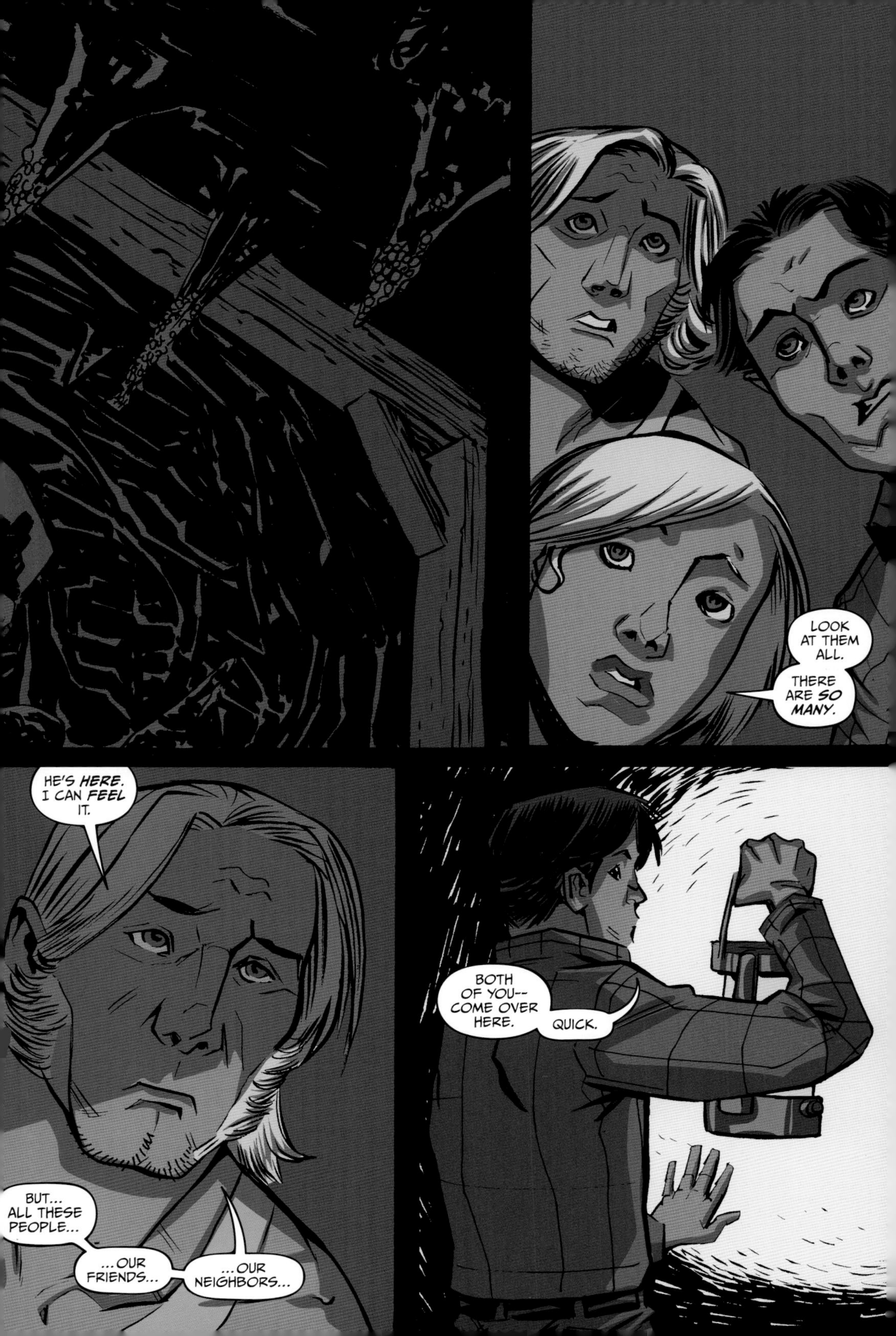
LOOK AT THEM ALL.
THERE ARE SO MANY.
HE'S HERE. I CAN FEEL IT.
BUT... ALL THESE PEOPLE...
...OUR FRIENDS...
...OUR NEIGHBORS...
BOTH OF YOU-- COME OVER HERE.
QUICK.

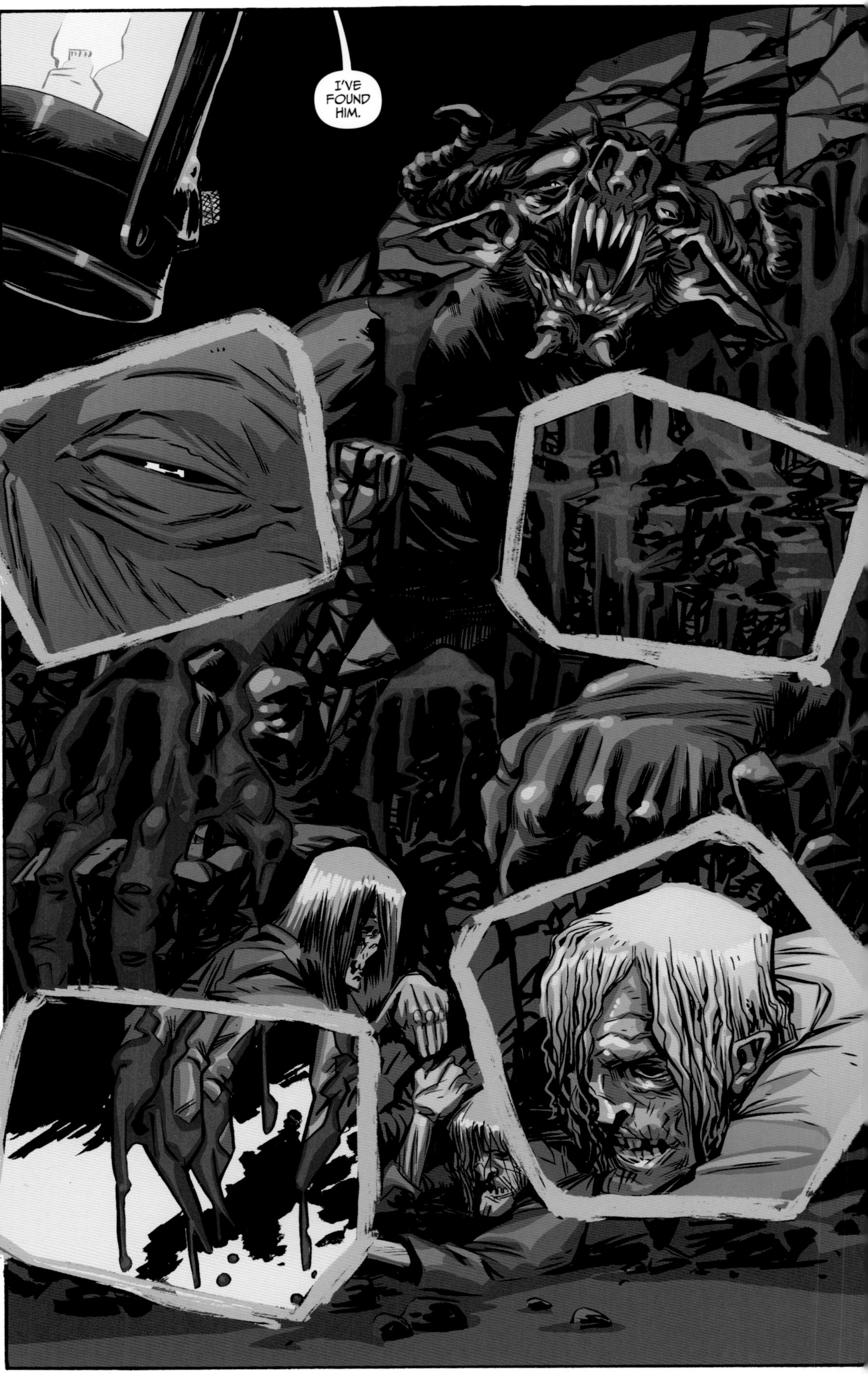
I'VE FOUND HIM.

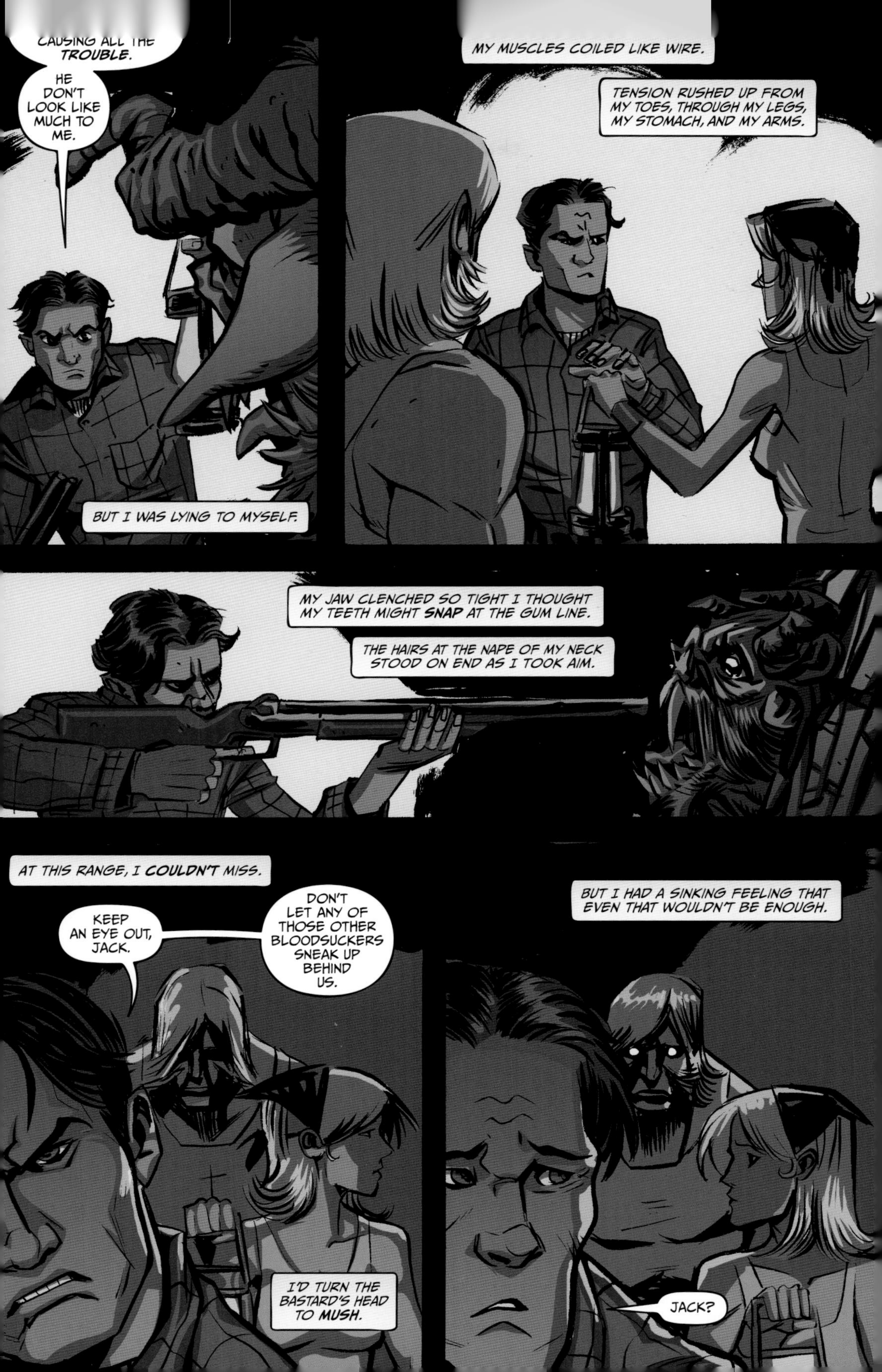
CAUSING ALL THE TROUBLE.
HE DON'T LOOK LIKE MUCH TO ME.
BUT I WAS LYING TO MYSELF.
MY MUSCLES COILED LIKE WIRE.
TENSION RUSHED UP FROM MY TOES, THROUGH MY LEGS, MY STOMACH, AND MY ARMS.
MY JAW CLENCHED SO TIGHT I THOUGHT MY TEETH MIGHT SNAP AT THE GUM LINE.
THE HAIRS AT THE NAPE OF MY NECK STOOD ON END AS I TOOK AIM.
AT THIS RANGE, I COULDN'T MISS.
KEEP AN EYE OUT, JACK.
DON'T LET ANY OF THOSE OTHER BLOODSUCKERS SNEAK UP BEHIND US.
I'D TURN THE BASTARD'S HEAD TO MUSH.
BUT I HAD A SINKING FEELING THAT EVEN THAT WOULDN'T BE ENOUGH.
JACK?

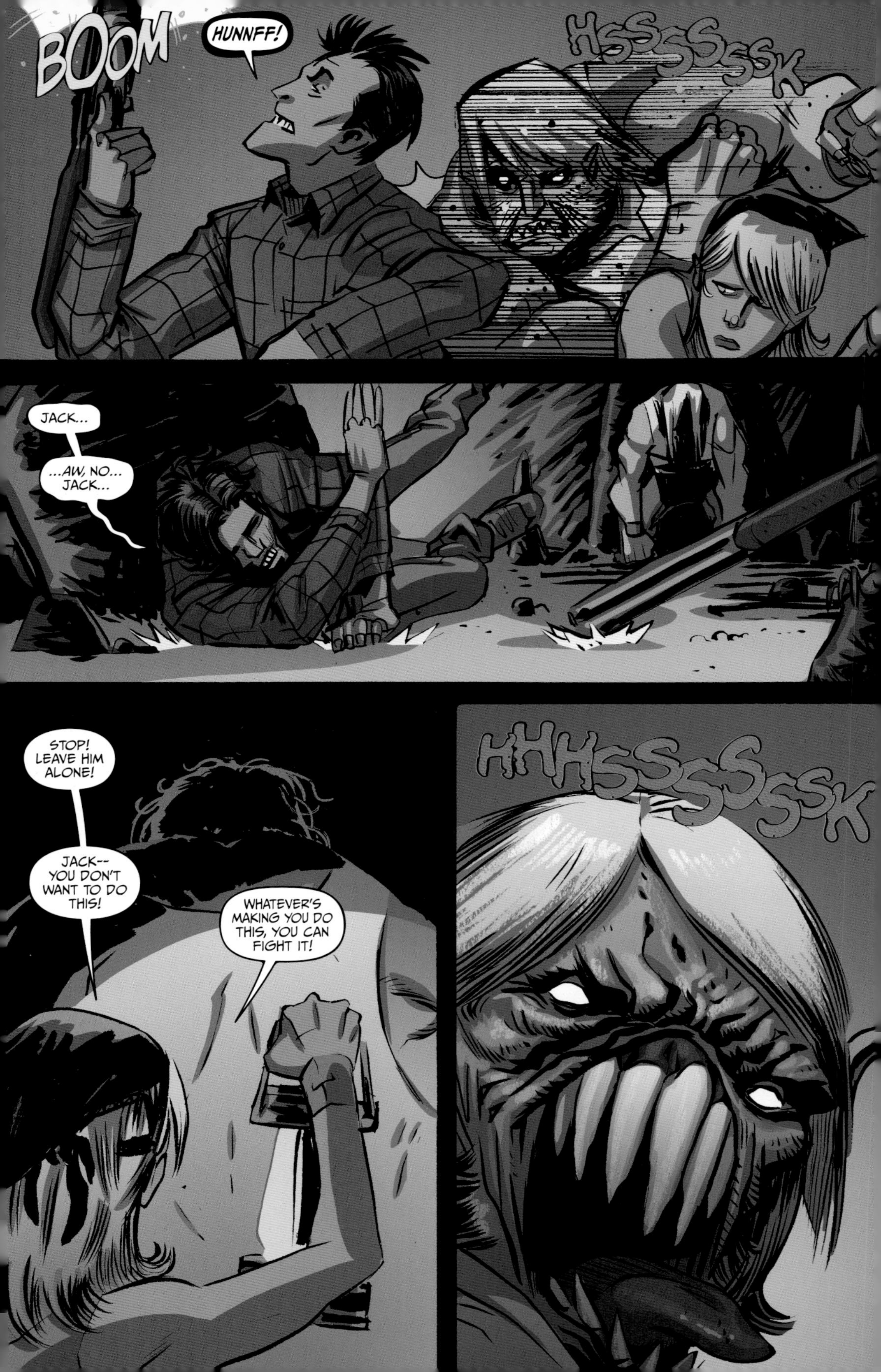

BOOM
HUNNFF!
HSSSSSSSK
JACK...
...AW, NO... JACK...
STOP! LEAVE HIM ALONE!
JACK-- YOU DON'T WANT TO DO THIS!
WHATEVER'S MAKING YOU DO THIS, YOU CAN FIGHT IT!
HHHSSSSSSSK

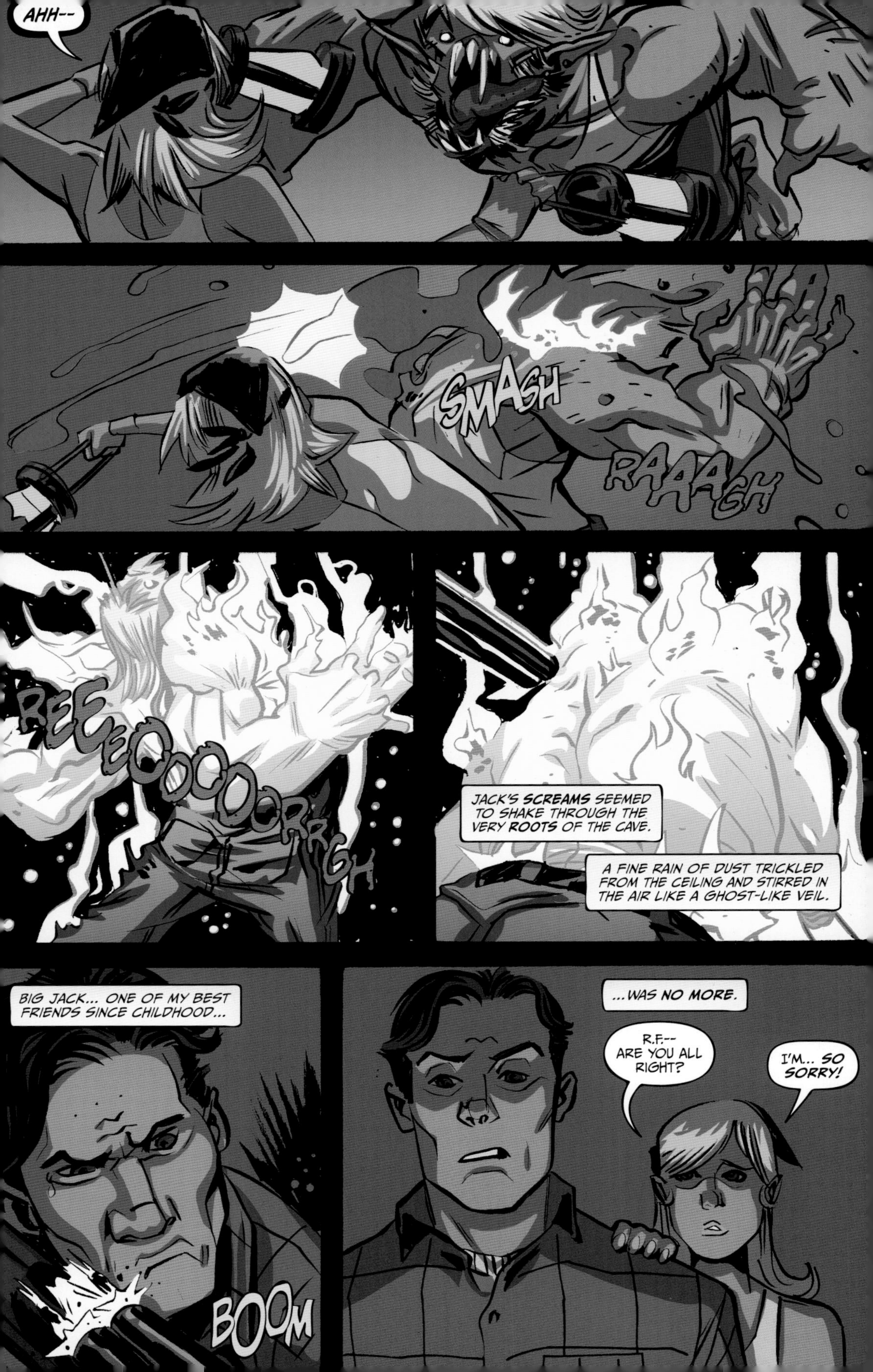
AHH--
SMASH
RAAAAGH
REEEOOOOORRRGH
JACK'S SCREAMS SEEMED TO SHAKE THROUGH THE VERY ROOTS OF THE CAVE.
A FINE RAIN OF DUST TRICKLED FROM THE CEILING AND STIRRED IN THE AIR LIKE A GHOST-LIKE VEIL.
BIG JACK... ONE OF MY BEST FRIENDS SINCE CHILDHOOD...
BOOM
...WAS NO MORE.
R.F.-- ARE YOU ALL RIGHT?
I'M... SO SORRY!

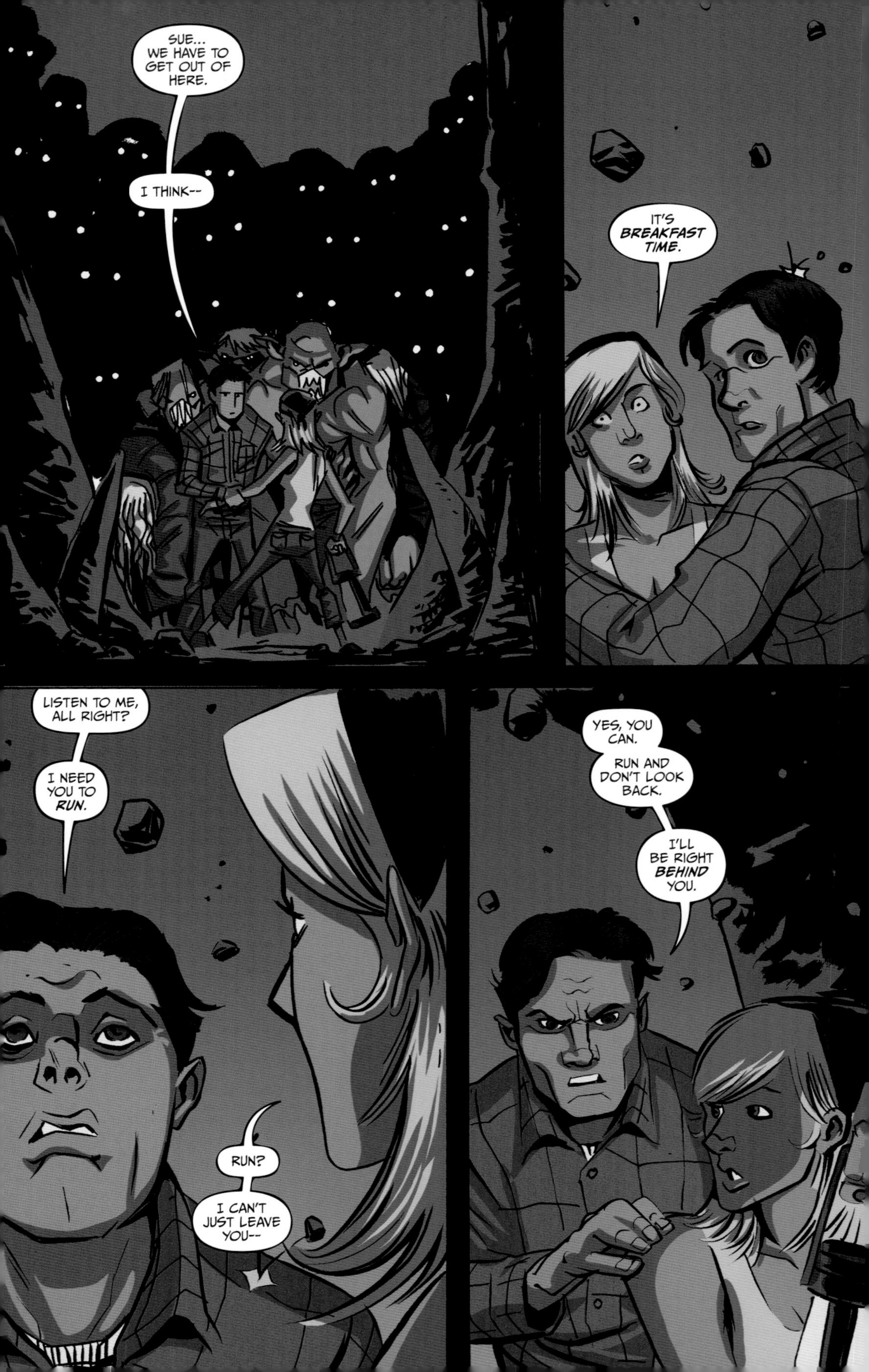
SUE... WE HAVE TO GET OUT OF HERE.
I THINK--
IT'S *BREAKFAST TIME.*
LISTEN TO ME, ALL RIGHT?
I NEED YOU TO *RUN.*
RUN?
I CAN'T JUST LEAVE YOU--
YES, YOU CAN.
RUN AND DON'T LOOK BACK.
I'LL BE RIGHT *BEHIND* YOU.

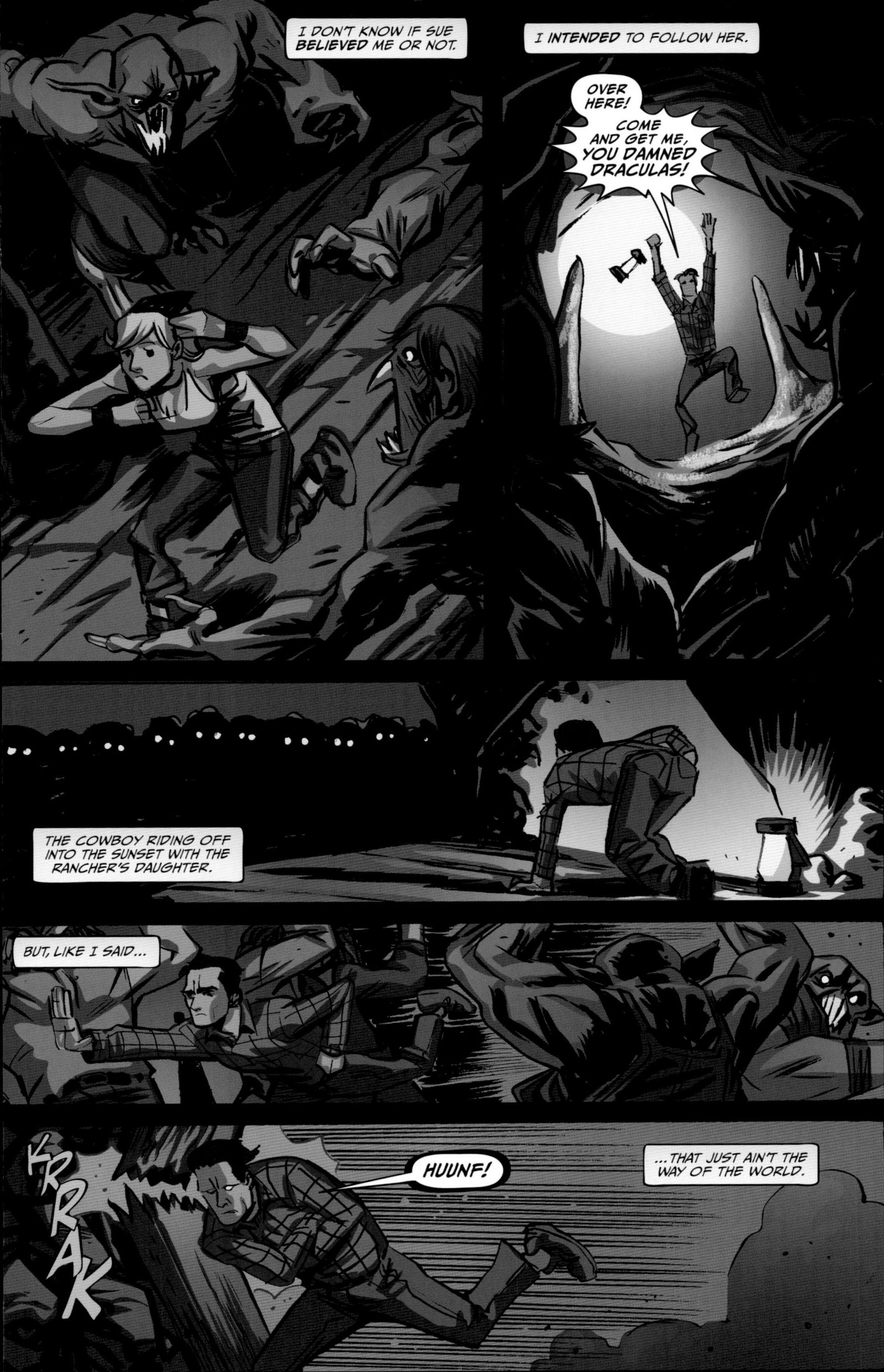
I DON'T KNOW IF SUE BELIEVED ME OR NOT.
I INTENDED TO FOLLOW HER.
OVER HERE!
COME AND GET ME, YOU DAMNED DRACULAS!
THE COWBOY RIDING OFF INTO THE SUNSET WITH THE RANCHER'S DAUGHTER.
BUT, LIKE I SAID...
KRRAK
HUUNF!
...THAT JUST AIN'T THE WAY OF THE WORLD.

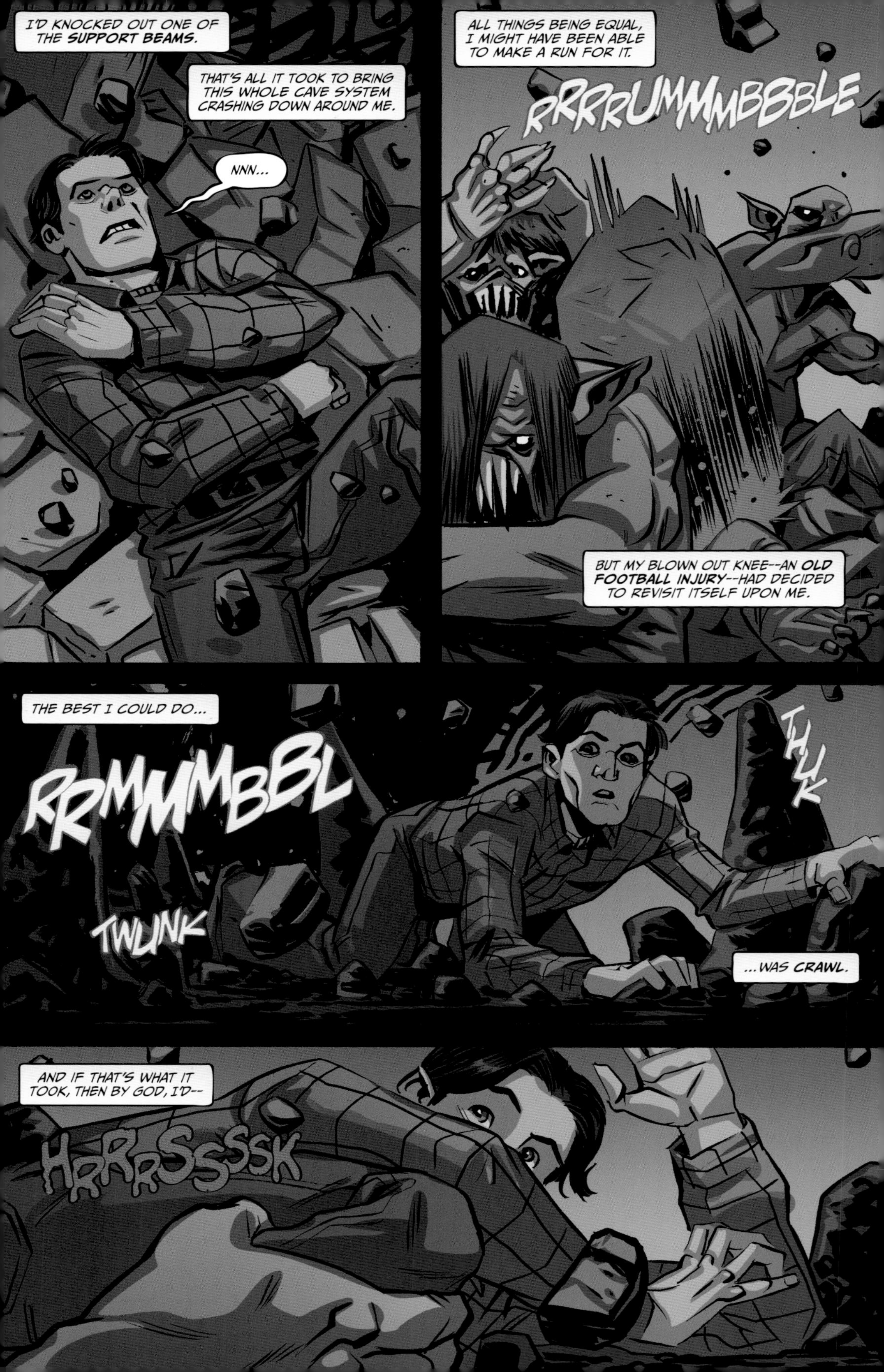
I'D KNOCKED OUT ONE OF THE SUPPORT BEAMS.
THAT'S ALL IT TOOK TO BRING THIS WHOLE CAVE SYSTEM CRASHING DOWN AROUND ME.
NNN...
ALL THINGS BEING EQUAL, I MIGHT HAVE BEEN ABLE TO MAKE A RUN FOR IT.
RRRRUMMMBBBLE
BUT MY BLOWN OUT KNEE--AN OLD FOOTBALL INJURY--HAD DECIDED TO REVISIT ITSELF UPON ME.
THE BEST I COULD DO...
RRMMMBBL
THUK
TWUNK
...WAS CRAWL.
AND IF THAT'S WHAT IT TOOK, THEN BY GOD, I'D--
HRRRRSSSSSK

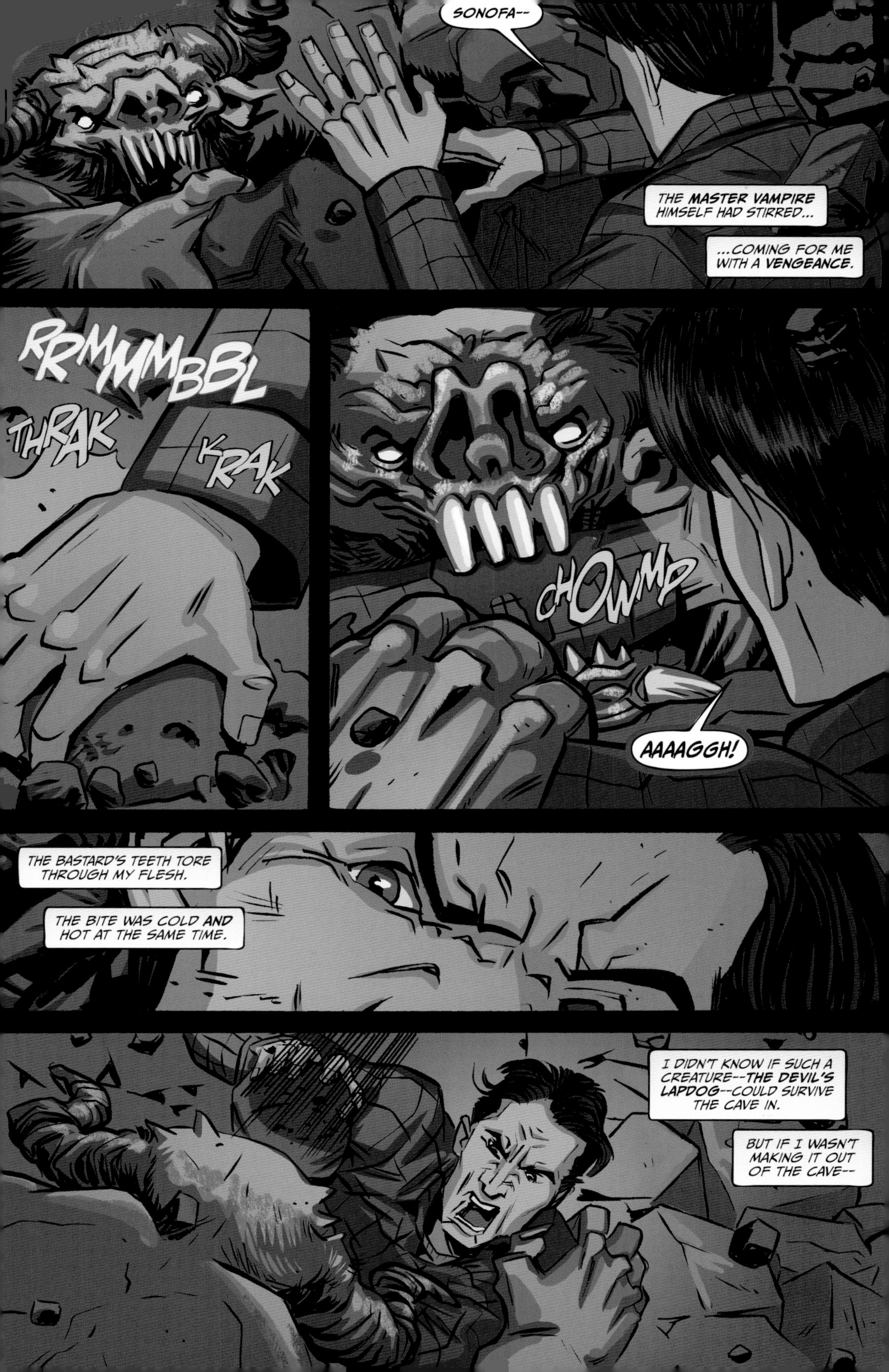
SONOFA--
THE MASTER VAMPIRE HIMSELF HAD STIRRED...
...COMING FOR ME WITH A VENGEANCE.
RRMMMMBBL
THRAK
KRAK
CHOWMP
AAAAGGH!
THE BASTARD'S TEETH TORE THROUGH MY FLESH.
THE BITE WAS COLD AND HOT AT THE SAME TIME.
I DIDN'T KNOW IF SUCH A CREATURE--THE DEVIL'S LAPDOG--COULD SURVIVE THE CAVE IN.
BUT IF I WASN'T MAKING IT OUT OF THE CAVE--

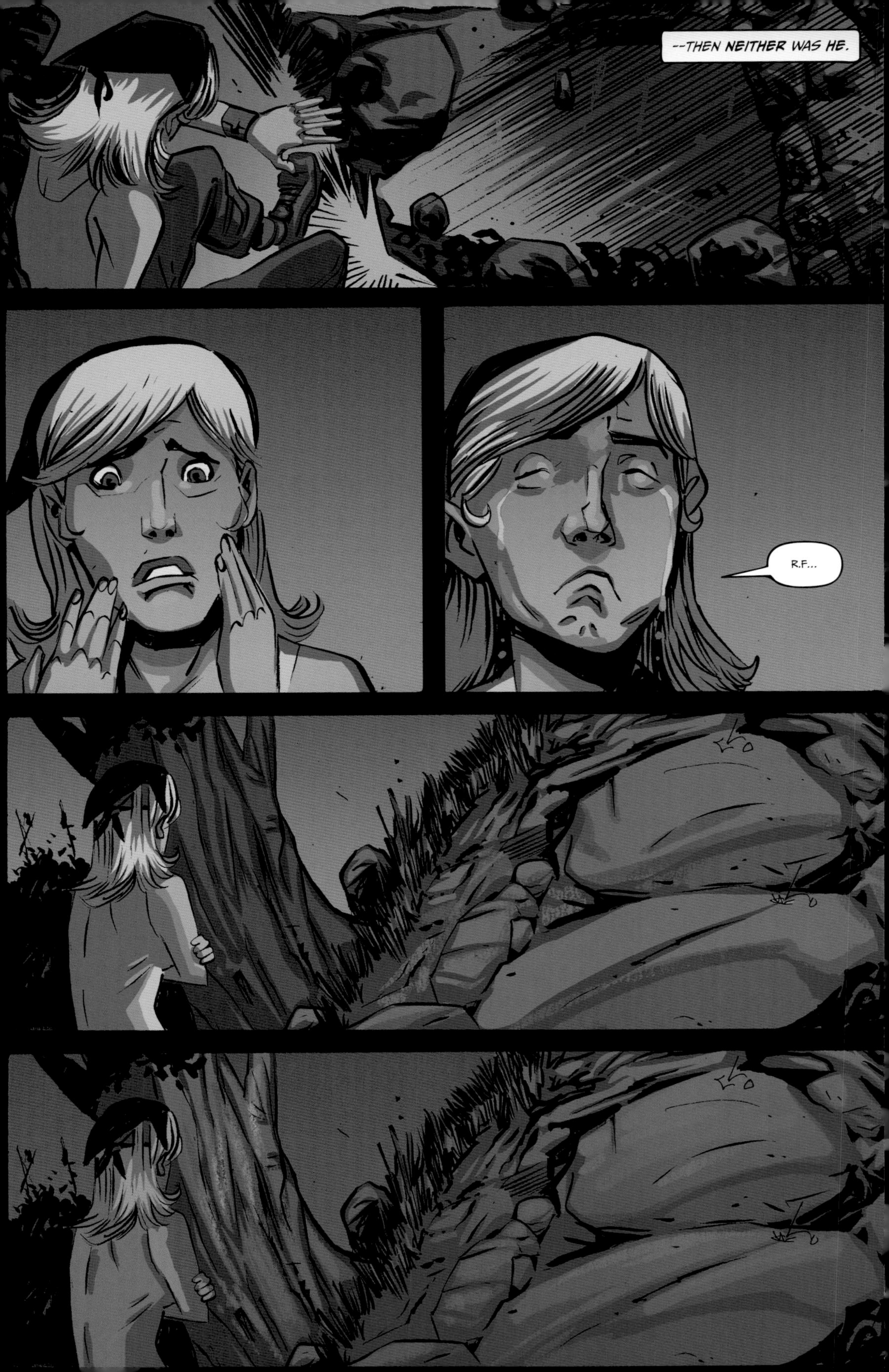
--THEN NEITHER WAS HE.
R.F...

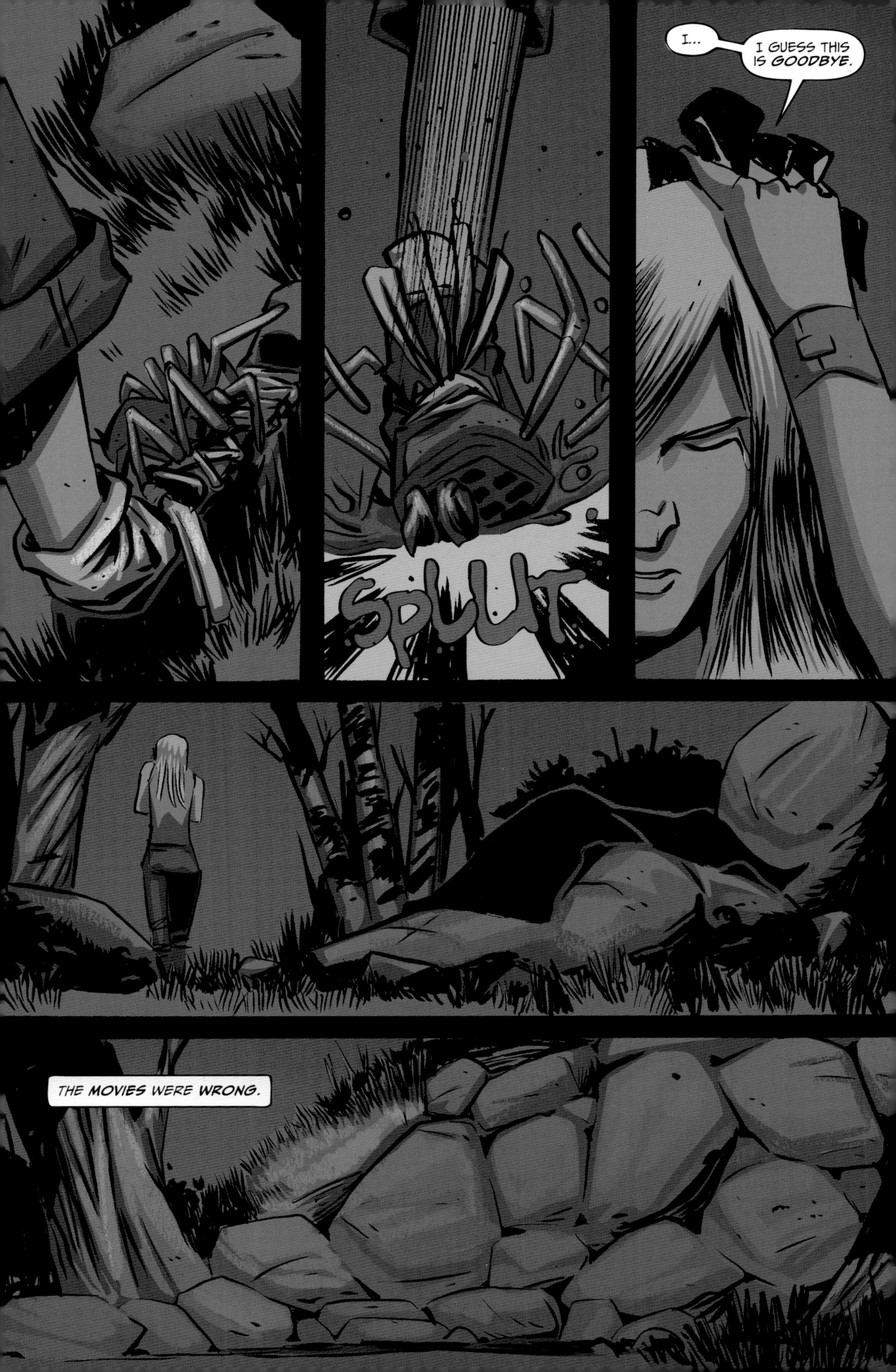
SPLUT
I...
I GUESS THIS IS GOODBYE.
THE MOVIES WERE WRONG.

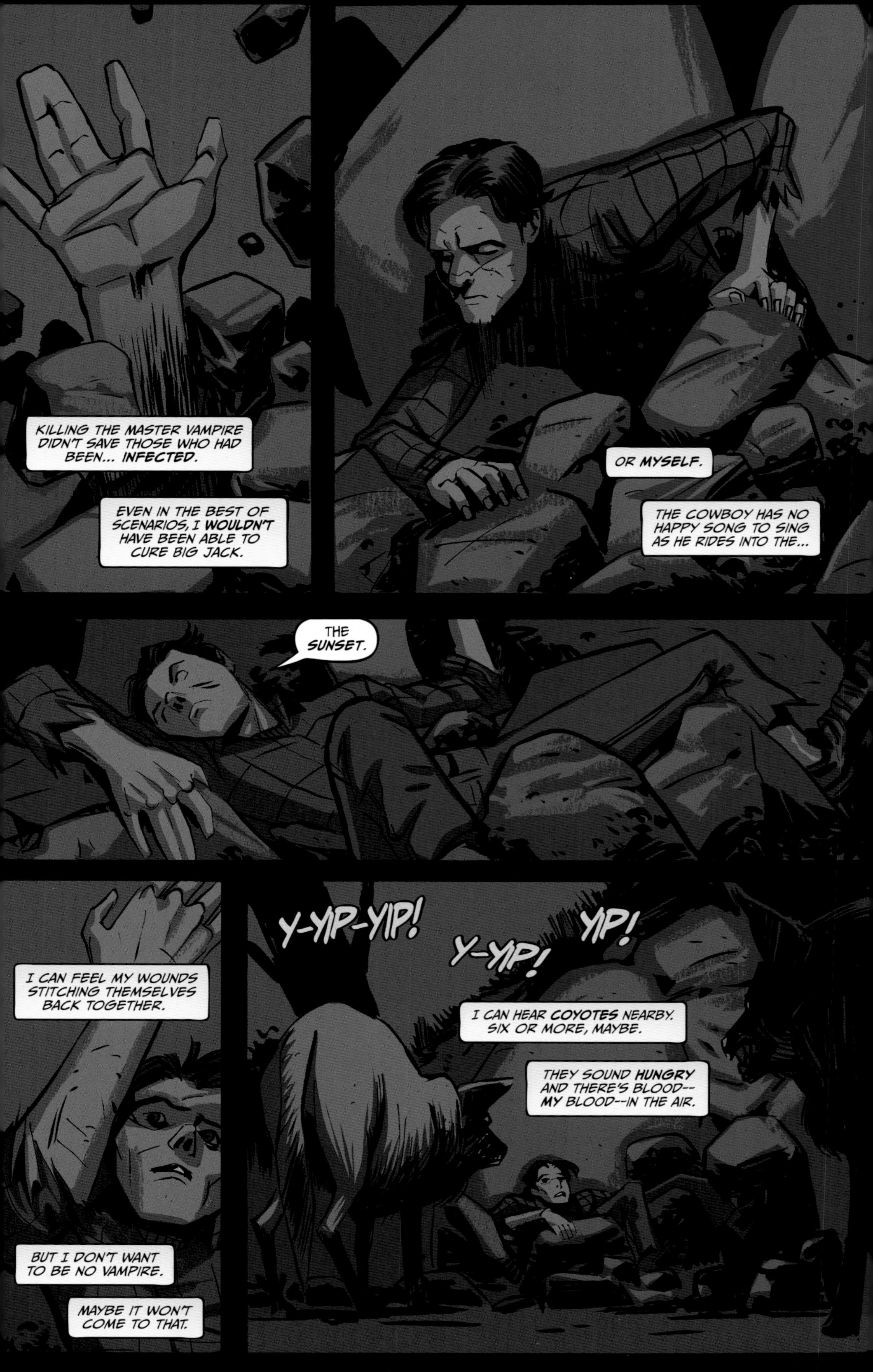
KILLING THE MASTER VAMPIRE DIDN'T SAVE THOSE WHO HAD BEEN... INFECTED.
EVEN IN THE BEST OF SCENARIOS, I WOULDN'T HAVE BEEN ABLE TO CURE BIG JACK.
OR MYSELF.
THE COWBOY HAS NO HAPPY SONG TO SING AS HE RIDES INTO THE...
THE SUNSET.
I CAN FEEL MY WOUNDS STITCHING THEMSELVES BACK TOGETHER.
BUT I DON'T WANT TO BE NO VAMPIRE.
MAYBE IT WON'T COME TO THAT.
Y-YIP-YIP!
Y-YIP!
YIP!
I CAN HEAR COYOTES NEARBY. SIX OR MORE, MAYBE.
THEY SOUND HUNGRY AND THERE'S BLOOD-- MY BLOOD--IN THE AIR.

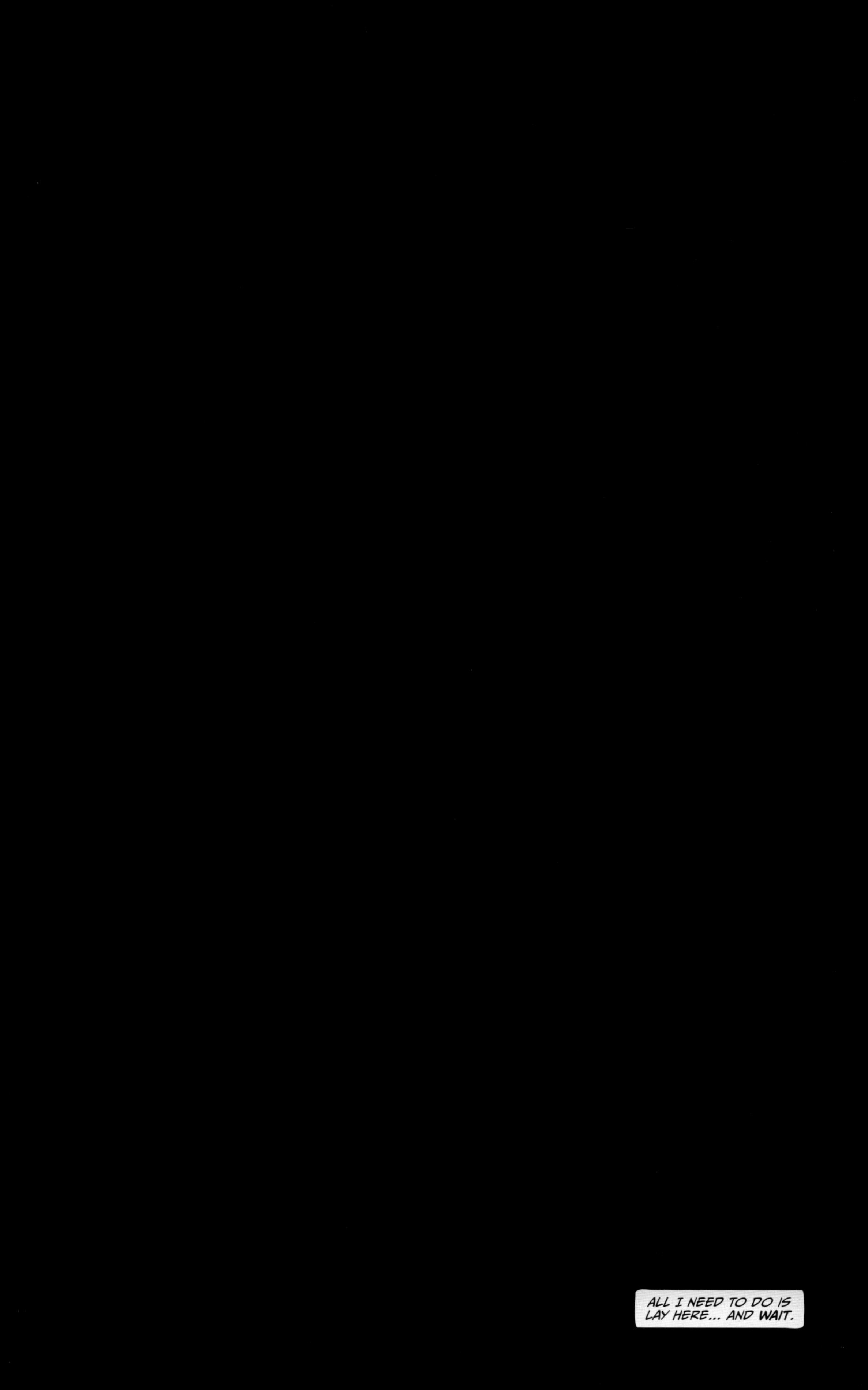
ALL I NEED TO DO IS LAY HERE... AND WAIT.

COVER GALLERY

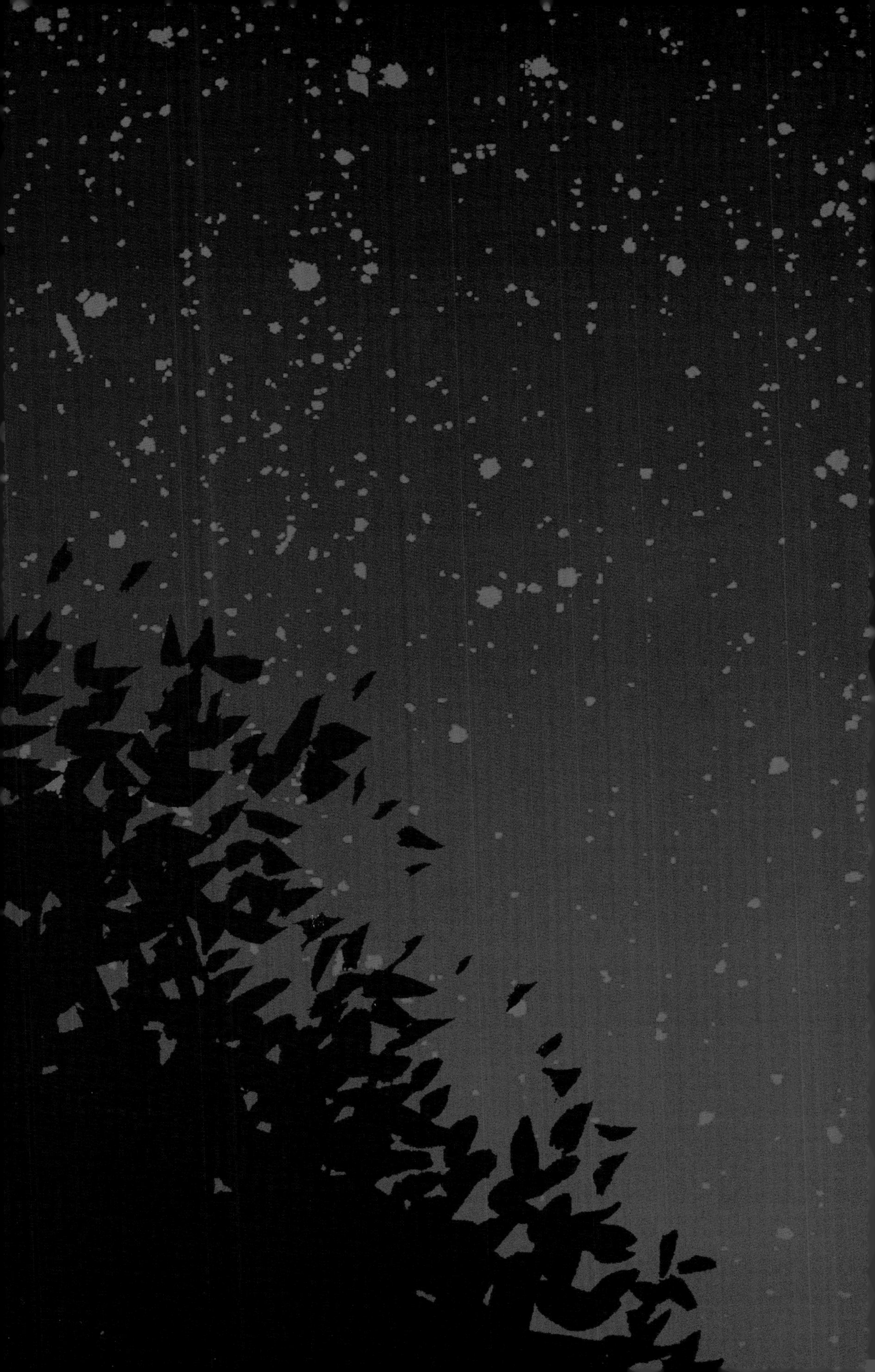

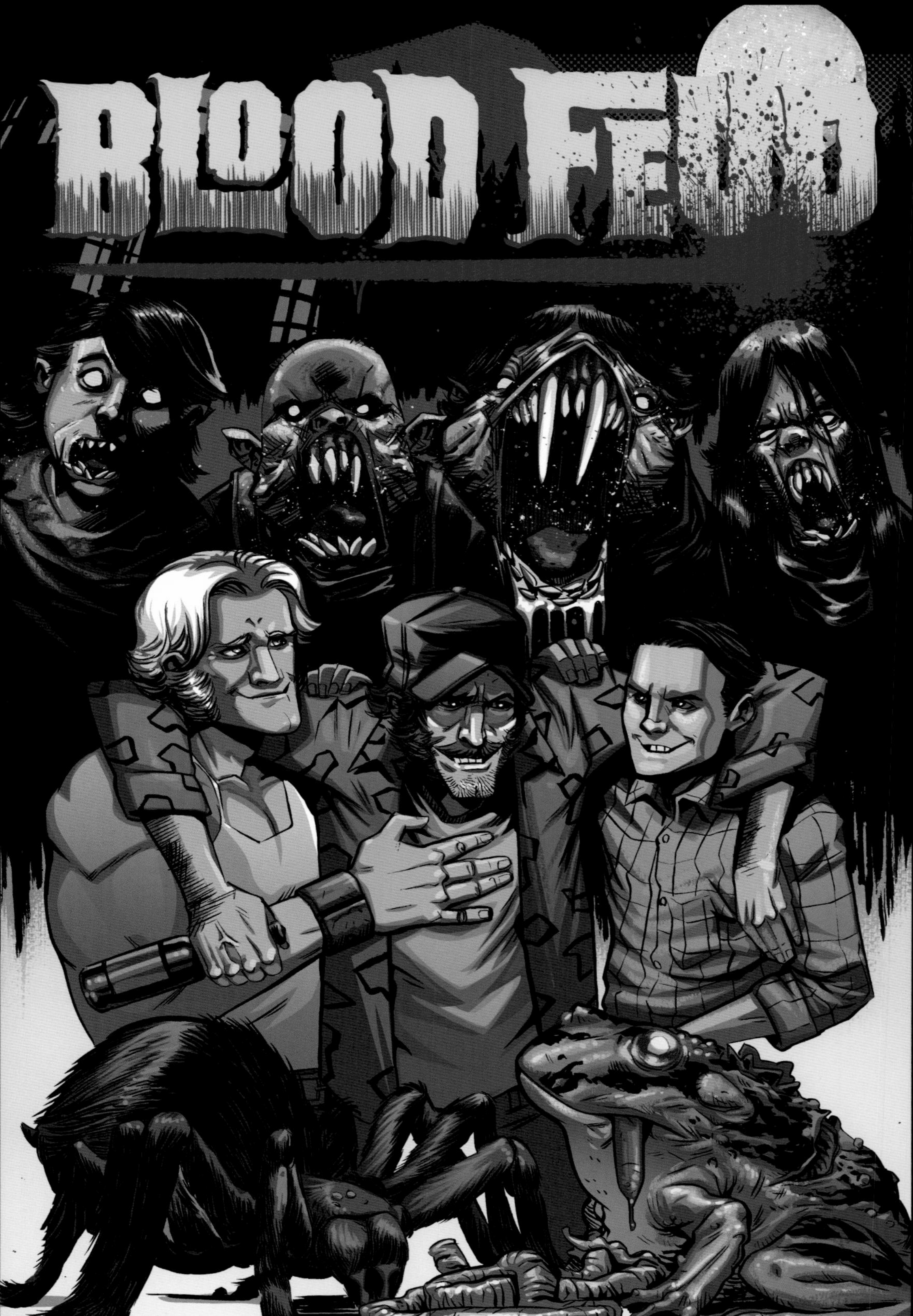
BLOOD FEUD

ISSUE #1 STANDARD COVER
ILLUSTRATED BY DREW MOSS, COLORED BY NICK FILARDI, DESIGNED BY DYLAN TODD

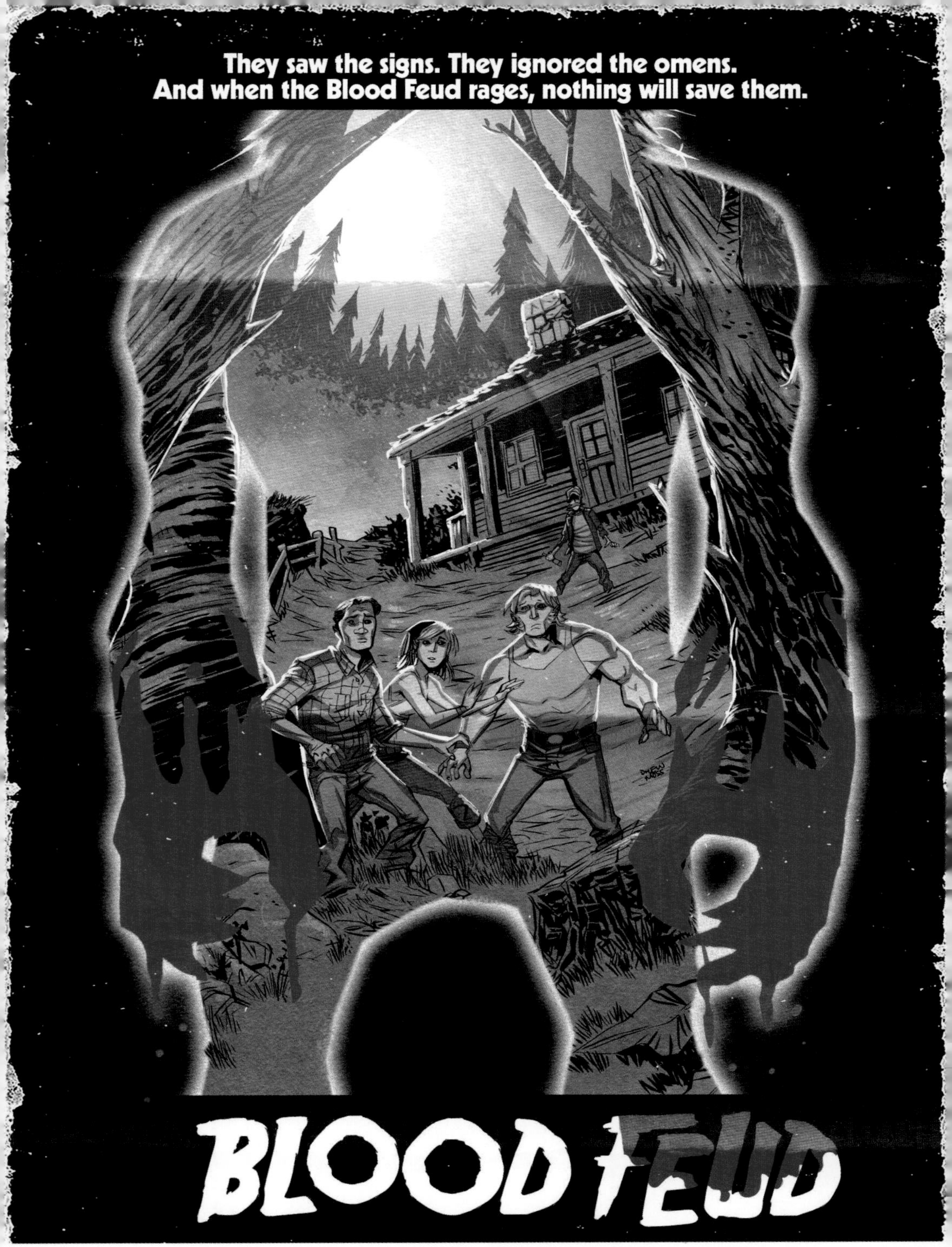
They saw the signs. They ignored the omens.
And when the Blood Feud rages, nothing will save them.
BLOOD FEUD

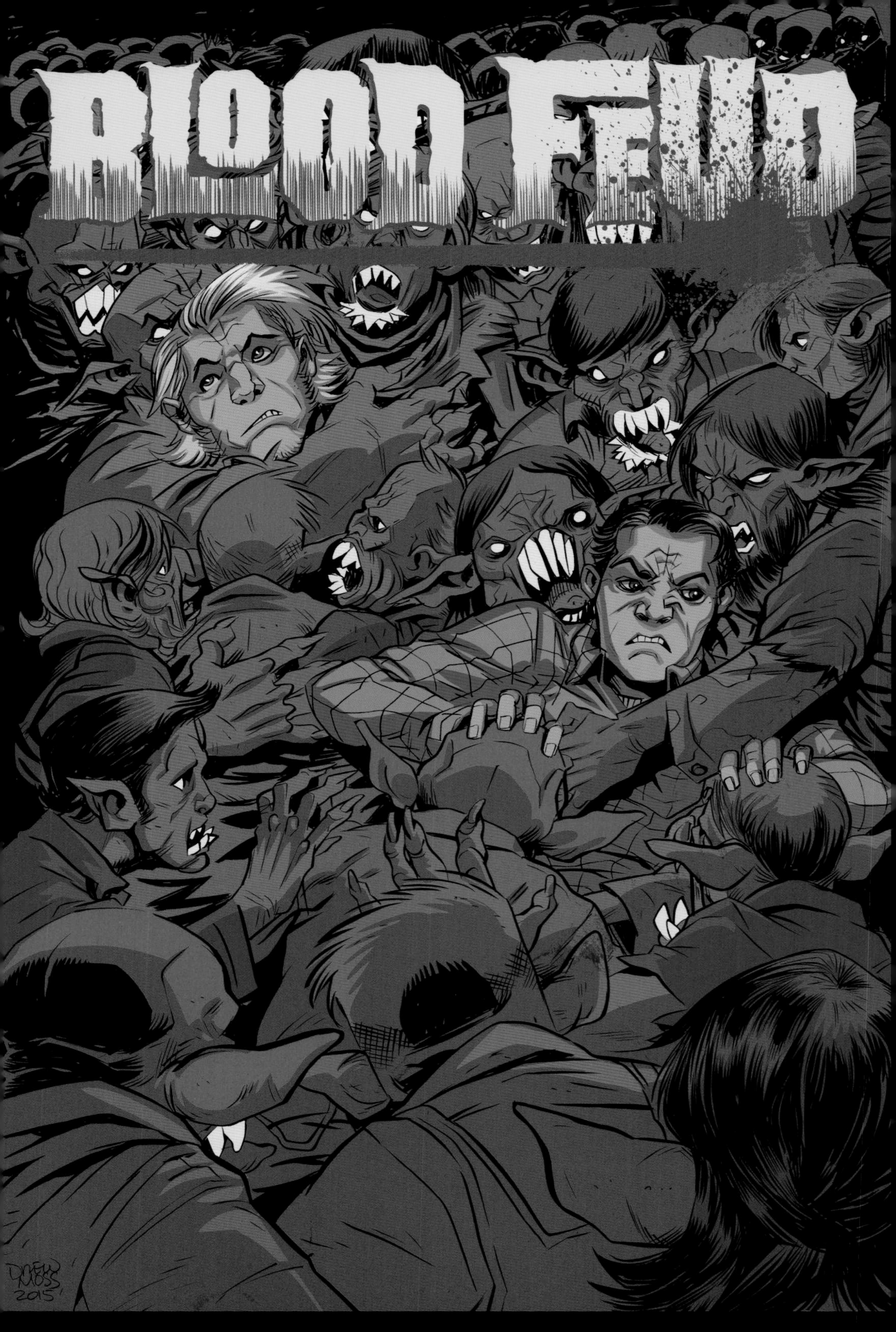
BLOOD FEUD
DREW MOSS 2015

ISSUE #2 STANDARD COVER
ILLUSTRATED BY DREW MOSS, COLORED BY NICK FILARDI, DESIGNED BY DYLAN TODD

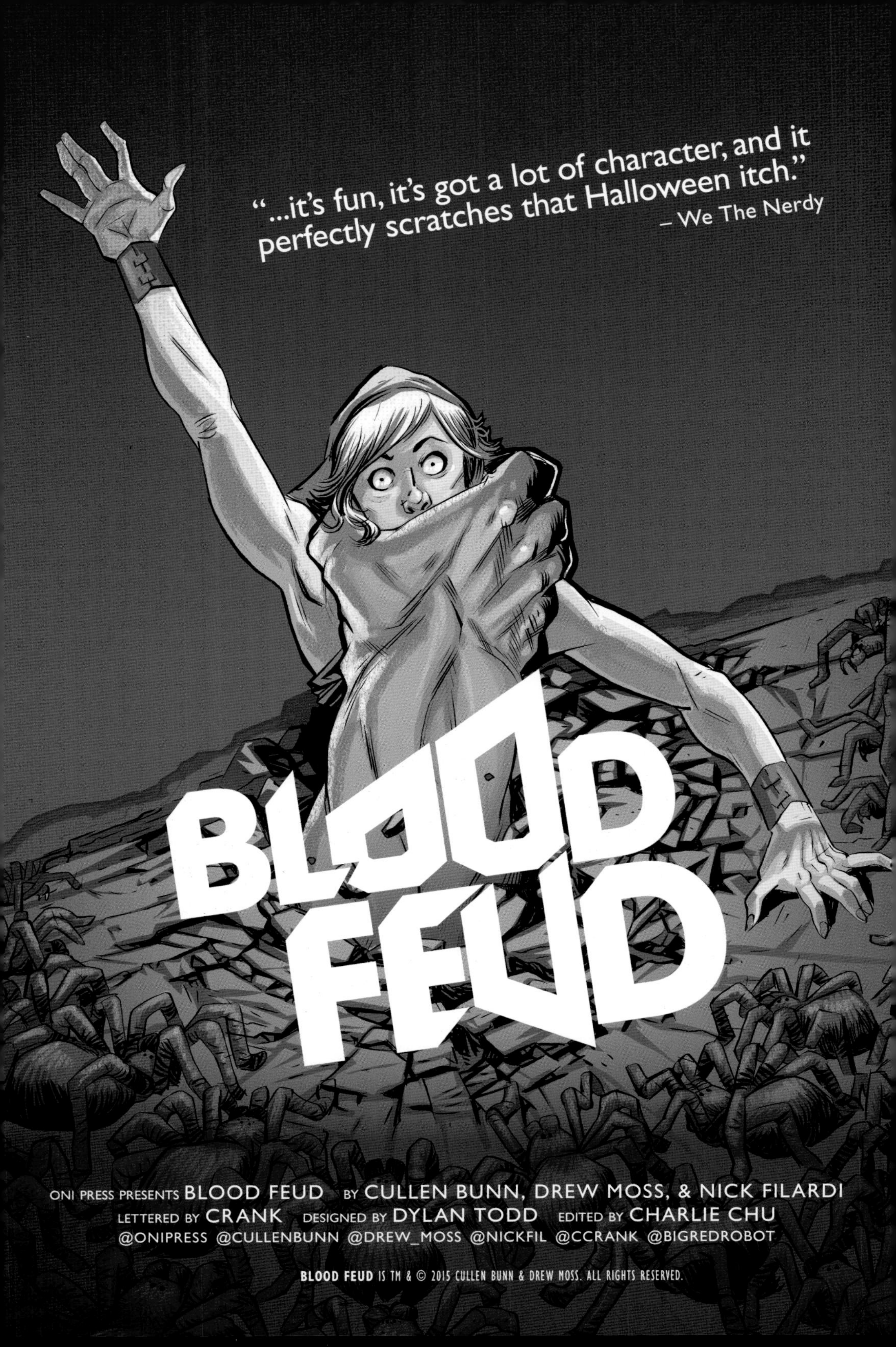

"...it's fun, it's got a lot of character, and it perfectly scratches that Halloween itch."
– We The Nerdy
BLOOD FEUD
ONI PRESS PRESENTS BLOOD FEUD BY CULLEN BUNN, DREW MOSS, & NICK FILARDI
LETTERED BY CRANK DESIGNED BY DYLAN TODD EDITED BY CHARLIE CHU
@ONIPRESS @CULLENBUNN @DREW_MOSS @NICKFIL @CCRANK @BIGREDROBOT
BLOOD FEUD IS TM & © 2015 CULLEN BUNN & DREW MOSS. ALL RIGHTS RESERVED.

ISSUE #2 **EVIL DEAD** HOMAGE COVER
ILLUSTRATED BY DREW MOSS, COLORED BY NICK FILARDI, DESIGNED BY DYLAN TODD

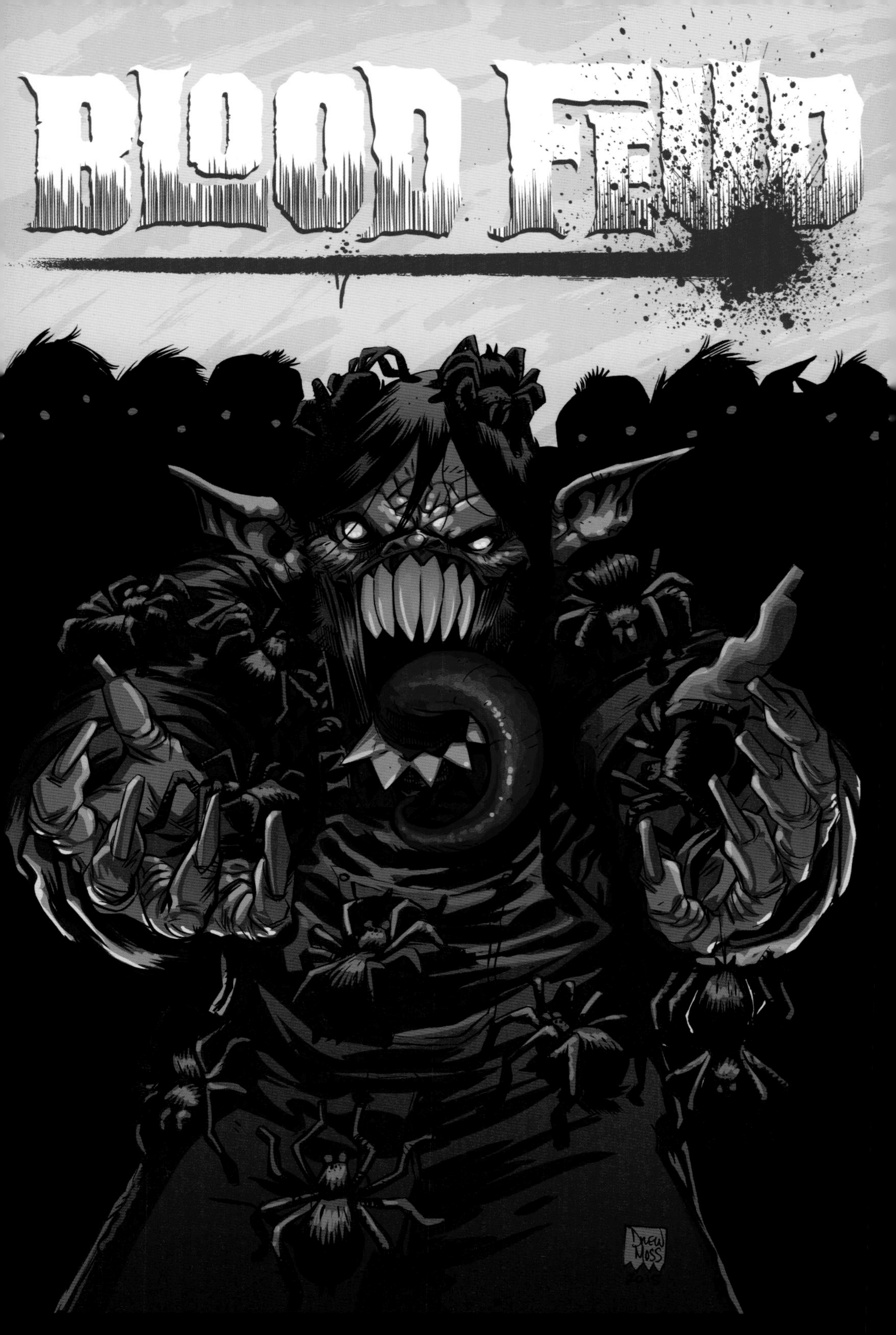
BLOOD FEUD
DREW MOSS

ISSUE #3 STANDARD COVER
ILLUSTRATED BY DREW MOSS. COLORED BY NICK FILARDI. DESIGNED BY DYLAN TODD

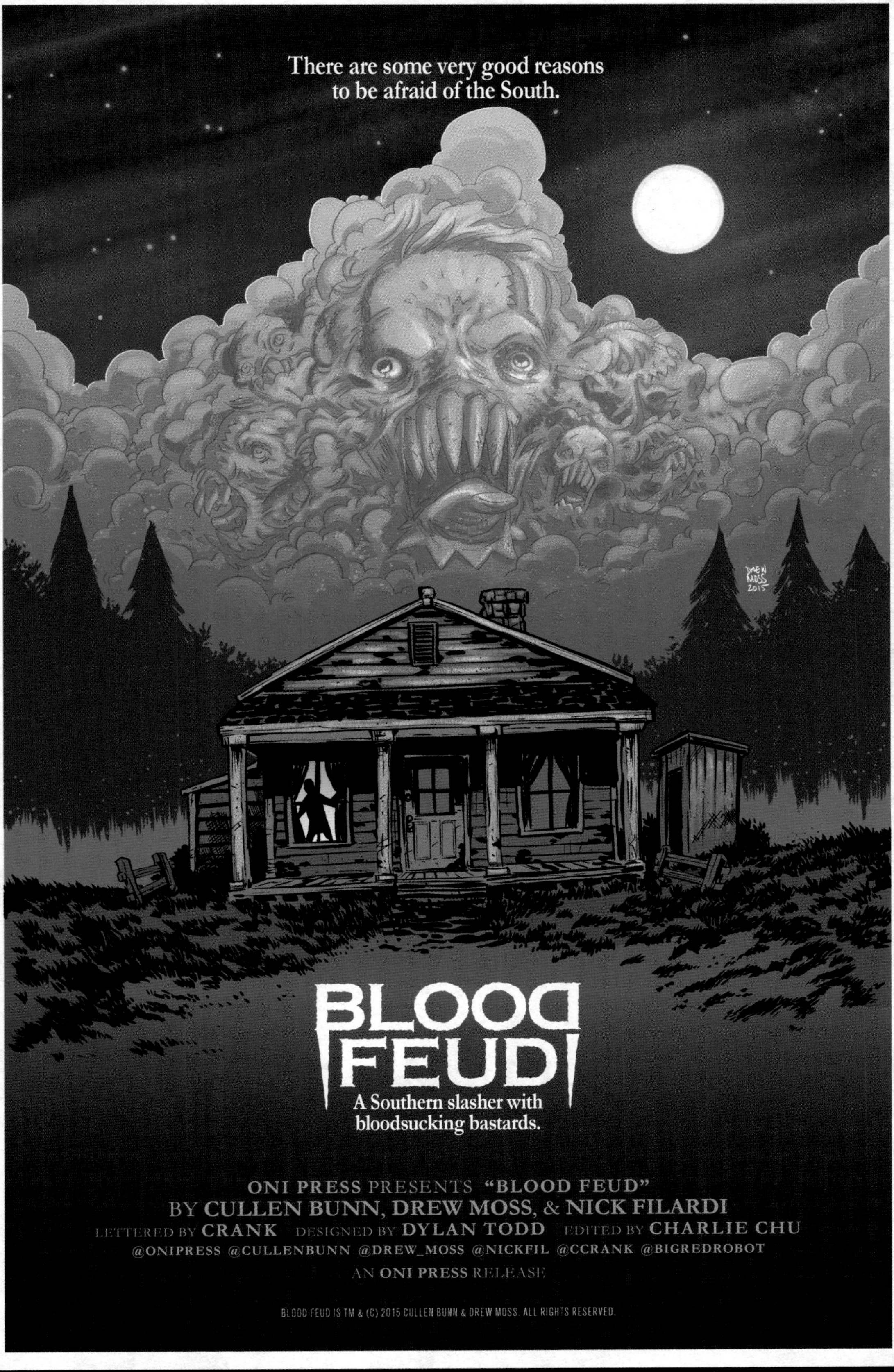
There are some very good reasons
to be afraid of the South.
DREW MOSS 2015
BLOOD FEUD
A Southern slasher with
bloodsucking bastards.
ONI PRESS PRESENTS "BLOOD FEUD"
BY CULLEN BUNN, DREW MOSS, & NICK FILARDI
LETTERED BY CRANK DESIGNED BY DYLAN TODD EDITED BY CHARLIE CHU
@ONIPRESS @CULLENBUNN @DREW_MOSS @NICKFIL @CCRANK @BIGREDROBOT
AN ONI PRESS RELEASE
BLOOD FEUD IS TM & (C) 2015 CULLEN BUNN & DREW MOSS. ALL RIGHTS RESERVED.

ISSUE #3 **FRIGHT NIGHT** HOMAGE COVER

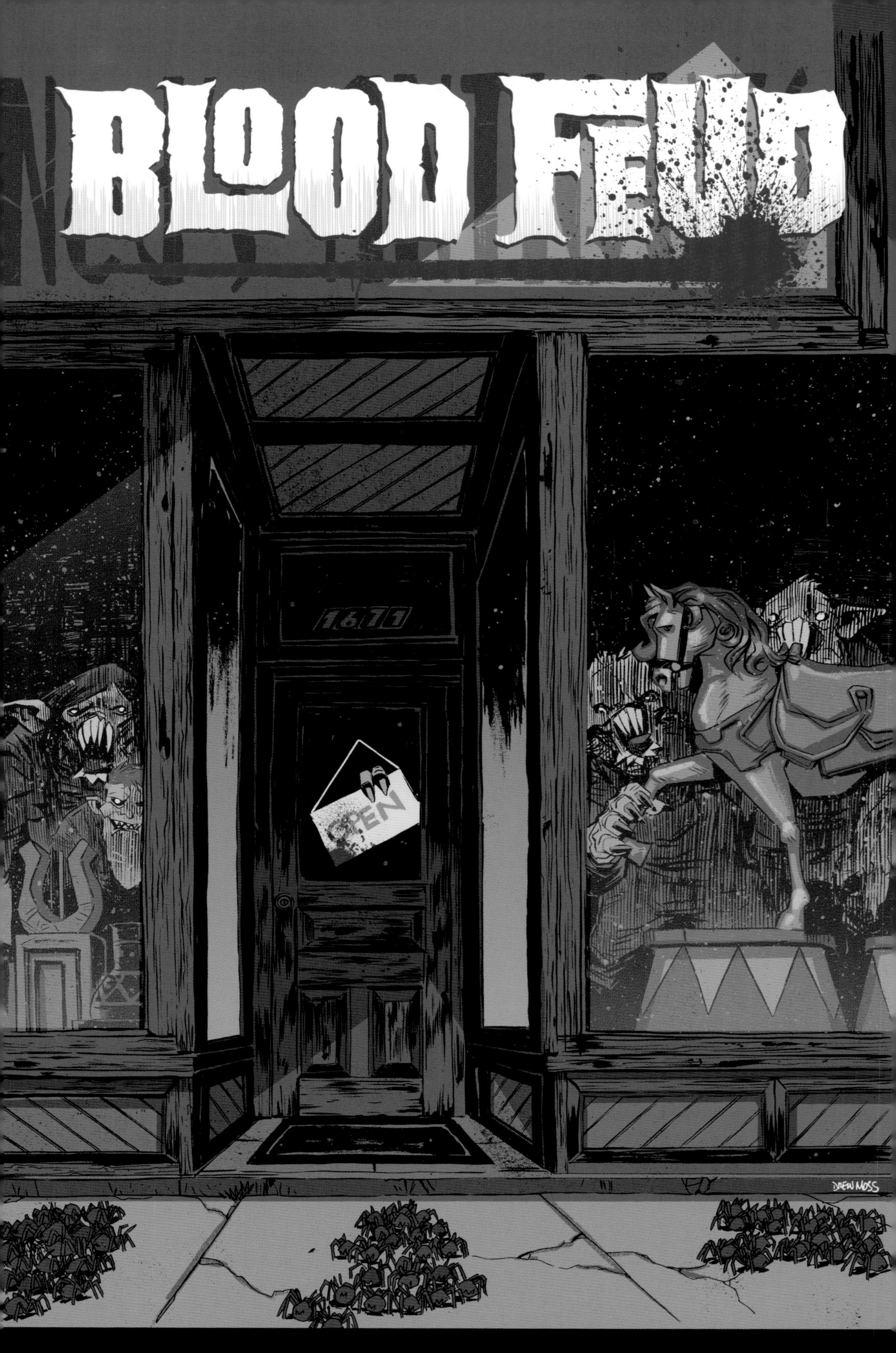
BLOOD FEUD
1611
OPEN
DREW MOSS

ISSUE #4 STANDARD COVER

Who will survive and what will be left after the feud?

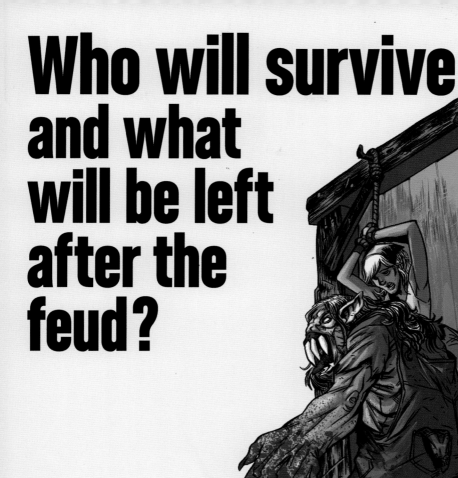

The South's most bizarre and brutal showdown!...

"THE SOUTHERN BLOOD FEUD MASSACRE"

What happened is true. Now the comic book that's just as real.

Oni Press presents "BLOOD FEUD" • BY CULLEN BUNN, DREW MOSS, & NICK FILARDI
Lettered by CRANK   Designed by DYLAN TODD   Edited by CHARLIE CHU
@ONIPRESS @CULLENBUNN @DREW_MOSS @NICKFIL @CCRANK @BIGREDROBOT

ISSUE #4 **TEXAS CHAINSAW MASSACRE** HOMAGE COVER

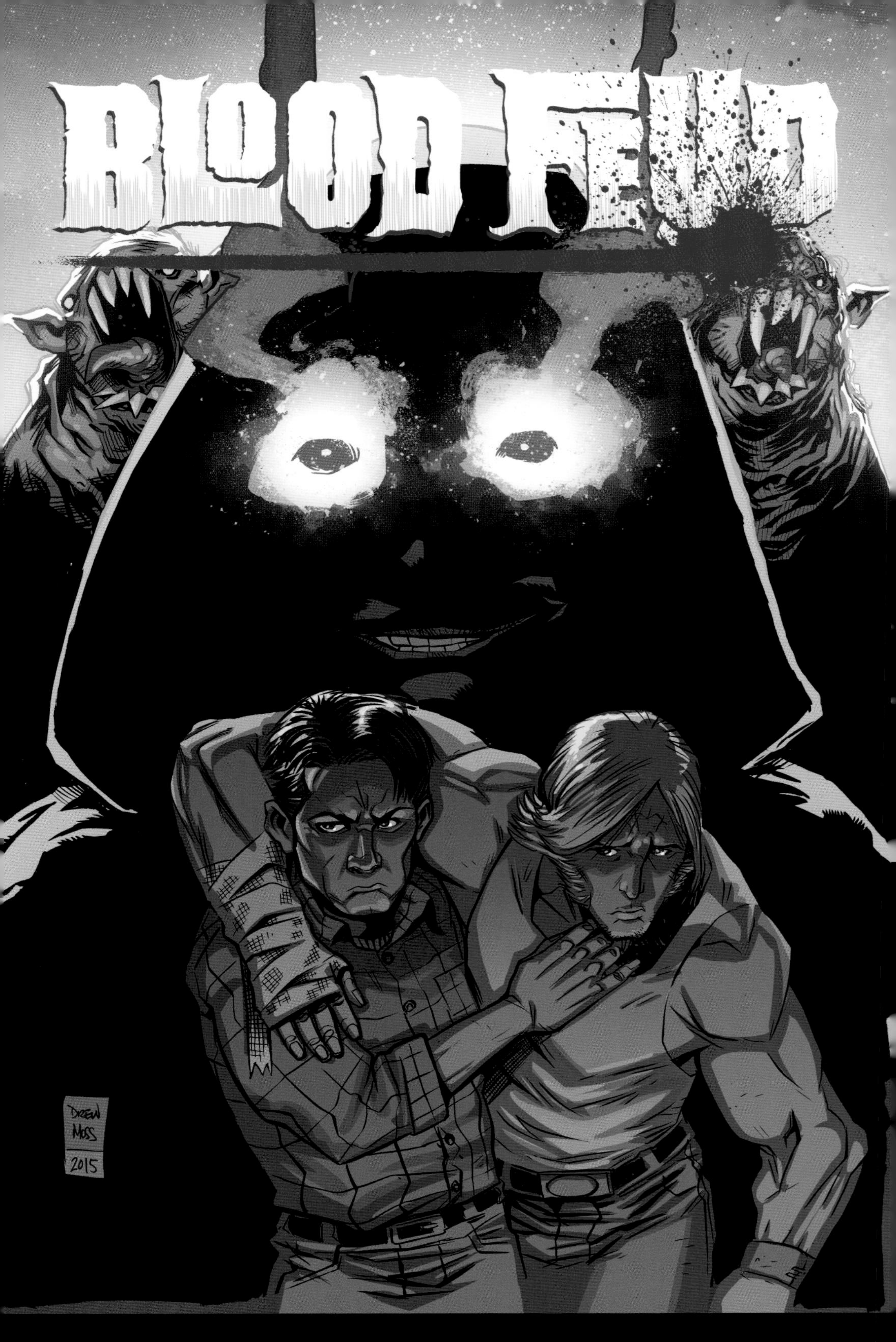
BLOOD FEUD
DREW MOSS
2015

ISSUE #5 STANDARD COVER

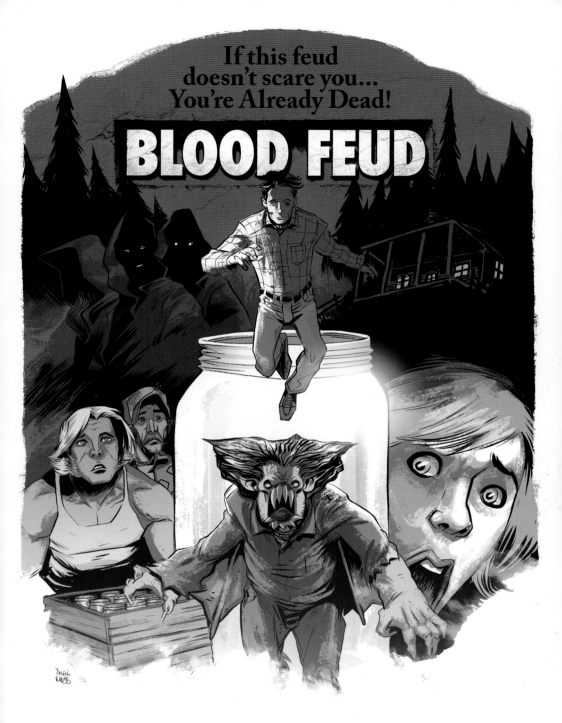

If this feud
doesn't scare you...
You're Already Dead!

BLOOD FEUD

ONI PRESS PRESENTS BLOOD FEUD   BY CULLEN BUNN, DREW MOSS, & NICK FILARDI

LETTERED BY CRANK   DESIGNED BY DYLAN TODD   EDITED BY CHARLIE CHU

@ONIPRESS @CULLENBUNN @DREW_MOSS @NICKFIL @CCRANK @BIGREDROBOT

ISSUE #5 **PHANTASM** HOMAGE COVER

IF THIS TOWN DOESN'T WAKE UP SCREAMING,
THEY WON'T WAKE UP AT ALL

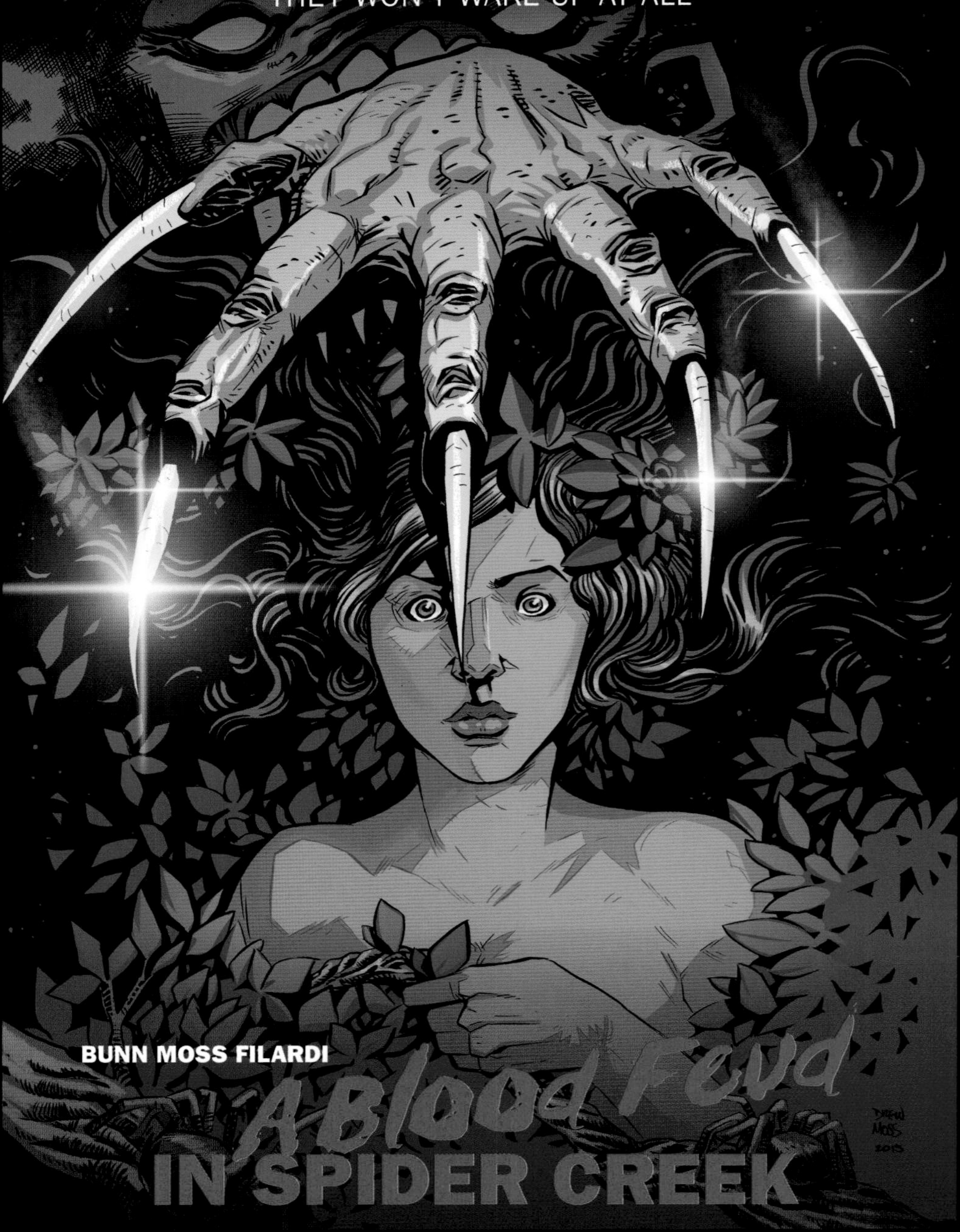
BUNN MOSS FILARDI
A Blood Feud
IN SPIDER CREEK
DREW MOSS 2015

ONI PRESS presents "BLOOD FEUD" By CULLEN BUNN, DREW MOSS, & NICK FILARDI

Lettered by CRANK Designed by DYLAN TODD Edited by CHARLIE CHU

@ONIPRESS @CULLENBUNN @DREW_MOSS @NICKFIL @CCRANK @BIGREDROBOT

ISSUE #1 BOOKS-A-MILLION EXCLUSIVE **A NIGHTMARE ON ELM STREET** HOMAGE COVER
ILLUSTRATED BY DREW MOSS. COLORED BY NICK FILARDI, DESIGNED BY DYLAN TODD

ABOUT THE CREATORS

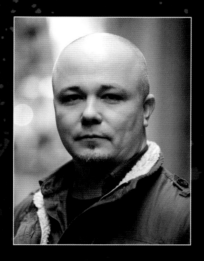

You know him, you love him: it's CULLEN BUNN!

Trudging deep out of the wastelands of Missouri, Cullen is the writer of comic books such as *The Sixth Gun*, *Helheim*, *The Damned*, and *The Tooth* for Oni Press. He has also written titles including *Harrow County* for Dark Horse and *Uncanny X-Men* for Marvel Comics.

Cullen claims to have worked as an Alien Autopsy Specialist, Rodeo Clown, Pro Wrestling Manager, and Sasquatch Wrangler. He has fought for his life against mountain lions and performed on stage as the World's Youngest Hypnotist. When he first wrote these words, he thought no one would ever believe them. Shockingly, people tend to put stock into those parts of the bio that aren't true, discrediting the factual bits.

In this way, Cullen continues to force you to rethink everything you thought was real.

His website is **cullenbunn.com**.

You can find him on Twitter at **@cullenbunn**.

DREW MOSS is an illustrator that has worked for various comic publishers, with work including *Creepy* at Dark Horse, *The Crow: Pestilence* and *Zombies vs Robots* at IDW, and *Outlaw Territory* at Image. He previously illustrated and co-created the Oni Press series, *Terrible Lizard*, with writer Cullen Bunn.

He is a lover of monsters, superheroes, cigars, and fine baked goods. Drew resides in southeastern Virginia with his lovely wife, amazing kids, and Mowgli the Shar Pei.

facebook.com / **DrewerdMoss** / **@drew_moss**

NICK FILARDI can be found coloring *Powers*, *Howling Commandos of S.H.I.E.L.D.*, *Slash & Burn*, *Helheim*, and the new series *Heartthrob* when he isn't tinkering with *Magic: The Gathering* decks. He resides with his 3-legged dog in sunny Florida.

He can be found on Twitter at **@nickfil**.